CW0664248

The Kurds

The position of the 19 million Kurds is an extremely complex one. Their territory is divided between 5 sovereign states, none of which has a Kurdish majority. They speak widely divergent dialects, and are also divided by religious affiliations and social factors. It has taken the tragic and horrifying events in Iraq this year to bring the Kurds to the centre of the world stage, but their particular problems, and their considerable geo-political importance, have been the source of growing concern and interest during the last two to three decades.

There is a remarkable dearth of reliable and up-to-date information about the Kurds, which this book remedies. Its contributors cover social and political issues, legal questions, religion, language, and the modern history of the Kurds in Turkey, Iraq, Iran, Syria and the Soviet Union. *The Kurds* will be an invaluable source of reference for students and specialists in Middle East studies, and those concerned with wider questions of nationalism and cultural identity. It also offers extremely useful background information for those with a professional concern for the numerous Kurdish immigrants and asylum seekers in Western Europe and North America.

Routledge/SOAS Politics and Culture in the Middle East Series

Edited by Tony Allan, Centre for Near and Middle Eastern Studies, School of Oriental and African Studies

Egypt under Mubarak
Edited by Charles Tripp and Roger Owen

Turkish State, Turkish Society
Edited by Andrew Finkel and Nukhet Sirman

Modern Literature in the Middle East
Edited by Robin Ostle

Sudan under Nimeiri
Edited by Peter Woodward

The Kurds

A Contemporary Overview

Edited by Philip G. Kreyenbroek
and Stefan Sperl

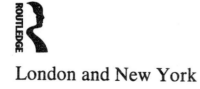

London and New York

First published 1992
by Routledge
11 New Fetter Lane, London EC4P 4EE

Simultaneously published in the USA and Canada
by Routledge
a division of Routledge, Chapman and Hall, Inc.
29 West 35th Street, New York, NY 10001

Printed and bound in Great Britain by
Biddles Ltd, Guildford and King's Lynn

British Library Cataloguing in Publication Data
The Kurds : a contemporary overview.
  1. Kreyenbroek, Philip G., *1948–*
  II. Sperl, Stefan, *1950–*
  305.89159

  ISBN 0–415–07265–4

Library of Congress Cataloging in Publication Data is available

To all Kurds forced to leave their homeland as refugees

Contents

Contributors

Hamit Bozarslan is a Member of the Equipe de Recherches sur la Turquie et l'Iran contemporain, CERI, Paris.

Martin van Bruinessen is a frequent visitor to Kurdistan and a well-known specialist on Kurdish affairs.

Jane Connors is a lecturer in the Law Department of SOAS, London. Kurdish affairs are among her special fields of interest.

Fereshteh Koohi-Kamali is an Oxford-trained specialist in the modern history of the Middle East generally, and of the Kurds in particular.

Philip G. Kreyenbroek is Lecturer in Modern Iranian Languages at SOAS; he is currently working on religious movements in Kurdistan, and on oral traditions in Iranian languages.

David McDowall is a specialist in Middle Eastern affairs, and author of several publications on the Kurds and the Palestinians.

Munir Morad is a Member of the Centre of Near and Middle Eastern Studies, SOAS.

A. Sherzad is a Kurdish researcher currently studying the influence of 'modernity' on Kurdish culture and politics.

Stefan Sperl is currently Lecturer in Arabic at SOAS; he worked for UNHCR for ten years, and has a special interest in Kurdish refugees.

Ismet Chériff Vanly has represented the Kurdish people at an international level for many decades, and has published widely on Kurdish affairs.

Sami Zubaida, a well-known specialist in Middle Eastern affairs, lectures at Birkbeck College, London.

Editors' preface

The aim of this volume, which contains articles about major aspects of the life and recent history of the Kurds by leading scholars, is to introduce the reader to the plight of the Kurdish people, and to generate greater understanding and support for the many Kurds who have been forced to abandon their homelands in recent years.

Most of the papers in this book were originally presented at an orientation seminar on the Kurdish problem organized in June 1989 for a group of United Nations Staff members by Dr Sperl and the External Services Division of the School of Oriental and African Studies, London (SOAS). The papers have since been revised and updated by the authors. Other contributions, in particular those on Turkey, Syria and the Soviet Union, have been especially commissioned for this volume.

In a book of this type transliteration is a major problem, as different conventions are normally used to transliterate Arabic, Kurdish, Persian and Turkish. The editors have sought to achieve some degree of consistency, but it proved impossible to reach complete uniformity. The use of diacritical signs has been kept to a minimum, and in some cases preferences of individual contributors have been respected.

The editors would like to extend their special thanks to Professor Tony Allan and to Ms Diana Matias, without whose help and encouragement the project would not have been realized. We also received much valuable help in editing the papers from Ms Jane Connors, and from Mr George Joffe, Dr Bengisu Rona and Mr Eralp Alışık. Some of the publication costs were met by the SOAS Research and Publications Committee and the SOAS Middle East Centre. The final typescript was compiled with the help of Ms Diana Gur and Ms Fiona McEwan of the Middle East Centre. We are very grateful for their expertise and for their unfailing good humour in dealing with the text.

NOTE

The material in this volume reflects the opinions of the contributors. Officials of the School of Oriental and African Studies, where the material appearing here was coordinated and edited, do not necessarily share the views expressed.

Introduction

Sami Zubaida

The collection of papers in this volume brings together many aspects of Kurdish history, politics and culture. They are valuable scholarly contributions. Their interest, however, at this particular point in time, goes beyond the scholarly. The Kurdish nation is living and suffering a particularly critical conjuncture in its history. At a time of advances in democracy and respect for human rights in many parts of Europe and elsewhere, the transgressions against Kurdish lives and liberties are getting worse. The outcome of the two recent regional wars frame the problems and the prospects for the Kurds.

The aftermath of the Iraq–Iran war brought calamity to Iraqi Kurdistan, which suffered the concerted savage onslaught of Iraqi forces, killing thousands with chemical weapons, uprooting and relocating even larger numbers, and razing towns and villages which have been Kurdish habitations for centuries. The face of Iraqi Kurdistan has been dramatically transformed, making the very territorial identity of the Kurds precarious. Hundreds of thousands of Kurds, uprooted by the war, by Iraqi deportations, first of Faili Kurds to Iran before and in the early years of the war (estimated at 130,000, see Morad in this book), then more recently of Kurds expelled from their towns and villages and resettled in government "new towns" with no tangible means of subsistence, and refugees in make-shift camps in Turkey estimated at 60,000. These are in addition to the many thousands deported to other parts of Iraq since the early 1970s.

In Iran, Kurds suffered the depredations of war, being in the border regions between the combatants, and coming in, in the earlier years of the war, for the special attention of the Revolutionary Guards fighting Kurdish insurgents, destroying villages and generally imposing a harsh and violent regime on civilians. Iranian authorities, however, did not pursue their persecutions with the degree of savagery of their Iraqi counterparts.

The end of the Iran–Iraq war signalled the increasing vulnerability of armed Kurdish resistance in both countries. Chemical weapon attacks in Iraq and the removal of Kurdish habitations and resources have confined Kurdish forces to bases across the borders with Iran, and drastically limited their activities. In Iran, Kurdish fighters are similarly limited. In both countries the only immediate prospect of any advances were confined to the possibility of some form of understanding with the authorities, negotiating from a position of weakness with capricious regimes. The assassination of Abd al-Rahman Ghassemlou in Vienna in 1989, by Iranian representatives with whom he was conducting secret negotiations, is a clear indication of the pitfalls of this course of action.

The conclusion of the last Gulf war, over the occupation of Kuwait, has brought even greater disaster to the Iraqi Kurds. Encouraged by Iraqi defeat in the war and the destruction of Iraqi military capacities, and deceived by American rhetoric during the war calling for the removal of Saddam Hussain and a democratic regime, Kurdish forces in the north of the country, and the Shi'i opposition in the south, staged simultaneous revolts against the regime. Both wings of the revolt formed parts of an Iraqi front which includes a wide range of Iraqi opposition forces committed to the establishment of a democratic and pluralist regime in Iraq and the recognition of Kurdish national rights within it. Initial successes of these revolts, especially on the Kurdish front, were soon reversed, with the regime marshalling its loyalist forces, equipped with heavy weapons and helicopter gunships against the rebels' light arms. The Americans stood aside allowing the massacre of populations which have become the hallmark of the Saddam regime, pleading that they had no mandate to intervene in Iraq's internal affairs. This uncharacteristic "neutrality" is clearly related to perceptions of the political interests of the USA and its clients in the region, principally Turkey and Saudi Arabia. At the time of writing, Iraqi Kurds are living through yet another nightmare, greater in scale and intensity than any which have preceded it. Millions are fleeing Saddam's terror in the directions of the Turkish and Iranian borders, both countries reluctant hosts, and the Turkish authorities actually forcing the refugees into high mountain camps inside Iraqi territory, with no protection against severe weather conditions and no food or medicine. The "international community" has woken up to the tragedy and is marshalling humanitarian aid. The European powers are initiating plans for UN intervention. It is not clear at this stage what the ultimate outcome will be, except that thousands more Kurds will have died, and millions been made homeless.

What Turkish Kurdistan has in common with its Iraqi and Iranian counterparts is that it constitutes the poorest and least developed part of the country. It is a border region defined by the state as a security area, with a more or less permanent imposition of martial law. Military rule is arbitrary and oppressive, with a high level of violence, arrests and deportations. The armed activity of the PKK (Kurdish Workers Party), and official reprisals add to the ambience of violence and insecurity. The large numbers of Kurdish migrants to the major Turkish cities and to western Europe occupy, for the most part, low socio-economic statuses, and suffer more than their fair share of urban poverty and insecurity. However, the Turkish situation is different from Iraq and Iran in important respects, and in particular, in the operation of a political process, however precarious. The monolithic regime in Iraq has eliminated political organization or contest outside its direct control. The only location for opposition or resistance within the country was provided courtesy of the Kurdish resistance and the territory it controlled, and came to an end with its demise. Iran has a more open political field, but one confined to factional strife between the Islamic forces, and which excludes any other form of politics, certainly any related to ethnic aspirations. Turkey, on the other hand does have a political process, including a limited measure of institutional democracy with party pluralism. It should be emphasized that this is precarious and subject to periodic military suppression. In between, Kurdish forces and interests do have some representation (see Bozarslan in this book), the significance of which will be examined presently.

It is often forgotten that there are indigenous Kurds in Syria and the Soviet Union, and that, in the era of nation-states in the twentieth century, they have suffered similar assaults on their identity, culture and territory as their brethren in the neighbouring states. Vanly's article in this volume is a timely reminder of their plight.

Given this catalogue of sorrows, what are the prospects for the Kurds? Are there any political solutions? There has been much debate on the question of self-determination, of Kurdistan as an independent nation-state as promised in the Treaty of Sèvres. But, I think, there is widespread realization among political Kurds and their friends that, under present circumstances, this is a Utopian dream. It is not so much the divisions of the Kurds along tribal, class, religious and even linguistic lines, illustrated in this book and elsewhere, which would impede the formation of a Kurdish nation-state. Such divisions are common and natural in a complex society, and the Kurds are no different in this respect from other nations. Other states in the region have faced and continue to confront similar problems. The state forges the nation, with different degrees of success. Rather, it is the realities of power in the region and the world which make a Kurdish state an unlikely outcome. It is only imaginable under conditions of the simultaneous weakness, nay near collapse of all three states of Iraq, Iran and Turkey. It would also require active sponsorship and support by the USA or a consortium of world powers. This conjuncture seems most unlikely. In any case, a separate Kurdish state does not seem to feature at the present time on anyone's agenda, and, as we have seen, the Iraqi Kurds are committed to a programme of autonomy within a democratic Iraq.

There then remains the solution of "autonomy", cultural and possibly political, the recognition of Kurdish identity and insti-tutional provision for its cultivation and expression. On the face of it, the 1970 autonomy decree in Iraq is an example of such procedure. Indeed, in so far as this decree is applied, it does provide for the cultural and educational (including linguistic) elements of the Kurdish identity. The patchy and ambivalent recognition of Kurdish identity by various Iraqi regimes since the years of the British Mandate, together with territorial institutionalization of the Kurdish resistance, have made Iraqi Kurdistan an important centre for the development of modern Kurdish politics and culture for the whole region. However, the scope and form of the application (or redundance) of autonomy provisions, as well as the definition of Kurdish territory and populations, have depended on the whims and interests of the government. And it has not prevented that government from committing savage atrocities against the Kurdish population, while maintaining some broadcasting in Kurdish and teaching the language in some schools. As Sherzad (in this volume) points out, the long-term strategy of the Ba'thist regime was aimed at the integration of Kurdistan into an Arab Iraq. The Iraqi case shows clearly that "autonomy" only makes sense in states where the government is subject to the rule of law, and where political and institutional constraints can be applied to the rulers. This is a good reason why political Kurds should make common cause with the democratic forces in their respective countries, as many of them have done and continue to do. However, unhappily, the prospects for democratic transformations in most countries in the region are dim. Iraq's defeat in the war over Kuwait has opened up possibilities for political transformations in the country. Dare we hope that this will lead to some degree of democracy, pluralism and the rule of law?

Turkey remains the most interesting country from a Kurdish point of view. As we have already noted, it is the only country which features a relatively open political process, however limited and precarious. Turkey has maintained a stubborn denial of Kurdish identity and has severely repressed cultural and linguistic expressions of Kurdishness. A hedged acknowledgement of Kurdish nationality was made recently by President Özal as part of his strategy for influencing the outcomes in a future Iraq. He has also taken steps to lift the interdiction on the use of the Kurdish language in private, though not in public spheres. At the same time, his government has "suspended" the application of elements of the European Convention on Human Rights in the Kurdish areas (as if it were ever applied), on grounds of national security arising from hostilities in the Gulf. The Turkish government has a history of atrocities against its Kurds no less severe than that of Iraq (short of chemical warfare), and the violence and repression in the Kurdish areas continue. Yet it has not been able to preclude its considerable Kurdish population from playing a part in its political arena.

Turkey can, perhaps, be said to have a more complex political and economic structure than Iraq or Iran. The Kurdish regions, being the poorest and least developed, have contributed a large number of migrants to the major Turkish cities. Kurds have entered Turkish society at many levels. In an electoral system, the numerical potential of the Kurds acquires great importance. Practically all the political parties now have Kurdish members and deputies (see the excellent analysis by Bozarslan in this volume). Parties recruit Kurdish support through their clientalistic networks, and as such become involved in the tribal, religious and class divisions of Kurdish society. The pressures on the ruling authorities engendered by this political participation, including parliamentary representation, as well as external pressures from the Western world with respect to human rights, have led to a weakening and subversion of the rules denying Kurdish identity. The conflicts which have arisen within political parties over the Kurdish issue, as in the case of the expulsion of some Kurdish deputies from the Social Democratic Party and the subsequent resignation of others in 1989, have only served to heighten the process of Kurdish visibility. The "Kurdish question" is now identified by its name in sections of the press, and even in parliamentary debates.

The Turkish case shows that when Kurds are able to participate in politics, they do not necessarily enter it on the same side. This is only natural in a complex and variegated society. But however divided they may be politically, they do create the overall effect of highlighting Kurdish identity and interests. As Bozarslan points out, Kurdish political participation represents integration, not separation, from the Turkish state. Yet it is not assimilation, because it renders Kurdishness more visible and pressing. Perhaps the best parallel to illustrate this situation is the example of Basques or Catalans in Spain. Their separate identities and regional political autonomy are only made possible through their participation in national Spanish politics and culture. And they enter the political and cultural arenas not as unified national forces, but with their political differences clearly marked. However, for these activities to proceed, minimal conditions of political democracy and pluralism must prevail, and that is just what is at issue in the region at the present time. In the absence of these conditions, does the answer lie in armed struggle?

Given the history and constitution of Kurdish societies, and the situation in which they found themselves at the inception of the twentieth century, armed resistance may have been inevitable. Indeed it was partly through the armed struggle that Kurds established their national identity and political presence in the region. What, however, can this armed struggle achieve now?

It is clear, in retrospect, that under conditions of modern warfare, and of the means of surveillance, control and violence available to modern states, Kurdish insurgents are only able to operate with the aid of one regional power against another, and under conditions of weakness of the state in question. Witness the destruction of the Kurdish forces in Iraq at the end of the Gulf war (see McDowall in this volume), and their ultimate defeat in the more recent uprising in March 1991. The fortunes of war and diplomacy can lead to the sudden withdrawal of support from a neighbouring state, or to the recovery of weak states. The lessons of 1975 and again of 1988–9 and 1991 for Iraqi Kurds should not be lost. The armed struggle can win particular battles, but ultimately it loses the war, with the familiar tragic consequences for the civilian populations. The late Abd al-Rahman Ghassemlou died in the process of trying to find a political alternative to a hopeless and destructive war. Yet, as we have seen, and as the assassination of Ghassemlou has shown, political solutions are difficult to achieve with capricious and despotic governments, especially from a position of weakness.

I should now like to examine the possible effects of the Islamic factor in Middle East politics on the Kurdish question. The spectacular spread of Islamic politics has been such that wherever any measure of political liberalization has been instituted (such as in Jordan and Algeria) Islamic forces have come to the fore in electoral contests. Even (or especially) secular, Kemalist Turkey is experiencing the assertion of Islamic politics. What are the implications for the Kurds?

In the early days of the 1979 Islamic Revolution in Iran, Ayatollah Khomeini dashed the hopes of Kurds aspiring to a democratic revolutionary Iran by asserting that the Kurds, being Muslims, should obey the Islamic authorities like other good Muslims. The Revolution did not change the situation of the Kurds, except in instigating conflicts between the Sunni majority and their Shi'i brethren in the south who supported Khomeini. Turkey, however, presents a different picture.

For political Kurds in Turkey and elsewhere Islam was associated with traditionalists and conservatives, with *aghas* and landlords. When religious leaders entered the nationalist struggle, as in the case of Barzinji in Iraq, they subordinated the language of religion to that of the national struggle. The Kurdish national struggle in Turkey, as elsewhere, was, in the 1960s and 1970s, characterized by secular ideologies of Marxism and neo-Kemalism (see Bozarslan). The PKK retains its Marxist rhetoric to the present time. Yet, the great majority of ordinary Kurds, living as they do in the most backward regions of the country, have retained Islamic identity and adherence. Right-wing religious parties, notably the Refah (Welfare) Party have had a Kurdish constituency through the 1970s and 1980s. Many, presumably religious, Kurds, however, continued to support secular nationalist and even leftist politics. The view of Islam as a political creed was not then so prevalent. The rise of political Islam on a world scale has altered this situation in important respects. Islam is now a "modern" creed of the intelligentsia, no longer identified with backward *aghas* and Mullas. What is more important, it ranges itself against the (secular-Kemalist) state and its agencies. It is now a vehicle for expression of social and economic grievances. This development coincides with the apparent collapse of communism on a world scale. Do not let us forget that the appeal of leftist affiliations in the Middle East depended to a considerable extent on its identification with a world power and its might. Now Islam appears to its adherents as a world political force against imperialism and corruption. It is too early to say what consequences this development will have for Kurdish politics in Turkey. It is likely, however, that more Kurds will turn to Islamism for political inspiration. But will Sunni Islamism be any more favourable to Kurdish aspirations than its Shi'i counterpart in Iran?

The potential of political Islam for nationalism is ambiguous. On the one hand pan-Islamism has an anti-nationalist logic. On the other, this logic is not usually followed in practice. The Iranian Revolution, followed by the Gulf War, has, if anything, reinforced Iranian nationalism, to the detriment of the Kurds. In the short term, Islamic agitations are likely to lead to communalist strife between Sunni and Alevi Kurds, a repeat of the episodes instigated by right-wing forces in the 1970s. As an opposition movement, Islamism may coincide with particular aspects of Kurdish struggles. But Islamists in power are no more attracted to democracy, pluralism and the rule of law than their secular counterparts. They can be self-righteous in their rejection of democracy and pluralism as imperialist, Western divisive poisons. The organicist emphases of Islamist ideologies preclude pluralism, including national pluralism. Note the antagonism of Algerian Islamists to Berber national expressions. Political Islam may be gratifying for some Kurds in combining an expression of their frustrations and grievances with their deep-seated faith and identity. But it is not likely to lead to any novel solutions to the Kurdish question. It is more likely to attempt to eliminate the question in the name of Islamic unity, much as Atatürk denied Kurdish ethnic identity in favour of a national unity.

The foregoing discussion of prospects and retrospects does not offer any immediate remedies for the sufferings of Kurds at the present time. While they continue to live under repressive regimes which consider the Kurds as security risks, their liberty, property and life continue to be under attack. The immediate task, therefore, for concerned democrats is the defence of the human rights of the Kurds. Jane Connors's clear analysis (in this book) of the issues involved in international law and human rights conventions shows that these provisions can only have effect through concerted international pressures on the offending states. Tragically, Western powers who have trumpeted their concern for human rights and national rights to self-determination when it has suited them, have not reacted with any vigour or consistency to the violations of these rights with respect to the Kurds (or other Middle Eastern peoples). Expediency with regard to political and economic interests in the region predominate. On the other hand, there is every indication that the plight of the Kurds strikes a sympathetic chord with enlightened public opinion, in the media, in educational institutions, in political parties and in parliamentary circles. It is essential to maintain, inform and mobilize these sympathies to exert pressure on governments and international organizations to act more decisively in defence of the Kurds. This book is a valuable contribution to informing such a readership.

Chapter 1

The Kurdish question: a historical review

David McDowall

INTRODUCTION

It is a sad feature of the Kurdish question that the only times it is brought to our notice is at moments of conflict, when Kurdish guerrillas attack government forces or vice-versa, or when some atrocity is committed: gas attack in Iraq, mass execution in Iran, or arbitrary arrest and torture in Turkey. Is this an accurate picture of the Kurdish place in today's Middle East order?

Undoubtedly the Kurdish people are currently undergoing one of their worst ordeals on record.

The purpose of this chapter is to set this ordeal in its historical perspective, and to challenge a widely assumed view that the Kurdish question is simple either in essence or in its solution, as the protagonists would sometimes have us believe. Many Kurdish nationalists argue for the establishment of a Kurdish state, while the states which embrace parts of Kurdistan insist that all would be well if only the Kurds acted as loyal subjects.

A natural corollary of periodic newspaper coverage of Kurdish insurgency is the assumption that the relationship between the Kurds and their neighbours has always been one of unremitting conflict. It is a view easily reinforced by the history we have, which records the exceptional and the dramatic rather than the norm. Consequently, report of disasters, military campaigns and battles and so forth rather than the normality of everyday life in between these "events" dominate our view of the past.

Indeed, our very first view of the Kurds, or "Kardu" is when they mauled Xenophon's Ten Thousand during their famous retreat to the Black Sea in 400 BC. During the Arab period and thereafter there are numerous references to Kurdish revolt and depredations.

By the time of the Crusades the Kurds had acquired a reputation for military prowess, not only giving trouble to those who interfered with them, but evolving a tradition of military service to the regimes in power. This tradition is epitomized in Islam's most famous warrior, Saladin, who though a Kurd, never lived in Kurdistan. Like many other Kurds, he grew up in the culture of the military camps which were to be found near the centres of power in the Fertile Crescent.

Another natural assumption about the Kurds, since they speak a separate language, is that they are ethnically different from their neighbours. The reality is more complicated. Perhaps the Kardu who attacked the Ten Thousand were really Medes, as Kurds themselves like to think, a distinct mountain tribal people of Indo-Aryan origin. But we also know that by the time of the Arab Muslim conquests of the seventh century AD, the ethnic term "Kurd" was being applied to an amalgam of Iranian and iranicized tribes, some of which may have been indigenous "Kardu", but many of which were of semitic or other ethnic origin. In Israel today there are Jews who describe themselves as Kurdish, and we can describe the Assyrian Christians who coexist with Muslims in Kurdistan and speak one of the Kurdish dialects, as Kurdish by culture also. Although the Kurdish people are overwhelmingly Sunni Muslim, they embrace Jews, Christians, Yazidis and other sects (e.g. the Alevis of central Anatolia, and the Ahl-e Haqq in southern Iranian Kurdistan). Furthermore, the existence of substantially different dialects cuts further lines of division across a simplistic idea of a Kurdish nation. So who are the Kurdish people? They are all those, I would argue, who as a consequence of the environment in which they live, feel a sense of Kurdish cultural identity.

The question of identity is also to do with imagined lineage and, as with other Sunni Muslims, lineage that can be traced back to the Prophet and other early Arab figures in Islam is important. Arab lineage among the Kurds is not all imagined. Arab descent had a very special practical role among the Kurds for both religious *shaykhs* and for the chiefs of tribal confederations. For the former, to be a *sayyid* and claim descent from the Prophet naturally enhanced their religious authority. For a paramount chief, the absence or diminution of blood relationship with the tribes under his authority placed him above and outside the politics of tribal kinship, and thus strengthened his credibility and authority as an impartial arbitrator among his tribes. If he could additionally claim the nobility of descent as a *sayyid* so much the better.

A brief word needs to be said about the basis of solidarity in Kurdish society. Apart from the population on the plain and in the foothills, most Kurds belonged to nomadic or semi-nomadic tribes. Tribalism was frequently a mix between the ties of kinship and those of territory, being neither purely one nor the other. In the mountainous heartlands of Kurdistan the sense of tribe has always – until today – been strongest, but in the low-lying areas in the foothills and on the plain many Kurds lost their tribal identity. Except in the matter of religion, a Kurdish mountain tribe would almost certainly feel more in common with an Assyrian mountain tribe than it would with non-tribal Kurds living on the plain or in the foothills of the mountains.

It is difficult to classify Kurdish tribalism since it has always been far from homogeneous and has always been revolutionary. At the risk of crude generalization one might say that traditionally the Kurds were largely organized into a rough hierarchy of sub-tribes, tribes and tribal confederations. Loyalties were not immutable, and a strong and determined leader of one tribe might well be able to acquire a sufficient following and perhaps territory to throw off previous loyalties and realign himself with another federation or group, or even with the government.

Traditionally Kurdish tribal leaders have necessarily been guided in their politics by the conflicting balance of power among neighbouring tribes and with the more distant government of the region. Needless to say, central government often saw advantage in supporting an up-and-coming chief who might act as a counterbalance or "policeman" against neighbouring tribes which were unwilling to do the government's bidding. Many chiefs were quite willing to act on behalf of the government against a neighbour if properly rewarded. As recently as the 1950s, when asked by a British diplomat what he would do about a Kurdish tribe that was in revolt, the Iraqi Prime Minister Nuri al-Said replied, "Oh, it's quite simple, I shall send a bag of gold to a neighbouring chief."

THE KURDS BEFORE 1918

A tension has always existed in the Middle East between the central government and those societies which live on the fringes of, or beyond the reach of, its authority. Two categories immediately come to mind, the respective dwellers in the deserts and mountains. Central government naturally wishes to extend its control to the greatest possible area, while the people who inhabit these areas frequently do so to avoid precisely this kind of government interference. The tension is understood. Mountain people have proved far harder to bring under control than the Bedouin, with Maronites and Druzes, Kurds and Afghans being present day examples of repudiation of central government.

From time to time this tension exploded into open conflict. But these explosions were the exception rather than the norm. Both in the case of the Bedouin and of the mountain people of the Middle East, a delicate *modus vivendi* usually existed at the point of balance between the respective strengths of government on the one hand and "the tribes" on the other. Unless the ambitions of a governor or tribal chief disturbed things, both parties preferred a quiet life in which goods and services could be exchanged.

In the Kurdish case, the tribes exported to the plain livestock, oak galls (for ink) and timber in return for their own needs, particularly metal artefacts. Furthermore, it suited government to make constructive use of the Kurds' martial propensities. Successive governors in the plains surrounding Kurdistan recognized the semi-autonomous status of certain chiefs in return for performing services. One of these services was the payment of tribute, always a tricky area since it was effectively an economic evaluation of the power balance between the two. The other service, the provision of troops, sometimes under the command of a close member of the chief's family, frequently satisfied the needs of both parties. The governor needed hardy troops such as Kurdistan offered, while many tribes were happy to "export" surplus manpower on account of population growth in an economically poor environment. Such arrangements became increasingly formalized during the Saljuq period (from the eleventh century onwards). One result of course was that the Kurdish chiefs, especially if they commanded the troops they provided, themselves became incorporated into the governing structure of the state.

In the upheavals in Anatolia caused by the Mongol and Turkoman invasions during the thirteenth and fourteenth centuries, the Kurdish tribes began to extend their territorial control northwards beyond the Zagros range, onto the eastern part of the Anatolian Plateau. With the struggle between the growing Ottoman and Safavid Empires in the sixteenth century, the Kurdish tribes were able to extend their powers and position even further. Both empires sought to stabilize the border after the decisive Ottoman victory over the Safavids at Chaldiran in 1514, and both sought the cooperation of the Kurdish tribes to achieve this. On both sides, Kurdish paramount chiefs, or *amirs*, were appointed and given fiefdoms, sometimes in areas hitherto unoccupied by the Kurdish tribes, in return for policing the border and ensuring its tranquillity. In an age when the mobilization of the imperial army was an expensive and lengthy undertaking, this arrangement was efficient and economical. Furthermore, by using the tribes to their advantage, the two empires avoided costly and recurrent revolts among the tribes beyond their immediate control. For their part, the tribes enjoyed considerable freedom, and were seldom disturbed so long as they ensured relative tranquillity in the Ottoman–Safavid border marches.

This relatively happy state of affairs continued undisturbed for three hundred years before it began to disintegrate. The immediate reason for this disintegration was the growing threat by the European powers to the integrity of the Ottoman empire, and the latter's attempt to respond to the challenge. Chastened by the loss of Greece (1828), trepidation concerning further unrest in the Balkans, and the dangers of Russian expansion into eastern Anatolia, the Ottoman government in Istanbul attempted to extend direct control over its eastern borders. Implicitly this undermined the hitherto accepted semi-autonomous status of the Kurdish emirates. The Ottoman government was able to contemplate such steps because of the advance in military technology during the early nineteenth century. Similar changes also began to take place on the Persian side of the border.

The extension of Ottoman control precipitated a number of revolts by Kurdish *amirs* during the rest of the century. Some tried to achieve complete independence, others merely to hang on to what they had previously enjoyed as of right, while one or two tried unsuccessfully to play off the two regional powers, neither of which was likely in the long run to welcome Kurdish independence. It is natural that some Kurds look back to these revolts as the beginning of the national struggle, but it must be borne in mind that the *amirs* acted individually, as reluctant to subordinate personal power to the greater opportunities of acting in concert with the other paramount chiefs as they were to accept the authority of government.

While the *amirs* had been responsible for peace and security, day-to-day power was usually wielded by the tribal chiefs, or *aghas*, in each valley. With the decline of the *amirs* during the middle years of the nineteenth century, the importance of the *agha* class grew. The source of power of these *aghas* was simple. Mountain villages depended upon strict discipline to ensure their economic viability and political security. The fair allocation and maintenance of agricultural terracing, and the equitable distribution of that most scarce of resources, water, was the responsibility of the *agha*. He alone handled contacts with the outside world, with the neighbouring tribes, with the paramount chief, and with the government itself.

These *aghas* enjoyed confirmation by government of their position, but this was a two-edged weapon. So long as an *agha* enjoyed it, his position both with his own tribe and with neighbouring ones was strengthened. But by the same token he also knew that his position was in part contingent on his doing the government's bidding. Unless he was secure enough to disregard the wishes of government he might well find the government backing one of his more ambitious relatives in an attempt to unseat him. The triangular rivalries between chief A, chief B and government is a long-standing one.

Following the destruction of the emirates in the middle of the century, secular power became more localized and devolved on the tribal *aghas* but in the absence of the mediation previously provided by the *amirs*, there was frequent disorder and conflict between the *aghas*. The vacuum was filled by the growing number of religious *shaykhs*. These *shaykhs* belonged predominantly to two religious brotherhoods, the Qadiriya and the Naqshbandiya, which began to spread rapidly throughout Kurdistan in the early nineteenth century. Popular loyalties, often on a village or tribal basis, were frequently directed towards the *shaykhs* of one order or the other. The spread of both orders was random, dependent upon the charisma of particular *shaykhs*. One valley population might be Qadiri while a neighbouring one might as easily be Naqshbandi. However, both brotherhoods transcended tribal borders and their respective *shaykhs* were thereby frequently able to act as intermediaries in inter-tribal disputes.

Even the poorest boy, if suitably gifted and studious, could become a *shaykh* and thereby acquire political as well as religious power. Shaykhly dynasties rapidly emerged, some connected with an *agha* family, while others rose to prominence from peasant origin. The importance of these *shaykhs* should not be underestimated. It was one of them, Shaykh Ubaydallah of the Naqshbandiya, who first called for an autonomous Kurdish entity in 1878. On that occasion the Ottoman and Qajar authorities found no difficulty in recruiting Kurdish *aghas* who felt threatened by his ambition to help in his defeat. The impact of the *shaykhs* is still felt. It is no accident that three of the greatest nationalist figures in the twentieth century, Mahmud Barzinji, Mulla Mustafa Barzani and Jalal Talabani, all hailed from shaykhly families, as do a number of other Kurdish leaders. Their religious antecedents, although now perhaps of diminishing importance, helped them into positions of secular leadership.

In 1908 the Young Turk revolution promised constitutional reform and representative government. All over the empire the event proved a catalyst in the nascent nationalism espoused by the intellectuals of the various ethnic or cultural groups which were part of the empire. A handful of educated Kurds, frequently the sons of *aghas*, began to form political clubs and even some schools. But such initiatives soon fell foul of inter-family rivalries, of *aghas* who suspected their own position might be undermined, and of the new Ottoman authorities who sensed the beginnings of separatism in such initiatives. In any case, in 1914 any thoughts of a political future for the Kurdish people were swept aside by world war.

The Ottoman Empire was defeated by the Allies in 1918, and an entirely new order was ushered in by this defeat. British forces occupied all Mesopotamia, including Kurdish areas around Sulaymaniya and northwards to the east and north of Mosul. The remaining Arab areas of Syria, Lebanon and Palestine had also been lost to the British and their Hashemite Arab allies.

Allied plans for a peace settlement had included the dismemberment of the remaining Turkish parts of the old empire, allocating parts to Greece, Russia, Italy and France. But the collapse of Tsarist Russia in 1917, and the internal upheaval inside Turkey provoked by the collapse of Ottoman authority rendered such plans impracticable. Nevertheless, a balance was proposed between the strategic interests of France and Britain, which were both concerned primarily with the Arab areas of the old empire, and the "principles of civilization" as proposed by the American President, Woodrow Wilson, in his Fourteen Point Program for World Peace, point twelve of which stated that the non-Turkish minorities of the Ottoman empire should be "assured of an absolute unmolested opportunity of autonomous development". In view of the Armenian genocide that had only just taken place at the hands of the Ottoman authorities, it was an admirable sentiment but one which was likely to excite unrealistic aspirations among the different and intermingled ethnic groups of the old empire. The appeal to ethnicity implicit in point twelve had unsettling implications for people used to living within a multi-ethnic and multi-confessional empire. Many, not least the *aghas*, still felt they were Sunni Muslim subjects of a fundamentally Islamic empire and had no interest in an unpredictable Kurdish entity in which their own status might change for the worse.

The outcome of the Allies' deliberations was the Treaty of Sèvres, signed reluctantly by the Ottomans in August 1920. As regards the Kurds, it envisaged interim autonomy for the predominantly Kurdish areas of Turkey with a view to full independence if the inhabitants of these areas wanted this, including those falling within the British-occupied province of Mosul. The Treaty of Sèvres was the nearest the Kurdish people ever got to statehood. However, while many Kurds today look back ruefully to the failure to implement the treaty, it is more than likely that the proposal would have triggered new conflicts, between the Kurds and those other groups, mostly notably surviving Armenians and also the Assyrian Christians, which aspired to a patch of their own and whose lands overlapped and intermingled with areas where Muslim Kurds predominated. Furthermore, one must ask whether the proposal would not have also triggered conflict between rival Kurdish tribes, each probably bent upon achieving predominance first in its own area, and then in the whole Kurdish region. One can also envisage the tension between *aghas* and others subscribing to the traditional social order who rued the passing of the old order on the one hand, and the "intellectual progressives" who hoped to forge a new nation on the other. Furthermore, given that the outcome would probably have been an entity in which tribal identity remained fundamental, neighbouring states would have found it tempting to entice any dissident and disconsolate *aghas* into rebellion.

In any case, the possibility for such a state never occurred, since a Turkish officer, Mustafa Kemal (Atatürk), repudiated his government's submission at Sèvres, raised the flag of revolt in the name of the Muslims of Anatolia, and drove out the

Christian forces in the west (Greece) and the east (Armenians and Soviets). Many Kurdish *aghas* and their tribes willingly helped Atatürk in this task, in the belief that they were fighting for the Muslim Patrimony in which they had a share. When victory was achieved, however, and the borders with Syria, Iraq and Iran were stabilized, they found their prospects, as with their Kurdish sister communities elsewhere, greatly altered. The one common feature in the new states of Turkey, Syria, Iraq and Iran was the determination of their governments to compel Kurdish submission to essentially non-Kurdish but ethnically nationalist governments. It was a recipe for recurring conflict.

THE KURDS IN TURKEY

Following his victory, in which the Kurds had played their part, it soon became clear that Atatürk did not have in mind the re-establishment of the old order, but the creation of a modern state along European lines with an identity that was explicitly Turkish. In other words, it was a state in which the Kurds – since they were not Turks – could not be citizens in the fullest sense. The abolition of the Sultanate (in 1922) and the Caliphate (in 1924) symbolized the destruction of the world order in which Kurdish society had a place. It challenged the role of the *aghas* as secular leaders, and of the *shaykhs* as religious ones, particularly since the new Republic was explicitly secular. It has only recently come to light that Atatürk toyed with the idea of autonomy for the Kurds in 1923, but the idea was never discussed publicly, let alone implemented.

Instead there were repeated and virulent revolts by the Kurds against the constraints of the new order, in the 1920s and 1930s. But these revolts themselves reflected the fragmented nature of Kurdish society, and that there was as yet no sense of national unity among them. The government's response to these revolts was to execute the leaders, and to raze offending villages, deporting their inhabitants out of the area. Such was the stringency of the government's policy that hundreds of thousands of Kurds perished in these pacifications, particularly in the Dersim (now called Tunceli) region of central eastern Anatolia. Kurdish parts of Turkey have remained under military or semi-military control almost continuously since. Although the presence of Turkish armed forces in eastern Anatolia is often officially ascribed to the defence of NATO's eastern flank, the reality has as much to do with Turkey's unresolved Kurdish question.

In order to increase its control the state endeavoured to incorporate the *agha* class into the ruling élite. This was done mainly by the award of Kurdish communal lands, and investing the *aghas* with village authority. The passage of land into the hands of the *aghas*, throughout all Kurdistan was already well under way before the collapse of the old order on both the Ottoman and Persian sides of the old border.

It is, perhaps, worth noting the importance of land control in the exercise of power. Although on the plains and foothills the Kurdish peasantry, like peasantry elsewhere, traditionally worked on lands held in fief or directly owned by landlords who shared neither common lineage nor common economic interest, in the mountains an entirely different attitude to land tenure had existed. Land belonged to the tribe, and its *agha* was responsible for its equitable use and the settlement of land disputes with neighbouring tribes. So long as tribalism underpinned the political economy of the Kurdish region, such a system was satisfactory. But in the second half of the nineteenth century the system began to disintegrate as government attempted to implement closer control of land rights and use. When land was registered it was usually in the name of the tribal chief, since he handled matters with government. Thus the legal landholder or owner ceased to be the customary one, the tribe, and passed into individual ownership. These *aghas* became increasingly incorporated into the state, and in some cases moved to town, becoming in effect absentee landlords whose sense of tribal obligation weakened over the years.

With the transition in the early years of the century from a subsistence economy to a market one, the process of socio-economic transition accelerated. Increasingly the *agha* class abandoned its economic responsibility to its tribespeople, the former becoming a landlord class, and the latter becoming a landless peasantry.

The process had begun before the First World War and was completed after it. As Turkey's agrarian economy shifted away from subsistence, so the landlord class saw its interest increasingly aligned with the government rather than with the landless or smallholding peasantry. The transition produced a situation by the mid 1960s in Turkey in which over 30 per cent of Kurdish farmlands were owned by 2 per cent of the farming population.

Unlike the Iraqi Kurdish context, and to a lesser extent the Iranian one, Kurdish nationalism in Turkey retained no tribal basis or traditional leadership. Whereas in both Iraq and Iran *aghas* still – to a greater or lesser extent – could identify with nationalist aspirations, the co-option of the acquiescent *aghas* into the ruling establishment of Turkey, and the removal of recalcitrant ones, denied this possibility in Anatolia. Since the state denied Kurds except as "mountain Turks", Kurdish political activists looked to leftist Turkish parties with which to make common cause. From 1969 into the 1970s the proliferation of leftist groups and the support they enjoyed in Turkish Kurdistan led to increasingly violent confrontations with rightist groups which often enjoyed the backing of the police. Following the army coup of 1971, repressive measures were implemented against Kurdish areas, a situation which has persisted.

For many outside observers, it seemed that the Kurdish problem in Turkey was shrinking in the face of relentless suppression by the state. This conclusion, however, must be in doubt. Inside Turkey a number of clandestine and specifically Kurdish parties emerged in the 1970s, most of which invoked the right to self-determination and secession from Turkey. By far the most important and extreme of these is the Kurdistan Workers Party (PKK) which in 1984 embarked upon a campaign of explicit violence against Kurds associated with the state system. As a result a number of *aghas*, landlords and petty officials viewed by PKK as quislings were assassinated, frequently with their entire families. Army and police units sent to reassert state authority were sometimes ambushed. At first most Kurds recoiled in horror at the activities of the PKK, but since 1985 the counter-brutality of state forces, particularly the widespread use of arbitrary arrest and torture, has increased the cooperation or neutrality of large numbers of Kurds in eastern Turkey.

Furthermore, the forced displacement and voluntary migration of many Kurds westwards in search of work has led to the creation of sizeable concentrations of Kurdish expatriate communities as guest workers in western Europe as well as Turkish cities. In such urban environments Kurds acquire a new kind of political culture. Indeed, it is a good deal easier for politically motivated Kurds to evolve and succour the national struggle from the free political climate of western Europe than it is living inside Turkey.

Such factors highlight the international dimension of Turkey's

Kurdish question. Kurdish political associations in western Europe and sympathetic human rights groups have repeatedly drawn attention to Turkey's human rights record particularly with regard to its Kurds. At a time when Turkey wishes to take its membership of the Western bloc beyond NATO into full membership of the European Community, its human rights record will come under increasing scrutiny. In other words, after more than half a century of oppressive policy, it will have to choose whether to persist in its oppression of a minority that constitutes 19 per cent of the population and pay an increasing price in terms of its international political and economic relationships, or whether to risk the dangers of Kurdish irredentism if it decides to liberalize. In fact, liberalization and open discussion of the "Kurdish question" pose a far greater threat to the PKK than the counter-insurgency campaign currently being waged.

Another international dimension should be noted. In 1979 it was reported that 5,000 Turkish Kurds had been recruited to fight alongside Iranian Kurds against the new Islamic regime in Tehran, and that an arms shipment had been intercepted by the army. These reports indicate that after fifty years of oppression a threshold has been crossed. There are now, apparently, an increasing number of Turkish Kurds who feel a common identity with Kurds beyond Turkey's borders. The danger the state faces, if it fails to satisfy Kurds within national life, is of increasing pan-Kurdish solidarity. Such pan-Kurdish feeling received a significant fillip when Turkey reluctantly accepted Iraqi Kurdish refugees fleeing the onslaught of Iraqi forces in August and September 1988. However much the authorities may have wished to keep their own Kurds physically separated from Iraq's fugitive ones, and however much the government may have tried to use its involuntary hospitality to these refugees as evidence of its basically humanitarian attitude even to Kurds, the event has reminded both Turkish and Iraqi Kurds that they share a common predicament in which a shared solution may be more productive than those they have sought within their own international boundaries in the past.

THE KURDS IN IRAN

Although the government of Iran has never employed the same level of brutality against its own Kurds, it has always been implacably opposed to any suggestion of Kurdish separatism. With greater reason than Turkey, it feared that other large minorities inside Iran would also clamour for autonomy: for example its Arab, Turkic and Baluchi minorities. Unlike Turkey, however, Iran has generally allowed its Kurds to use the Kurdish language and to give open expression to its culture. It must be borne in mind, however, that Kurds are probably only 10 per cent of the population, far lower than the demographic share in Turkey or Iraq.

Following his accession to power after the First World War, Reza Shah held together the diffuse ethnic components of modern Iran by the incorporation of pliant chiefs, the extirpation of rebels and the forcible settlement of some of the large nomadic tribes. The danger of fragmentation in modern Iran became evident in the Second World War when Soviet and British troops occupied western Iran to prevent Reza Shah from giving material expression to his outward sympathy for Germany. Under Soviet influence, both the Azerbaijanis and the Kurds of north-west Iran proclaimed independent republics in December 1945.

The Kurdish republic of Mahabad was pitifully small, unable to incorporate the Kurdish towns of Saqqiz, Sanandaj and Kermanshah to the south, which fell inside the Anglo-American zone, and unable to attract the tribes outside Mahabad itself to the nationalist cause. The chiefs of these tribes were reluctant to jeopardize the relationship they had been encouraged to cultivate with Tehran during the 1930s. As a result, when the Soviets withdrew from Iran in December 1946, government forces were able to enter Mahabad unopposed.

Like the Treaty of Sèvres, the Mahabad Republic is regarded wistfully by many Kurds as a moment of great promise. But against the transient moment of genuine nationalist sentiment under the leadership of the new Kurdistan Democratic Party of Iran (KDPI) must be set less promising factors. Barely one-third of Iranian Kurds fell inside the republic, and of these a large number, perhaps a majority, remained passively neutral. Most, tribal Kurds still had no interest in Kurdish nationalism. Beyond the republic few Kurds demonstrated their willingness to fight on its behalf. More, indeed, entered Mahabad as auxiliaries of the government forces at its downfall. Finally, the fickle behaviour of adjacent powers (in this case the Soviet Union, but on previous occasions in Anatolia, Iran) was yet to be fully understood by Kurdish political leaders.

Kurdish nationalism went underground after the fall of Mahabad. It continued to be perceived as a threat not only by the government but also by the Kurdish landlord class, into whose hands three-quarters of the lands of Kurdistan now passed, leaving only some 2 per cent of what a century earlier must all have been tribally held. In the late 1960s a sporadic guerrilla campaign was conducted by KDPI from Iraqi territory, but this was brought to an unhappy end by the intervention of the Iraqi KDP at the bidding of Tehran (which was supplying it with war materials for its own war against Baghdad), an unfortunate precedent which continued to damage relations between the Kurds of Iran and Iraq into the 1980s.

The downfall of the Shah in 1979 gave the Iranian Kurds a real opportunity to negotiate a new relationship with Tehran. Although one or two tribal chiefs attempted to seize the initiative, they quickly found that their own constituency was not strong enough to throw off state control without the help of KDPI, unquestionably the strongest Kurdish political grouping. KDPI was emphatically opposed to tribalism in its nationalist policy. Its popular base confirmed the value of quiet solid work done at the grassroots level over years of suppression by the state security apparatus. Its only real challenger was Komala, the Kurdish Communist Party, which enjoyed a following on account of its literacy and health work, in spite of its "progressive" and atheistic flavour.

However, the Islamic revolutionary government was bound to reject the Kurdish request for autonomy because of the danger that autonomy for the Kurds would excite similar demands from other minorities, threatening the break-up of the country. At an ideological level also, the Islamic Republic was necessarily predicated upon the unity of the Islamic community, and was unwilling to grant special status for an ethnic group. It is worth noting in this context, that the minority of Kurds who are Shi'i (and live in southern Kurdistan) vigorously rejected autonomy, preferring direct rule from Shi'i Tehran.

During the summer of 1979 the Iranian Army reasserted its control over dissident Kurdish towns but was less successful in the countryside. In December Tehran tried to settle its differences with the KDPI and other Kurdish nationalist groups with the offer of the right to constitute a local Provincial Council and certain rights as a Sunni (there being relatively few other Sunnis in Iran apart from the Kurds) community. For the Kurds, however, such an offer fell short of the autonomy they sought, and they rejected it, a decision they must subsequently have regretted.

Iran's Kurds were able to take advantage of Iraq's surprise attack on Iran less than a year later to secure a substantial part of Iranian Kurdistan, but by 1983 Iran had not only regained territories captured by Iraq but had virtually pushed KDPI out of Iran except for Hawraman. KDPI was reduced to desultory guerrilla warfare, much of it after nightfall, when the army had greater difficulty maintaining control.

With the end of the Iran–Iraq war, Iran's Kurds are in as poor a position as ever in their struggle for a greater say over their communal affairs. Tehran has dealt severely with members of Komala, executing those who have fallen into its hands, presumably on the grounds that communists are by definition apostates. It has been more tolerant with KDPI, partly because the leadership – at the cost of a split in the party – has sought an accommodation with Tehran. Nevertheless, in July 1989 KDPI's veteran leader, Abd al-Rahman Ghassemlou was assassinated during secret talks with government representatives from Tehran in Vienna. Almost certainly this was the work of Iranian government agents, possibly to prevent Ghassemlou soliciting Western, particularly US support, for his struggle with Tehran.

THE KURDS IN IRAQ

With a higher proportion of the national population (23 per cent) than in either Turkey or Iran, the Kurds have repeatedly challenged state authority in Iraq. While Iraqi Kurds have had good reason to claim a greater say in their own and national affairs, the government in Baghdad can also claim it has gone further than its neighbours in offering formal autonomy. However, the level of distrust on both sides has so far destroyed any progress in this direction, and led instead to savage conflicts in which the Kurdish civil population has been the primary victim.

When Britain captured Mesopotamia from the Turks in 1918 it was unsure what to do with the Kurdish mountainous areas on the north and eastern borders. Its uncertainty was compounded by the Kurdish claim to Kirkuk, which was a mixed city, but set in a predominantly Kurdish hinterland. Because of its substantial oil deposits Britain (or any other authority in Baghdad) could not conceivably abandon control of this valuable area. Among the Kurds themselves there was deep disunity. Some of the tribes to the north of the Greater Zab river wished to be reunited with the Kurdish tribes north of the new Iraqi–Turkish border. This reflected the major dialect divide between those speaking Kurmanji Kurdish (Turkey and northern Iraq) and those speaking Sorani Kurdish south of the Greater Zab (eastern Iraq). Furthermore, while some tribes looked forward to complete freedom and independence of action (in their eyes a return to the freedom under the Ottomans until the nineteenth century), others – who had profited by helping extend government authority among lawless neighbours – looked forward to cooperation with the government in Baghdad. There was an economic argument against Kurdish separatism: beyond the self-sufficiency of subsistence the Kurdish population related economically to the market towns and cities of the Tigris valley, which were predominantly Arab or Turkoman.

Finally, there was broad geographical disunity among the Iraqi Kurds. When Britain sought reactions to its proposal of making the Hashemite Amir Faysal King of Iraq, the Kurds of Mosul and Arbil favoured the idea. The Kurds of Kirkuk, however, demurred, finally accepting the idea only on condition they formed a separate province which would *not* be incorporated with the Kurds of Sulaymaniya. The Kurds of the latter area were wholly hostile to accepting Faysal as King of Iraq.

The British plan to control Kurdistan through its tribal leaders quickly came unstuck. Within months, Shaykh Mahmud Barzinji rejected British authority, and repeatedly did so whenever the British were rash enough to release him from detention. Meanwhile, further north, Kurdish chiefs responded to the call of the Kemalist Turks to throw off British authority and join in the new Turkish republic.

It was not long before Britain found it easier to administer Kurdistan directly. Despite its own pledge to allow the Kurds to use their own language, both in schools and in the local administration, Britain did not include these pledges in the Anglo–Iraqi Treaty of 1930 whereby Iraq became an independent Arab state (in 1932). During the 1930s Barzinji and a growing number of other chiefs and more significantly perhaps, a growing number of urban Kurds, began to demand greater freedom.

Easily the most important of Barzinji's supporters was Mulla Mustafa Barzani of the northern area of Bahdinan. Barzani is an interesting character, not only on account of his intrinsic importance but also because his career highlighted the internal contradictions of Kurdish nationalism. From the mid 1930s until his death in 1979 his name became synonymous with the Kurdish struggle for independence. His grandfather had been a prominent *shaykh* of the Naqshbandi order. Mulla Mustafa combined the secular authority of an *agha* with the religious aura he also inherited from his father and grandfather, so that, given his charismatic character, it was not difficult to rally the tribes of the Kurmanji speaking parts of Iraqi Kurdistan, and then extend his appeal beyond. Driven with his forces from Iraq in 1945, Barzani played an important part in the defence of Mahabad before retreating into the Soviet Union.

Barzani was given amnesty by Brigadier Qasim, following the latter's *coup d'état* in 1958, and for a while they worked amicably together. Barzani was able to use Qasim's support to settle scores with mutual enemies, neighbouring "anti-government" tribes. These "anti-government" tribes, it should be noted, were in fact supporters of the old Hashemite regime, and some of them had been in feud with the Barzani clan for thirty or more years. Barzani was also able to secure his own predominance in the KDP, which he then persuaded Qasim to legalize.

Qasim demanded favours in return. In addition to the punishment of mutual Kurdish enemies, he used Barzani to assist in the suppression of anti-Qasim insurgents in Mosul in 1959, and of Turcoman in Kirkuk. By 1960 Qasim began to recognize that his failure to maintain a Kurdish counterweight to Barzani was mistaken, and he quietly began to arm some of the latter's enemies. But it was too late. Barzani soon got wind of what was happening and relations between the two rapidly deteriorated through 1960–1. Qasim was now in a weak position. Barzani could count on many *aghas* to support him against Qasim, including some old pro-Hashemite chiefs, and many others who stood to lose their land in Qasim's widely publicized agrarian reforms designed to break the power of the landlords.

However successful he was against Baghdad, it was not long before Barzani fell out with Jalal Talabani and Ibrahim Ahmad, the intellectual leadership of the KDP, urban leftists who wanted to build an ideological framework in which to foster a form of nationalism that would make tribal politics obsolete. Barzani's whole style ran counter to their consultative approach, but appealed far more to the mountain Kurds who formed the backbone of the Kurdish forces. Inevitably it was Barzani who came to personify the KDP.

The 1960s were characterized by repeated conflict between Barzani and the various regimes in Baghdad. In 1968 the Ba'th Party resumed power through a coup (it had briefly and precariously held power in 1963) and made the conclusion of a stable peace with the Kurds a central plank of its domestic policy. Barzani was deeply sceptical, particularly since he knew his rival Talabani was far more likely to appeal to the Ba'th as representative of the Kurdish people. However, he need not have worried. The Ba'th thought Talabani was insufficiently strong to bring peace to Kurdistan. Willy nilly, Barzani was their man.

The negotiations for autonomy, however, proved fruitless despite an initial agreement between Barzani and Baghad. Many Kurds believed that in practice what the Ba'th was offering would be a mere fig leaf for real autonomy. The almost complete absence of trust led both sides to act with duplicity. Barzani started to raise his demands, as Iran, Israel and the CIA all egged him on with the provision of military hardware. The Ba'th found it harder to bring negotiations to an acceptable conclusion, it made repeated but clumsy attempts to assassinate Barzani. But it also began to believe that Barzani did not actually want a negotiated settlement, since a regularized political settlement might leave him and his tribal style of leadership without a role to play. At the beginning of 1974 things came to a head with the nationalization of Kirkuk oil production, and Barzani's demand for "proportional distribution of oil revenues". Baghdad announced an autonomy law unilaterally, giving the KDP fourteen days in which to accept it – autonomy, one might say, by ultimatum.

Barzani raised the banner of revolt, and the Iraqi army began a major assault on KDP-controlled Kurdistan. The Iraqi army was unexpectedly successful, and it was clear by the end of summer 1974 that the KDP could only survive with massive Iranian support. By the winter Iraqi troops were close to the Iranian border, but the use of Iranian ground to air missiles and long-range artillery against Iraqi forces meant that any final offensive to drive Barzani out of Iraq threatened direct and formal war with Iran. It was something Baghdad could not afford, and in March 1975 it ceded to Tehran its claimed share of the Shatt al Arab waterway, a long running dispute between the two countries. With the withdrawal of Iranian support, Barzani's forces collapsed within a week. It was a major defeat from which Barzani himself never recovered. He died in the United States in 1979.

Kurdish nationalists were deeply divided over Barzani's decision to abandon the struggle after his defeat in 1975, and Talabani was able to make use of this division to start a new party, the Patriotic Union of Kurdistan (PUK), to carry on the struggle for Kurdish autonomy, from the border marshes of Turkey.

When the Shah was overthrown in 1979 both the PUK and the KDP, now led by Mulla Mustafa's son Mas'ud, competed for the new regime's favour. The latter was successful, partly because of the long-standing relationship with Tehran, but more practically because Mas'ud was willing to support Tehran against its own Kurdish insurgents led by KDPI. Mas'ud held KDPI responsible for the desecration of his father's grave at Ushnavia in Iranian Kurdistan. As a matter of principle, PUK refused to act against the interest of Iranian Kurds whom it considered to be an intrinsic part of the Kurdish struggle.

Iraq's surprise attack on Iran in September 1980 gave Iraq's Kurds a unique opportunity to obtain by war what they had failed to achieve in 1974. A number of Kurdish nationalist parties, of which KDP and PUK in Iraq, and Komala and KDPI in Iran were the most significant, all tried to exploit the situation in order to drive governmental forces out of Kurdistan. The KDP was able to capitalize on Iran's counter-offensive against Iraq in 1983 to capture Hajj Omran and border area in the north of the country.

PUK, however, unsuccessfully supported KDPI against Iranian forces, while itself conducting a war single-handed against Iraqi forces on the west side of the border in the area of Panjwin. By summer 1983 PUK, in contrast with Iranian-backed KDP, was seriously concerned about its strategic future, in spite of its own modest success in pinning down large numbers of Iraqi troops. In May Turkey had demonstrated its willingness to act on Iraq's as well as its own behalf by sending troops across the border to destroy Kurdish bases (used by Turkish as well as Iraqi Kurds). If the Kurdish national movement found itself fighting on three fronts at once, it could not possibly become strong enough to negotiate a new deal for the Kurdish people.

The war at this juncture was also going badly for Baghdad with a high number of desertions from the army, and Talabani was able to commence secret negotiations with a view to securing a substantial autonomy agreement. Both sides were pleased with the ceasefire that ensued in December 1983. But it was not destined to last. PUK demanded more than Baghdad was prepared to concede. More importantly, Western alarm at the prospect of an Iranian victory led to substantial military support for Baghdad. By March 1984 Baghdad no longer felt so urgently the need to parley with PUK. Furthermore, in October Turkey reportedly warned Baghdad that if it came to an agreement with the PUK, it would cut the vital Iraqi oil pipeline that ran through Turkey to the Mediterranean.

Hostilities between Baghdad and PUK recommenced, but for PUK the whole episode had been a damaging setback. Many Kurds were dismayed by its secret negotiations – believing it to be surrenderist at a moment when the Kurdish national movement's prospects had never been brighter. PUK's loss was KDP's gain, and by spring 1985 the two parties were probably of equal strength after some diminishment of PUK and a resurgence in the KDP. Each controlled large swathes approximating to the two dialect areas, KDP the northern (Kurmanji) areas and PUK the Sorani-speaking areas south of the Greater Zab.

Throughout the period a bitter relationship had persisted between the Barzanis of KDP and Talabani of PUK. In view of their common struggle and the slowdown in Iran's offensives, it was a feud they could no longer afford to have. PUK was accepted back into the Iraqi opposition forces' fold during 1986, and in early 1987 a formal Iraqi Kurdistan Front (IKF) was formed, comprising KDP, PUK and three smaller parties. That year and the early part of 1988 saw the high tide of Kurdish military success, with the capture of a number of Kurdish towns, culminating in the capture of Halabja in March 1988.

There seemed to be a real prospect of Kurdish forces driving the Iraqi army out of the mountains altogether. But Baghdad demonstrated its willingness to respond ruthlessly against the Kurdish military threat, with a gas attack on Halabja, which left approximately 6,000 inhabitants dead. It was clear that Baghdad had a weapon against which all the martial skill and valour of the Kurdish forces could be of no avail. When Iran, which by this time had run out of steam, agreed to a ceasefire in August, Baghdad turned its forces onto Kurdistan where it routed the Kurdish forces in the space of a fortnight, by gas attack, artillery, air strikes and armoured troop assault.

By the autumn 1988 the IKF was in a worse situation than ever, with mass deportations, resettlement of populations and the razing of mountain villages in full swing. Reportedly over three-quarters of Kurdistan's villages and hamlets have been destroyed with a view to resettling their erstwhile inhabitants in suburbs around large centres like Sulaymaniya and Arbil, or in "model villages", in practice, state supervised settlements. This policy was originally commenced following the end of the 1974–5 war.

Neither KDP nor PUK have abandoned the struggle, but there must be a serious question about their military and political future. The prospect has seldom been so gloomy for Kurdish nationalists, for the Iraqi Kurdish people as a whole have suffered during this war as never before, and Kurdish society (as it was known in the mountains) may never recover.

One of the questions that must be asked is the effect these events will have on those Kurds who support Baghdad. For both in the 1974–5 and 1980–8 wars Baghdad was able to call on certain Kurdish tribes, for example the Zibari and Miri Shaqlawa, to act as auxiliaries to the army. The proportion willing to act for Baghdad has been diminishing over the years. Will the number now willing to cooperate with the state increase as a result of the nationalists' defeat, or will the wholesale destruction of much of Kurdish society intensify the sense of nationalism and erode old tribal political traditions?

THE PROSPECTS

It is impossible to believe that Kurdish nationalism is finally defeated, or that the respective governments may now rest in the knowledge that they have nationalist aspirations firmly under control. Iraq has now done what Turkey did to its Kurds fifty years ago. But the razing of villages and mass relocation has not brought an end to the Kurdish movement in Turkey. On the contrary, despite the unpromising prospects, it is the Kurds of Turkey who are the most wholeheartedly in favour of independence rather than autonomy. Furthermore, there are modest signs that Kurdish nationalism in Turkey is growing, as a result of increased awareness of state manipulation and perhaps more significantly the growing awareness that they share a common problem with the Kurds of Iraq, some of whom are now refugees in their country.

As "pan-Kurdish" nationalism begins to grow, so one also senses the recession of the tribal loyalties which still dominated much of the Kurdish scene as late as the 1960s. Tribalism has not yet disappeared, as Baghdad's ability to call on Kurdish tribal auxiliaries indicates. But it does currently seem to be in retreat since its social function is so greatly diminished. Ironically the forced relocation of Kurdish villages may well accelerate that process and advance a more proletarian form of nationalism which will prove harder for government to contain.

In all three countries the Kurdish story is by no means over, but one must doubt whether Kurdish nationalism can ever prevail against three hostile governments willing to apply ruthless methods to contain the challenge. One must equally doubt the capacity of the governments of the region to achieve the stability all three need. The Kurds in each country will remain a potential cat's-paw for those wishing to foment unrest in the region, whether it be one of these three governments acting against another, or whether it is an external contestant, like Israel or the United States.

If there is to be a solution other than a grumbling continuum of the conflict – possibly with urban warfare as a new expression of Kurdish frustration – the three governments of the region must be persuaded (and helped) to evolve a more fruitful relationship with their Kurdish minorities. Suppression may commend itself as a short-term answer, but in the longer term the substantial Kurdish communities will only be mollified and reconciled to their situation if they feel they are being reasonably dealt with.

One need only look at the size of the Kurdish community by the late 1980s, even by a conservative estimate, to recognize the need for a more constructive approach to their predicament than these governments have so far pursued (see Table 1.1). Whatever one may think about the nation-state system fostered in the Middle East by the Great Powers in 1918, it is unlikely to disappear in the foreseeable future. The creation of a state for the Kurds, even if it were a possibility, would be unlikely to solve the problem, for minorities in their midst (for example Turcomans, Assyrians and Yazidis in Iraq) might themselves clamour for independent statelets. The isolation of different ethnic and religious communities can hardly produce solutions for the fundamental problems of inter-community existence which have bedevilled the Middle East since 1918.

Somehow, a balance must be found between state and community requirements. If the Kurdish communities remain disconsolate because they are denied adequate expression and control over their internal affairs, the political and economic future of the states they inhabit, particularly Turkey and Iraq, is bound to be impaired.

Table 1.1 Size of Kurdish communities, late 1980s

Country	Percentage of population	No. of Kurds (millions)
Iran	10	5.0
Iraq	23	3.9
Turkey	19	9.6
Syria	8	0.9
USSR		0.3
Estimated total for 1987		19.7

If the international community is to grasp the nettle, it must seek ways in which to support the sovereignty and stability of Iran, Iraq and Turkey, but also use either carrot or stick to persuade them to allow their Kurds the community freedoms that will in themselves diminish the appeal that nationalism currently holds for the Kurdish people.

Chapter 2

Kurdish society, ethnicity, nationalism and refugee problems

Martin van Bruinessen

Over the past years, we have seen large numbers of people fleeing Kurdistan. The Gulf War and the Kurdish armed rebellions in Iraqi and Persian Kurdistan (or rather, the violent repression of the Kurdish movement for autonomy) have dislodged hundreds of thousands of Kurds. Those who succeeded in crossing international borders became visible as political refugees; the numbers of less visible internal refugees and deportees are probably much higher. Apart from the dramatic events of 1991, the only recent instance of flight from Kurdistan which received much media coverage took place in August 1988 after the Iraqi-launched chemical attacks on Kurdish-held valleys in northern Iraq when tens of thousands fled across the Turkish border. Much larger numbers of Iraqi Kurds have fled into Iran during the past few years. In both cases the refugees include political activists and guerrilla fighters, although the vast majority are displaced villagers. Numerous Kurdish political activists from Iran and Turkey have fled Kurdistan and sought asylum in western (and, to a lesser extent, eastern) European countries.

War and political persecution by governments are not the only reasons why people have fled. Most of the tens of thousands of Turkish Kurds who have applied for asylum in western Europe are commonly thought of as "economic" refugees, not fleeing political persecution but seeking economic betterment. It is true that the relative economic underdevelopment of Kurdistan and the relatively high birth rate have resulted, in all countries concerned, in a considerable labour migration away from Kurdistan. Among the "push" factors in this migration process, however, the economic motive is only one, and in many cases it is partly conditioned by the political situation. This is most clearly so in the case of those belonging to religious minorities such as the Yazidis and the Syrian Christians, who claim persecution by their Muslim neighbours, or Alevis who feel threatened by the Sunni majority. But many Sunni Kurds too have felt forced to flee from various forms of local oppression or political conflict.

It would be fallacious to consider the Kurdish problem simply as a conflict between Kurds and Arabs or Turks, or between Kurds and central governments, although the rhetoric on both sides may give that impression. Kurdistan is a complex society, with many internal conflicts and rivalries, which tend to be exacerbated both by economic changes and political conflict at the state level. Local power relations and conflicts have become linked up with those at the state and inter-state levels, and various forms of intensive cooperation between local power holders and the state apparatus (or the Kurdish movement, another state-like actor) have developed. These make it difficult to make a sharp distinction between persecution by the state and purely local forms of oppression.

KURDISH SOCIETY: HETEROGENEITY, STRATIFICATION, MINORITIES

For the past few centuries at least, the Kurds have had a general awareness of being a separate people, distinct from Persians, Turks and Arabs as well as from the various Christian groups living in their midst. There was also, at least among the literate, a quite concrete idea of who were and who were not Kurds, and of where they lived. This awareness of identity and unity is surprising, given the many things that divided (and still divide) the Kurds. Language and religion are, to many Kurds, essential aspects of their identities, but neither do all Kurds adhere to the same religion, nor do they speak the same language. Kurdish society is highly stratified, a tribal elite dominating settled peasants. Conflicts between tribes and exploitative relations between the dominant and subject strata have long divided Kurdish society. Conflicting interests have always prevented collective action, even if only by all Kurds of a particular district. Furthermore, there are various non-Kurdish minorities living among the Kurds and tied to them by intricate networks of social and economic relations.

Linguistic diversity

The Kurds speak a large number of different dialects, many of which are not mutually intelligible. The chief dialect groups, gradually shading into one another, are *Kurmanji*, or northern Kurdish, spoken in Turkey and the northernmost parts of Iraqi and Persian Kurdistan, and *Sorani*, spoken in southern Kurdistan. Both Sorani and Kurmanji have a written literary tradition. Besides these dialects of Kurdish proper, two other Iranian languages are spoken in Kurdistan; *Zaza* in the north west, in a large area north and west of Diyarbakir, and *Gurani* in various parts of southern Kurdistan. Zaza and Gurani speakers consider themselves (and are considered by others) as Kurds, in spite of minor cultural differences with the Kurdish-speaking Kurds.[1] As a result of forced or voluntary assimilation, moreover, there are quite a few Kurds who speak no or only a poor Kurdish, preferring to use Turkish, Arabic, or Persian. And in each of the countries concerned, the spoken Kurdish shows, in vocabulary and even in syntax, a strong influence of the dominant official language.

The influence of the states into which the various parts of Kurdistan have been incorporated is not restricted to this impact on the Kurdish language alone. The different educational systems of these countries, their mass media and their distinct political cultures have inevitably left deep imprints on Kurdish culture as well. Iraqi Kurds are Iraqis as well as Kurds, and often find it easier to relate to other Iraqis than to Turkish Kurds. The political discourse in each part of Kurdistan is different, and so are the forms of political action.

Religious diversity

If language can thus hardly be thought of as the real basis of the ethnic unity of the Kurds, religion is not a major uniting factor either. The vast majority of the Kurds, it is true, are Sunni Muslims, adhering to the Shafi'i *madhhab*, but there are numerous Kurds of other religious persuasions. The Sunni Kurds, moreover, differ widely in the degree of their devotion and in ritual practices. Traditional religious education, in the *madrasa*, was rather widespread until the beginning of this century, and may have contributed to Kurdish self-awareness. The students here studied, besides religious texts in Arabic and Persian, also works by Kurdish authors, including the "national" poet Ahmad Khani and the mystic Mulla Ahmad Jaziri (Melê Cizirî). These two seventeenth-century poets were later adopted by nationalist intellectuals as their precursors, and their work has inspired much national pride.

Important to note is the popularity, among the Sunni majority, of mystical orders (*tariqa*), notably the *Naqshbandiyya* and *Qadiriyya*, and the almost superstitious veneration in which the shaykhs of these orders used to be held by the peasantry and urban lower classes (van Bruinessen 1978, pp. 249–339). Several shaykhs acquired great economic and political powers, surpassing those of many tribal chiefs. In the early period of Kurdish nationalism, roughly 1880–1930, these mystical orders played a crucial part in popular mobilization. The orders were independent of the tribal structure with its rivalries and feuds, and could therefore coordinate action even by traditional rivals. Most leaders or figureheads of the Kurdish rebellions during this period were *tariqa* shaykhs.

In Kemalist Turkey, both the *madrasa* and the *tariqa* were banned, being obstacles to modernization and Westernization. The oppression of religious expression and of Kurdish ethnicity there strengthened the association of Kurdishness with Sunni Islam (at least among the Sunni Kurds). Both *madrasa* and *tariqa* continued to function underground, though on a small scale. In all parts of Kurdistan, secular education has by and large replaced the traditional religious education. Though never banned in Iran and Iraq, the *madrasas* there now have a marginal function at best. The mystical orders too, have declined much in importance, although in all parts of Kurdistan there are still families of *tariqa* shaykhs that command great political influence.

By a rough estimate, only 80 per cent of the Kurds are Sunnis. In the southernmost part of Kurdistan, among the Kurds of Khaniqin, Mandali and Kermanshah, not Sunni Islam but "Twelver" (*Ithna'ashari*) Shi'a is the dominant religion. This includes the *Fayli* Kurds living in Baghdad (see Morad in this volume). There is a large Kurdish enclave in Iran's north-eastern province of Khorasan, all of whom are *Ithna'ashari* Shi'is too (van Bruinessen 1978, pp. 215–20). Unlike the Shi'is of southern Kurdistan, they never played any part in the Kurdish movement.

Furthermore there are numerous heterodox minority groups and sects among the Kurds (for a survey see Müller 1967). A quite significant minority, in Turkish Kurdistan, are known as Alevis. This is a blanket name for various syncretistic, extremist Shi'i sects, which have in common the deification of Ali and various beliefs of pre-islamic Turkish and Iranian origins (Mélikoff 1982). An important sub-group of Kurdish Alevis, those of Dersim (Tunceli), speak Zaza, but there are also numerous Kurmanji and even more Turkish-speaking Alevis (and most of the Zaza, it should be noted, are Sunni). In the Ottoman Empire, the Alevis were often persecuted, both for their heterodoxy and because they were suspected of pro-Iranian sympathies. This is the reason why many Alevi communities chose to live in inaccessible mountain villages, relatively isolated from their Sunni neighbours. Since the 1950s many have migrated to the towns, where they compete for housing and jobs with the local Sunnis. Since then there have in many central Turkish towns been increasingly violent conflicts between Sunnis and Alevis (about which more below). There are no official statistics on the Alevis, but altogether (Turkish and Kurdish Alevis) they must number at least 4 or 5 million. Recent estimates vary from 4.5 to 18 million (Andrews 1989, p. 57).

A similar sect is that of the Ahl-e Haqq or Kaka'i in southern Kurdistan (speaking Sorani and Gurani dialects, while in Iraq there are also Turcoman Kaka'i). Ali, to them, is only one in a series of divine incarnations, the most important among which is the founder of the sect, Sultan Sahak.[2] This sect emerged among the Guran, and has since spread all over Iran and parts of Iraq. Kurds are no longer the majority of its devotees. Like the Alevis, the Ahl-e Haqq often live in an uneasy relationship with their orthodox Muslim neighbours, who in this case include both Sunnis and Shi'is. The Shah's government exploited this religious animosity by enlisting many members of the Ahl-e Haqq Qalkhani tribe into its paramilitary border police. These could be relied on not to make common cause with the Sunni Kurdish tribes.

Another syncretistic sect, even further removed from orthodox Islam, is that of the *Yazidis*, who are often incorrectly called "devil-worshippers". The Yazidis seem initially to have been an extremist Sunni sect, and later to have incorporated many elements of old Iranian and Anatolian religions, including sun worship and belief in reincarnation. The Peacock Angel (*Malak Tawus*) whom they worship may be identified with Satan, but is to them not the lord of evil as he is to Muslims and Christians.[3] The

Yazidis speak Kurmanji, but some of the more pious Muslims nevertheless refuse to recognize them as Kurds because of their religious peculiarities. In the seventeenth century, the Yazidis were still quite numerous, but their numbers have dwindled due to physical oppression, forced conversion and emigrations. There are still four major regional clusters of Yazidis: in the Kurd Dagh ("Kurdish mountain") district north of Aleppo, in the Sinjar mountains on the Syrian–Iraqi border, in the Shaykhan district north of Mosul, and in the south-western Caucasus. In Turkish Kurdistan, only a few pockets persist, mainly in the provinces Urfa, Mardin and Siirt. Large numbers of Yazidis from Turkey, feeling persecuted by their Muslim neighbours and not protected by the state, have during the past decades sought refuge in West Germany (Schneider 1984; Andrews 1989, pp. 118–20). The Yazidi communities in the Soviet Caucasian republics are the descendants of nineteenth-century refugees from west and central Kurdistan, and probably make up the majority of the Kurds there (Guest 1987).

Non-Kurdish minorities

Living amidst the Kurds, we find various Christian communities, of different languages and creeds. The most numerous of these used to be the Armenians. These traditionally had their own church, the Gregorian, but by the end of the nineteenth century many of them had, through the efforts of European missionaries and promises of European protection, converted to Roman Catholicism or Protestantism. Greater Armenia, where the largest concentration of Armenians lived, coincides with present eastern Turkey (or northern Kurdistan). The majority of Armenians were peasants, but most of the craftsmen and many traders in this region were Armenians too. The relations between Kurds and Armenians were usually politically unequal, the latter often being economically exploited and at times violently oppressed by Kurdish chieftains. In order to avoid oppression, unknown numbers of Armenians in the late nineteenth century became Muslims and opted for a Kurdish identity. A European visiting the Dersim district (present Tunceli) in the early twentieth century noted that many of the local Alevis or Qizilbash were in fact recently converted Armenians (Molyneux-Seel 1914).

Due to the mass deportation and massacres of 1915 (during which some Kurds participated in the killings, while others attempted to save their Armenian neighbours' lives), very few Armenians are left in Kurdistan now. Most of the survivors of the massacres left either for the Caucasus, where an Armenian republic was established, or emigrated to Europe or America. There are still small communities in the towns of Diyarbakir and Derik (near Mardin), and a few remaining Armenian villages (see Andrews 1989, pp. 127–8). I have, moreover, come across small groups of half-Kurdicized Armenians in villages south of Siirt; they were kurdophone and called themselves Kurds without attempting to hide their Armenian origins.

Smaller Christian minorities are the "Syrians" (Suryani) of the Tur Abdin district east of Mardin (Anschütz 1984), and the Assyrians of Central Kurdistan (Joseph 1961; Chevalier 1985), both of whom speak Aramaic dialects. As in the case of the Armenians, many members of these communities have also converted from their original churches (the Jacobite and Nestorian, respectively) to Protestantism or Catholicism. The Uniate Assyrians, most of whom live in the districts north of Mosul, are called *Kaldani* "Chaldaeans". The Nestorians used to be concentrated in Hakkari near the present Turkish–Iraqi border; tribally organized and fierce warriors, they formed political alliances with Kurdish tribes against rival Assyrian and Kurdish tribes. Since the mid nineteenth century, massacres and wars have reduced their numbers and dispersed them over northern Iraq and the neighbouring districts of Iran. Many of the survivors have fled Kurdistan altogether for Baghdad, Tehran or the United States. Until the early twentieth century, the Suryani of Tur Abdin also took part in Kurdish tribal alliances and oppositions and held their own quite well. They suffered much in the First World War, however, and many left the Tur Abdin for French-occupied Syria in the following years. Migration to Istanbul and, from the 1960s on, western Europe, in search of employment and greater security, further drained the resilience of the communities remaining in the Tur Abdin.

Outside the heartlands of these various Christian groups, small numbers of each (and even smaller numbers of Greek Orthodox Christians) are found in the towns throughout Kurdistan. There also used to be small Jewish minorities, mainly urban, throughout Kurdistan, but almost all of these have left for Israel. Over the past century, all non-Muslim communities in Kurdistan have very significantly declined in numbers due to massacres, flight and, to a lesser extent perhaps, religious conversion. The position of those remaining has become precarious, and the Suryani and Yazidis of Turkey, at least, have apparently decided that their communities have no future there, and are making efforts for all their members to move to western Europe. A result is that Kurdistan has become more homogeneous and that a nation state based on Kurdish ethnicity has become at least conceivable. This very idea, however, forebodes numerous new potential conflicts.

Finally, there are numerous pockets of non-Kurdish Muslims in Kurdistan. In Iraqi Kurdistan there is an entire string of Turcoman towns and villages, including the important town of Kirkuk (which forms one of the arguments in Turkish irredentist claims on northern Iraq). In Turkish Kurdistan, there are important Arab enclaves in Mardin and Siirt and various old Turkish communities in many towns (speaking Azeri dialects mostly). There are also small pockets of Caucasian and Central Asian refugees, the oldest of them Qarapapakh and Circassians, the most recent Turcoman and Kirghiz from Afghanistan, resettled in the 1980s (near Diyarbakir and Van, respectively). The relations between these minorities and their Kurdish neighbours have also been very tense at times, especially during periods of rising Kurdish nationalism, which they perceived as a threat. In 1959, a political conflict in Kirkuk gave rise to heavy bloodshed between Kurds and Turcomans, and in revolutionary Iran a similar incident took place in 1979 between the (Shi'i) Qarapapakh of Naqadeh and (Sunni) Kurds of the neighbourhood (van Bruinessen 1981).

Social stratification, tribal and non-tribal population

The complexity of this ethnic-religious mosaic is further compounded by an intricate social and political stratification, which can only be sketched in its barest outlines here (cf. Barth 1953; van Bruinessen 1978, 1989b). Before effective central government control was established all over Kurdistan, nomadic and semi-nomadic (transhumant) tribes were the militarily, and therefore politically, dominant social category in the countryside. They commonly dominated communities of settled peasants, who were not tribally organized, Christians as well as Kurdish-speaking Muslims, who were often the virtual serfs of the tribal chieftains. The larger and more powerful a tribe was, the more hierarchical its internal structure, and the more "feudal" the relationship between the tribal chieftains and the subjected peasantry.

Not all rural Christians belonged to the subject stratum; there were important exceptions, notably the Assyrians of Central Kurdistan and at least some of the Suryani of the Tur Abdin. These openly carried arms – an anomaly in a Muslim state – and their leaders were on a par with any Kurdish chieftain. Actual intermarriage between these Christians and Muslim Kurds was rare, but it appears that cases of ritual co-parenthood were not uncommon: a Kurdish father could ask a Christian friend to sponsor his son's circumcision, after which he would remain the boy's "godfather" (*krîv*; Tu.: *kirve*).[4] There was until recently, moreover, a small Armenian nomadic tribe that was part of a Kurdish tribal confederacy.[5] Not all Kurds, on the other hand, were tribesmen. Pastoral nomads have probably never represented more than a fraction of all Kurds.[6] Many of the tribes were and are semi-nomadic (i.e. they spend the winter in permanent villages, practising some agriculture in combination with animal husbandry, and in summer take their flocks to mountain pastures a few hours or days away from their villages). Besides these, there have always been large numbers of fully sedentary Kurdish-speaking peasants who were not organized into tribes, and a large proportion of whom lived in subjection to a tribal élite. The tribes and the non-tribal population were almost like two castes; social mobility between these two strata was not entirely absent but quite rare. Within the tribal "caste", the chiefly families (*aghawat*) form a distinct sub-caste, rarely intermarrying with common tribesmen. Until the mid twentieth century, it was almost uniquely Kurds from the *aghawat* stratum who received a modern education.

Impact of the central state on social stratification and social conflicts

This vertical stratification of Kurdish society was consolidated and even reinforced by the central governments. The Ottoman and Persian Empires and their successor states were never strong enough to directly control all of Kurdistan. Various forms of indirect rule therefore developed, in which tribal chieftains were left in control of large areas in exchange for formal allegiance and symbolic taxes, or members of the tribal élite were given bureaucratic and military functions.

A notorious case was that of the Hamidiye, the mounted militias formed by (and named after) Sultan Abdulhamid II (1876–1908), which were almost uniquely recruited among Kurdish tribes. Selected tribal chieftains and their men were given arms to police the countryside, and granted virtual impunity in the face of complaints about their behaviour. In this way, the powers of these chieftains over their subjects, as well as *vis-à-vis* rival chieftains, were much enhanced. The Hamidiye gained a bad reputation in Europe because of their involvement in the Armenian massacre of 1894, but it should be remembered that other Kurds were just as often the victims of theft, oppression and killings by Hamidiye regiments as Armenians. (It may be added that in the subsequent deportations and large-scale massacres of Armenians in 1915, the Kurdish tribal regiments do not seem to have taken part. It was the regular army that did most of the killing, although some of the Kurds no doubt did their share of looting).

Recently, the Turkish government has established a rather similar paramilitary force, the village guards (*köy korucular*), in its efforts to combat the violent guerrilla of the Workers' Party of Kurdistan (van Bruinessen 1988a). One hears the same complaints as in the time of the Hamidiye: local chieftains use these village guards as their private armed thugs, fighting rival chieftains, extorting and oppressing the peasantry and bullying the population into obedience. The Iraqi government had earlier taken recourse to the same method. When Mulla Mustafa Barzani took to the mountains in 1961, the central government armed tribes that were traditionally hostile to the shaykhs of Barzan and sent them against the rebels. Throughout the 1960s and 1970s, the government employed such tribal militias, which proved more effective than the regular army against the nationalist Kurdish guerrilla.

The cooperation of the state with local Kurdish chieftains did not always have such immediate military objectives. More commonly the chieftains simply became extensions of the civil administration. In the Ottoman Empire there were formal arrangements, until the first decades of the nineteenth century, between the state and autonomous Kurdish emirates. As long as they upheld Ottoman law, paid the taxes, did not conspire with Iran or trespass into others' territories, these local rulers (*amir*) were formally recognized by the central government, and their authority, when necessary, backed up by troops stationed in the region. When these emirs were replaced by centrally appointed governors and a gradually expanding provincial bureaucracy, more informal power-sharing relations developed between these civilian and military officers and the tribal chieftains and shaykhs of the region.

Chieftains cooperated with the administration in exchange for various forms of patronage. Ambitious chieftains found that such cooperation could be extremely useful in consolidating or expanding their local authority and power. The rivals of chieftains favoured by the administration often had little choice but to become rebels or seek political alliances elsewhere. In the past there was always the neighbouring Persian empire with which they could ally themselves; in the present century, the Kurdish movement became another state-like actor to which the rebels could rally. (Conversely, the traditional rivals of chieftains who took part in the Kurdish rebellions often took the side of the government in putting down these rebellions).

In the 1920s and 1930s, both Atatürk in Turkey and Reza Shah in Iran attempted to eliminate this intermediary stratum of *aghawat* and to establish effective direct rule. Numerous chieftains, and sometimes entire tribes, were physically removed from the area and settled in other parts of the country (Beşikçi 1972; Salzmann 1971). A rural police force (*gendarmerie*) and modern civil administration, both recruited from other parts of the country, were to bring the villagers into direct contact with the state. These policies were only partially successful, since the civilian and military authorities found that they needed the cooperation of local influential people in order to carry out their duties. Later, many chieftains returned and regained much of their former influence. Much later, in the 1960s and 1970s, two other government measures, the establishment of schools for the villagers and the Iraqi and Iranian land reforms, did more to reduce the power of the *aghawat*. Modern education and the employment opportunities this provided, however limited, made the younger generation of villagers less dependent on the chieftains, while land reform significantly reduced the economic power of these chieftains (most landlords in Kurdistan belong to the *aghawat*). In Turkey, incidentally, landlords have thus far successfully resisted all serious attempts at land reform.

After the Second World War, Turkey became a multi-party democracy. This again strengthened the position of the *aghawat*, who were major votegetters. Rival chieftains allied themselves with the two major parties. Those whose party was in power could control the flow of patronage, development funds and facilities, and naturally used this to back up their own local authority and economic position. Because the bureaucracy is also highly politicized, the chieftains allied with the opposition party may get a modest share of patronage through fellow party members in the administration. Association with one of the major parties, moreover, lends a chieftain political protection against prosecution for offences. The same mechanism of political patronage caused the failure of land reform.[7]

Symbiotic relations between *aghawat* and the civilian and military authorities at the local level also continue. Many officials posted in Kurdistan found that they could not do their jobs without establishing good working relations with some of the local chieftains, and soon ended up getting involved in the tribal structure and its numerous conflicts. Thereby, they strengthened the power of some chieftains over the commoners as well as their traditional rivals. Smuggling, long an important economic activity in the border regions, is a case in point. It used to be an activity in which everyone with sufficient courage could take part, and by which many commoners earned some additional income. Every month large flocks of sheep and a wide variety of commercial goods illegally crossed the borders. When the borders came to be more effectively guarded by the military, only those who made a deal with the chief of the border guards or the local military commander could stay in the game. This was usually some local chieftain who, in exchange for a share of the spoils, could thus establish his monopoly over this lucrative activity.

Another instance is land registration. Traditionally the rights of farmers to their land were not clearly defined. Land registration by the state was begun in the nineteenth century but is still not completed. Often several people lay claims to the same land. By cooperating with, and sometimes bribing officials, many chieftains managed to have much land registered in their names at the expense of the actual cultivators – even where they could not even lay traditional claims. In this way, many peasants – especially, it seems, those belonging to the minorities, who enjoyed no political protection at all – have been robbed of their lands.

In various other ways, centrally appointed officials have connived, if not participated more actively in, the chieftains' continued exploitation and oppression of the peasantry. Officials who refused to cooperate were at times made to comply by threats. In other cases, chieftains managed, through connections elsewhere in the bureaucracy, to have uncooperative officials removed from the districts. As long as chieftains did not openly oppose the administration as such, they have been able to maintain and even strengthen much of their feudal powers.[8]

ETHNIC IDENTITY AND THE EMERGENCE OF NATIONALISM

In 1975 I asked a young man with whom I had been talking in a coffee house in a small town in north-west Iran, whether he was a Kurd or an Azeri. Kurds and Turkish-speaking Azeris are the major ethnic groups living in that district. His answer baffled me: "I am both a Kurd and an Azeri, and I am a Persian as well." I thought he was being sophistic and went on questioning him to find out what he really was. What language did he speak at home? That depended; his mother spoke only Kurdish well, but with his father he conversed in both Kurdish and Turkish, and sometimes in Persian. So his father was an Azeri and his mother a Kurd, I ventured, glad to have understood his reaction. No, he objected, his father was also a Kurd and an Azeri and a Persian. These terms were for him purely linguistic, not ethnic labels as I defined them. It did not occur to me then to ask him whether he was a Sunni or a Shi'i (Azeris are generally Shi'is and Kurds Sunnis), but I am not sure whether that would have yielded a more unambiguous answer, for young people there were not very religious at that time.

My question was of course prompted by my own belief in the objective existence of ethnicity. Most of the people whom I met, in fact, even those of mixed ancestry, defined themselves unambiguously as Kurds or Turks or Arabs. But there were others who, like the said young man, refused to be pigeonholed by a single ethnic label. Many pious elderly men, especially in Turkey, defined themselves as Sunnis only, claiming that language is unimportant. There were also people (in Agri province, eastern Turkey) whom I thought to be objectively Kurds but who insisted that they were Turks – they spoke both languages. The last two cases are no doubt at least partly a result of Turkey's policy of forced assimilation and the official doctrine declaring all Kurds to be really Turks who have unfortunately lost the purity of their language. But in earlier times too, there were many people in the region who apparently had no clear-cut ethnic identity.

Although most people must have had only one mother tongue, they did not necessarily define themselves by it. It has often been observed that the élite in the Ottoman Empire defined themselves as "Ottomans" rather than by ethnic labels (because, it has been suggested, "Turk" and "Kurd" carried overtones of boorishness). Large sections of the peasantry were simply called *ra'yat* ("subjects"), without any ethnic label attached: in different parts of Kurdistan they were variously called *guran, miskên, klawspî* and *kurmanj*, which were used as class rather than ethnic labels.[9]

Even in the case of those who had a definite ethnic label attached to them, ethnicity was not always a very stable trait. Entire tribes which were once recorded as being Turkish were at a later stage Kurdish, or vice versa (van Bruinessen 1989b, pp. 618–19). Individuals may have changed their ethnic identity within a lifetime. I met a man who was born a (Kurdish) Yazidi and had, like a significant number of members of this sect, become a Syrian Christian (Suryani) in order to escape religious oppression. When the Suryani community also grew weak and came to be subject to increasing oppression, he converted to Islam and "became a Kurd again".

The Armenians who turned into Zaza-speaking Alevis in Dersim and those who claimed to have become Kurdish Sunnis in Siirt have already been mentioned. In Hakkari I came across Kurds who told me that "originally" they were Nestorians, and who spoke of the Christian district of Kumkapi in Istanbul as "ours". Such recent converts, some of whom should perhaps be called "crypto-Christians", are still recognized as different from the Kurds proper, but they are acceptable as marriage-partners and those who wish can easily be integrated. Somewhat different again is the case of numerous young Turkish Alevis who, in the 1970s, redefined themselves as Kurds out of political sympathies. It was a shift easily made, for intermarriage among Turkish, Kurdish and Zaza-speaking Alevis has long been relatively common, and all use Turkish as their ritual language. In all these cases, as in those of Kurds forcibly assimilated to the Turkish majority, the major factor in the change of ethnic identity was political.

The emergence of a Kurdish nationalist movement (and the earlier nationalist movements of Armenians, Arabs and Turks) clearly strengthened people's tendency to define their identity in ethnic terms. But we should be aware that a strong ethnic identity and participation in ethnic nationalism are only very loosely correlated. In the First World War and the subsequent liberation struggle in Turkey, urban Kurdish intellectuals found that the Kurdish tribes were not at all interested in their nationalist message. They were mobilized as Muslims, at first by the Sultan's proclamation of jihad, later by Atatürk's call to save the Muslim nation.[10] It was only after Atatürk had started defining the new Turkey as a Turkish state and abolished the caliphate that large numbers of Kurds could be mobilized on a specifically Kurdish platform against that state (van Bruinessen 1985). Because of tribal rivalries and for various other reasons, most Kurdish nationalist rebellions were opposed and even fought by other Kurds who were equally aware of their Kurdish identity. In the 1970s, there were even Kurds in Turkey who affiliated themselves with the fascist and pan-Turkist Nationalist Action Party.

On the other hand, from the 1960s onwards, Chaldaean and Nestorian Christians of nothern Iraq took an active part in the Kurdish movement there without giving up their separate identities (although the Kurds preferred to call them "Christian Kurds"). Several of the founders of the most radical Kurdish organization in Turkey, the Workers' Party of Kurdistan (PKK), were ethnic Turks, while Armenians took an active part in several other Kurdish organizations. I had one friend of Armenian extraction who vacillated between left-wing Turkish and Kurdish political organizations and, depending on the political context, defined himself as an Armenian, a Kurd, or a Turkish citizen. When he was murdered, both Armenians and a Turkish left-wing organization claimed him as a martyr.

To sum up, ethnicity is a fluid thing and, to some extent at least, voluntaristic. It is not nature-given, one does not necessarily belong unambiguously to a specific ethnic group. Everyone has a number of partially overlapping identities, and it depends on the situation which ones he or she will emphasize or de-emphasize. A Sunni Zaza speaker is a Zaza, a Kurd, a Sunni Muslim and a citizen of Turkey. He also belongs to a specific social class and probably to a specific tribe, is an inhabitant of a specific village or valley, and may be the follower of a specific shaykh or an active member of a political organization. Each of these identitities is appealed to at one time or another. At present, most Zaza define themselves

first and foremost as Kurds, but their social and political behaviour
is more often defined by narrower loyalties. In areas where there
have been many Sunni–Alevi conflicts, people define themselves
primarily as Sunni or Alevi rather than as Turk or Kurd. The
emergence of Kurdish nationalism as a significant political force
compelled many people to opt for an unambiguous ethnic identity.
Many who had been partly or even entirely arabized or turkicized
began to re-emphasize their Kurdish ethnic identity. I often wonder
what happened, after more than a decade of armed struggle
between the Kurds and the central government of Iran, to the
young man who called himself a Kurd and a Turk and a Persian.
Will he still be able to maintain this triple identity?

KURDISH ETHNICITY AND KURDISH NATIONALISM

Nationalism is an essentially modern development, and the above
examples suggest that the emphasis on Kurdish ethnicity is
also a relatively new phenomenon. There is much to say
for the arguments of such authors as Anderson (1983) and
Gellner (1983), that the nation is a product of relatively recent
technological and economic developments. Gellner's observations
on the cultural gap that separated the elite from the rural producers
in "agro-literate" societies are certainly relevant for the Kurdish
case. Kurdish nationalism, if not engendered by the social and
economic upheavals and labour migration which Gellner sees
as the major factors, certainly owed its mass appeal to them.
Modern communications, printing, radio and the cassette recorder,
contributed much to the creation of the Kurdish "nation" as an
"imagined community", that is, as a community of people whom
one never meets face to face but whom one knows to exist and to be
like oneself (Anderson 1983). But Kurdish ethnicity is much older
than Kurdish nationalism. An "imagined community" of Kurds,
a well-defined Kurdish *ethnie*[11] has existed for many centuries,
although its definition was perhaps less inclusive and populist
than the present one.

   In 1597 the Kurdish ruler of the emirate of Bitlis, Sharaf Khan,
completed his famous *Sharafname*, a history of the Kurdish ruling
families. He distinguishes the Kurds from Ottomans (*Rūm*),
Persians (*'Ajam*), Arabs, Armenians and Assyrians. His Kurds
include Zaza and Guran as well as speakers of Kurdish proper,
Alevis and Yazidis as well as Sunnis. All the Kurds he mentions,

however, are urban aristocrats or tribesmen; the subject peasantry, irrespective of their religion and language, are never called Kurds. The Turkish author Evliya Çelebi, who travelled extensively in Kurdistan in the mid seventeenth century, also speaks of the Kurds as a well-defined, distinct people, and enumerates many tribes and dialect groups, including again Zaza, Alevis and Yazidis (van Bruinessen 1988b).

In the Kurdish epic poem *Mem û Zîn*, by the poet and scholar Ahmad Khani (1650–1706), we even find utterances which are very reminiscent of modern nationalist sentiment. In the prologue he explains that, in rebellion against common learned practice, he did not write this work in Persian but in Kurdish, "so that people would no longer say that the Kurds are devoid of wisdom and lacking in culture, that all peoples have their own books but that the Kurds alone cannot boast a single one". Khani laments the political divisions of the Kurds, which caused them to be ruled over by the Ottomans and the Persians. If only the Kurds were united under a strong ruler, he sighs, learning and the arts would flourish among them, and they would reduce all the Ottomans, Persians and Arabs to vassalage.[12]

Khani's strong ruler never appeared, but his opus served the purpose for which he says he wrote it. It became – in the twentieth century at least – a major source of Kurdish cultural pride. Significantly, it was the Bedirkhan family, scions of the Kurdish rulers of Jazira Botan and prominent nationalists in the early twentieth century, who first adopted *Mem û Zîn* as the Kurdish national epic. The story of Mem and Zîn was situated in Jazira Botan and associated with the court of that emirate; it could therefore also be made to legitimate the Bedirkhans' hoped-for leading role in the Kurdish nation. It is a work of court literature, and Khani's Kurds are not peasants but belong to the "feudal" élite. There is also a Kurdish folk literature, recorded instances of which date back to the seventeenth century, but this does not show the same awareness of the Kurds as an "imagined community" that we find in Sharaf Khan, Ahmad Khani and Evliya Çelebi's aristocratic Kurdish informants.

A clear awareness of Kurdish ethnicity has thus existed among the Kurdish rulers and tribal élite at least since the late sixteenth century (and probably much earlier). This concept of ethnicity encompassed only the courts and the tribes and apparently ex- cluded the subjected peasantry and lower urban strata. At this stage the Kurds thus formed what Smith (1986, pp. 76–83) has termed a "lateral-aristocratic *ethnie*" (as against the "vertical-demotic *ethnie*", which is not based on common "class" interests but on a strong sense of cultural, especially religious, commonality). Language and religion are obviously not the main determinants, although the Sunni speakers of Kurdish proper formed the central core of this *ethnie*. Religion, especially, was not very important: several ruling houses of emirates switched from Sunnism to Shi'ism and back again, apparently depending on their political alliances with the Ottomans or Safavids (for examples see van Bruinessen 1981). The commonality was based on habitat (the Zagros chain and the high mountains of eastern Asia Minor), a common tribal culture and ethos, a shared historical experience, the integrating role of the basically similar emirates, and linguistic and other cultural differences with the neighbouring Arab and Turkish tribes. There were myths of common origins, while marriage alliances cemented the ties between the ruling families.

The commonality, however, never led to political integration of the *ethnie*. Conflicts between the tribes were perpetual. The emirates could hold tribal conflicts in check to some extent, but when they were abolished in the eighteenth and nineteenth centuries, the Kurdish *ethnie* further fragmented. A British political officer, who served in central Kurdistan immediately following the First World War and who had an interest in seeing the Kurds unite against Turkey, observed that:

> as a race they are not a political entity. They are a collection of tribes without cohesion, and showing little desire for cohesion. They prefer to live in their mountain fastnesses and pay homage to whatever government may be in power, as long as it exercises little more than nominal authority.
>
> (Hay 1921, p. 36)

Like many of his colleagues, he conceived a romantic admiration for the Kurds, and predicted (had he heard of Ahmad Khani?) that, "The day that the Kurds awake to a national consciousness and combine, the Turkish, Persian and Arab states will crumble to dust before them. That day is yet far off" (*ibid.*).

By Hay's day, however, a process working towards integration had already set in. The mystical orders, especially the Naqsh-bandiyya, became widely influential in the course of the nineteenth century. Membership in the orders cross-cut tribal boundaries;

their shaykhs therefore emerged as arbitrators and peace-makers in tribal conflict, and could if necessary coordinate collective action by previously rival tribes. The shaykhs were linked together in a network of teacher–disciple relations that spanned large parts of Kurdistan. This is why, as already observed above, most of the Kurdish rebellions between 1880 and 1930 were led by *tariqa* shaykhs. The unity forged by a shaykh rarely outlasted a short surge of enthusiasm, but the orders did generate a more general awareness of ethnic unity overriding tribal and regional differences. More importantly, the orders had their followers among the peasantry and urban craftsmen and workers as well as among the tribes. They were an important vehicle whereby these lower classes were gradually integrated into the Kurdish *ethnie*. The other side of the coin was, of course, that the Kurdish *ethnie* became more strongly associated with Sunni Islam, and that Shi'is, Alevis and Yazidis were marginalized. Kurdish participation in the Armenian and Nestorian massacres may also have been prompted, at least in part, by this development.

In the very beginning of the twentieth century, the first Kurdish cultural and political associations were founded in Istanbul. There were two clearly distinguishable wings in these organizations, one led by the Bedirkhans, the other by Shaykh Sayyid Abdulqadir, a scion of one of the most venerable families of shaykhs. The Bedirkhan faction consisted of urbanized aristocrats with a modern, secular education; it included Zaza as well as Kurmanji and Sorani speakers, and Alevis as well as Sunnis. Later this faction was to conceive a fascination for the Yazidi religion, and to idealize it as the original Kurdish religion. Sayyid Abdulqadir's faction, on the other hand, though equally aristocratic, consisted of pious Sunni Muslims. Significantly, the Kurdish guilds of Istanbul, whose members were poor migrants of peasant and tribal origins, unambiguously declared that Sayyid Abdulqadir was the only person whom they wished to speak for them. The religious reformist and moderate nationalist Sa'id-i Kurdi (Sa'id Nursi), who belonged to neither faction, also directed his activities much more towards the lower classes than the secular nationalists did.[13]

When the idea of autonomy or even complete separation of Kurdistan from the remains of the Ottoman Empire gained ground among the urban nationalists (i.e., when they began to conceive of a Kurdish nation in territorial terms), they began to include the lower strata more explicitly into their Kurdish "imagined community". This vertical social integration initially led to a degree of alienation between Sunni and Alevi Kurds. In 1920 and 1921, Alevi tribal chieftains of western Dersim, speaking of themselves as Kurds, without reference to their religious affiliation, petitioned the Turkish National Assembly for administrative autonomy, at first for all of Kurdistan, later for their own districts. In 1925, a large Kurdish rebellion broke out in the Diyarbakir region. It was planned by nationalist officers and intellectuals, but they had to surrender leadership to Naqshbandi shaykhs, because only these had sufficiently wide influence. The participants were almost exclusively Sunni Zazas, both tribesmen and urban poor. The Alevis of Dersim kept aloof; a few small Alevi tribes in the region of the rebellion even actively fought it, because the Sunni character of the rebellion was threatening to them (Firat 1970; van Bruinessen 1985). In 1937 the Alevi tribes of Dersim rose in a rebellion with Kurdish nationalist overtones; this time none of the Sunni Kurds came to their support.

In Iran and Iraq too, Kurdish nationalism could initially only mobilize the masses under religious leadership, which turned it into a specifically Sunni movement. In Iraq, it was the Qadiri Shaykh Mahmud Barzinji of Sulaymaniya and the Naqshbandi Shaykh Ahmad Barzani (Mulla Mustafa's elder brother) who mobilized poor peasants as well as tribesmen in nationalist rebellions against the British and later the royal government. In the short-lived Kurdish republic of Mahabad (1946), the religious authority of Qazi Muhammad was essential to guarantee the participation of the various urban classes as well as the tribes. The Shi'i Kurds of southern Kurdistan stayed completely aloof from the Sunni-led Kurdish rebellions. Only during the 1960s, when the Kurdish movement in Iraq was no longer led by religious authorities but by a secular party, did Shi'i Kurds begin to take part in it.

Socio-economic changes setting in or speeding up in the 1950s – the mechanization of agriculture, industrialization, rural–urban migration, political mobilization in competitive party politics, the expansion of public education and mass communications – uprooted the traditional social structure of Kurdistan. Tribal loyalties, though by no means disappearing, weakened not only because of migration but also because of sharpening class-type conflicts within the tribe. The Kurdish urban population of large cities such as Istanbul, Ankara, Baghdad and Tehran, as well as the secondary cities in Kurdistan itself, swelled. Competition for jobs and resources made most of the migrants dependent on networks of patronage that were no longer based on single tribes but on wider regions of origin, and strengthened in at least some of the migrants an awareness of their Kurdish identity and ethnic solidarity. Where Kurdish organizations still existed, as in Iraq, their membership rapidly increased. In Turkey, where everything Kurdish had been suppressed, various new Kurdish associations, formal and informal, were founded in the 1960s – significantly in Istanbul and Ankara first, and only later in Kurdistan itself.

The ideological influences of Kemalism, pan-Arabism and various currents of left-wing thought combined with these socio-economic changes in fostering a secular and populist conception of the Kurdish *ethnie*, that largely replaced the earlier aristocratic and religious ones. Significantly, the term "Kurmanji", which initially referred to the subject peasants in northern Kurdistan, became synonymous with "Kurd". Although most if not all the intellectuals who led these organizations originated from the *aghawat* stratum, they explicitly addressed the lower strata of Kurdish society as well, and spoke up for their interests. Their attempts at vertical integration of the Kurdish nation were only partially successful. Virtually every Kurdish organization spoke in the name of all classes and even emphasized its identification with Kurdish peasants and workers, but most of the peasantry long remained aloof from the Kurdish movement. In the Iraqi Kurdish movement – in which, because of the long guerrilla war, the tribes came to play crucial parts again – virtually none of the non-tribal peasantry ever took part. They found that their interests were often better served by the central government, which offered land reform. The same, to some extent, was true of Iran under the Shah. Only in Turkey did the Kurdish movement, in the late 1970s, make significant inroads among the rural and urban poor. A part of the movement here, notably the Workers' Party of Kurdistan, turned against the *aghawat* as a class (although at times cooperating with individual chieftains).[14]

Since the 1970s Kurdish nationalists have been more successful in integrating religious minorities into the Kurdish nation. Alevis in Turkey, Yazidis, Shi'is and even Christian minorities in Iraq took an active part and gained leading positions in Kurdish political organizations. Only in Iran did the Shi'is of southern Kurdistan remain aloof from, or even oppose, the Kurdish national movement. There have been numerous sectarian conflicts during the past decades, but the Kurdish organizations have consistently attempted to play a moderating and conciliatory role.

Not all Kurds, to be sure, have come to identify themselves with the Kurdish nation. In the first place there are those persons of Kurdish descent who have become completely turkicized or arabized (or, less frequently, persianized). In most respects, these people have become Turks, Arabs and Persians, although the development of Kurdish nationalism has recently caused some of them to reassert their Kurdish identity. There are also many who have not entirely shed their Kurdish cultural identity, but whose primary political orientation is towards Turkey, Iran or Iraq, and who dissociate themselves from all forms of Kurdish separatism. In Turkey especially, there is a strong pressure on these people to deny their Kurdish identity. During the past two decades many people have vacillated between such an orientation towards their country and its "national" culture on the one hand, and a more regional, ethnic or Kurdish nationalist orientation.

Finally, there are those who identify primarily with Islam. Most of them see themselves as Kurds as well as Muslims, but feel little sympathy for the secular Kurdish organizations. The Iranian revolution inspired the emergence of several minor Islamic Kurdish political formations in both Iran and Iraq (van Bruinessen 1986, pp. 22–4). In Turkey, several country-wide Islamic movements found much support among the Kurds. In the major one of these, the *nurcu* movement, Kurdish national sentiment clearly surfaced during the 1970s and 1980s. Turkey's sole Muslim party, the National Salvation Party (after a ban in 1980 re-emerging as the National Welfare Party), also saw itself forced to appeal to regional and ethnic grievances in order to win votes in Turkey's Kurdish provinces. As a political force, Islam is not very significant in Kurdistan, and an Islamic orientation rarely implies a negation of Kurdish ethnicity. But it is not impossible that in the near future, under the influence of developments in both Turkey and Iran, more Kurds will insist on their Muslim as opposed to their ethnic identity.

VIOLENT CONFLICTS, FORCED DEPORTATIONS AND REFUGEES

It is not my intention to recount here the history of the Kurdish movements in Iraq, Turkey and Iran, nor to describe in detail the measures taken by the central governments to pacify or suppress these movements. Chronological and detailed information is available from other sources.[15] I shall only make a few general observations, concentrating on those developments which resulted in involuntary population movements (deportation or flight).

Armed nationalist struggle

A sustained guerrilla war against the central government, with the aim of obtaining some form of autonomy began in Iraqi Kurdistan in 1961 and lasted, with short interruptions, until 1968, when negotiations started that led to a peace agreement in 1970. When the Kurds, enticed by Iranian and American promises of large-scale support, refused to content themselves with the limited autonomy proclaimed by the government in 1974, a new war of unprecedented scope broke out. The following year, the Shah signed an agreement with Iraq by which he gained important border concessions in exchange for giving up his support for the Iraqi Kurds. Within weeks the movement collapsed, and tens of thousands of *peshmerges* (Kurdish guerrilla fighters) fled across the Iranian border, joining many more civilian refugees already there. As early as 1976, new guerrilla activities were reported from northern Iraq, though on a limited scale. The two major Iraqi Kurdish nationalist parties, the Patriotic Union of Kurdistan (PUK) and the Kurdistan Democratic Party (KDP), initially clashed more often with each other than with government forces.[16] When the Iran–Iraq War forced the Iraqi army to concentrate its efforts on the Iranian front, the Kurdish organizations stepped up their activities. The KDP from the beginning allied itself closely with the Islamic government of Iran, while the PUK, which found itself facing the Iranian army as well as the KDP and Iraqi troops, opened negotiations with Baghdad in 1983. These negotiations broke down, and in 1986 Tehran engineered a pact of military cooperation between the various Iraqi Kurdish factions.

The fighting between the Kurdish nationalist and government forces, the infighting among the Kurds, and later the frontal war between Iranian and Iraqi troops, resulted in the dislodgement of large numbers of Kurdish villagers. In the 1970s, bombardments and large-scale army operations caused tens of thousands to flee to less accessible Kurdish-held regions in the mountains or to Iran, while perhaps even larger numbers fled to the relative safety of the towns. By 1980, when the Iran–Iraq War broke out, there were still tens of thousands of Iraqi Kurds living dispersed in Iran; they were a major source of recruitment for the KDP. During the 1980s, many Iraqi Kurds who had returned to, or still remained in, their villages found it was impossible to remain neutral there; they had to take sides in the inter-Kurdish and Kurdish–government conflicts. To avoid this choice, they moved in large numbers to the towns, to Kurdish-held valleys in the north or to Iran; numerous others were forcibly deported by the government (about which, more below). Many young Kurds, moreover, fled abroad to escape military service. After the 1988 ceasefire in the Iran–Iraq War, Iraq concentrated its military efforts on the submission of Kurdistan. Its use of poison gas forced tens of thousands of *pershmerges* and civilians across the Turkish border, where they were initially welcomed but soon suffered less friendly treatment. International organizations were prevented from lending humanitarian aid to these refugees. Increasing pressure was put on them to either return to Iraq or move to Iran.[17]

After the Iranian revolution, the Kurds of Iran almost unanimously demanded some form of autonomy. Only the Shi'i Kurds of Kermanshah remained untouched by the general nationalist ferment, and some of them were later recruited by the government to fight the nationalists. Several charismatic leaders came to the fore and many political organizations competed for popular support, but only two parties consolidated themselves in the first clashes between government forces and Kurds. The Democratic Party of Kurdistan in Iran (KDP-Iran), led by Abd al-Rahman Ghassemlou, and with its centre of gravity around Mahabad, is the most significant of these. The other one is the Revolutionary Organization of Toilers of Kurdistan (Komala), with its zone of influence further to the south. The leadership of both is in the hands of the educated urban classes, their following includes peasants as well as townspeople, but very few tribesmen. Both received a measure of financial and logistic support from Iraq but carefully retained their political independence.

Throughout 1979 there were several bloody clashes between Shi'i minorities and their Kurdish neighbours, and also violent conflicts between peasants and landlords attempting to regain the feudal rights they had lost under the Shah's land reform (van Bruinessen 1981). The Barzanis, armed and supported by the Islamic government, became a significant political force in Iranian

Kurdistan and clashed several times with Iranian Kurds. In the summer of 1979, the Iranian army was sent against the Kurds and attempted to reassert central government authority. This signalled the beginning of a long guerrilla war, in which the Kurds were at first surprisingly successful. The Kurds kept control of the major towns until late 1980, and of vast rural areas, until in 1983 their guerrilla forces were finally pushed across the Iraqi border by a combined offensive of the Iranian army, revolutionary guards and the Barzanis' KDP, which had become Iran's dependable ally. Since then both parties have continued guerrilla activities inside Iran from their bases in the no man's land across the Iraqi frontier. The relations between the two organizations kept deteriorating, Komala declaring the KDP-Iran the "class enemy" and the latter retaliating with armed violence.

The rural population of Iranian Kurdistan does not seem to have suffered so much as its Iraqi neighbours, although localized conflicts as well as indiscriminate bombing by the Iraqi air force resulted in the temporary evacuation of many villages. The Iranian reprisals against the Kurds hit especially the town populations. The numerous summary executions of suspected Kurdish activists created terror, and many members and sympathizers of the Kurdish organizations fled the towns, at first to the "liberated territories" inside Iran, later across the Iraqi border. Unknown but large numbers of Iranian Kurds now live in Iraq; a minority has been able to find its way from there to Europe.

The KDP-Iran has for years been seeking a peaceful solution for its differences with the central authorities through direct negotiations. The murder of its leader Ghassemlou at the negotiating table in Vienna in July 1989, has no doubt greatly diminished the possibility of a negotiated settlement for some time to come.[18] The party, operating from headquarters in Iraqi Kurdistan, continues a low level of guerrilla activity, with little prospect of success. The 1991 Gulf War and the beginnings of Iranian–Iraqi rapprochement underline its precarious position.

During the 1970s, Turkey experienced an unprecedented political polarization, hand in hand with increasing political violence. Rival organizations of the left and the right fought for control of squatter settlements in the cities and later also of rural districts. Kurds could be found both among the right- and left-wing groups, but from the middle of the decade on increasingly in separate Kurdish organizations. The demands formulated by Kurdish intellectuals and politicians were very moderate at first: official recognition of the existence of the Kurds as a distinct people with their own culture, and economic development for Turkey's eastern (largely Kurdish-inhabited) provinces, which had too long been neglected. The first of these demands touched a raw nerve. Since the establishment of the Republic, the military and civilian elite have been obsessed by threats to its territorial integrity, and the Kurds, as the largest non-Turkish ethnic group, have been perceived as the most serious potential danger. All expressions of Kurdish cultural identity were banned and severely punished. This demand for recognition – initially supported by a left-wing Turkish party – caused great concern, and the state responded with severe repression. This in turn led to a gradual radicalization of Kurdish demands. No longer supported by Turkish parties or organizations, they began to organize themselves separately, while their demands moved towards political separatism: autonomy or even independence for the Turkish part of Kurdistan.

Personal rivalries and ideological discord caused the Kurdish movement to split into a large number of competing parties and associations, each of which carved out minor territorial bases in the cities and countryside. Class and tribal conflicts in Kurdistan became exacerbated as political organizations allied themselves with the parties to these conflicts and vice versa. By the end of the 1970s several parts of Kurdistan were the scene of enduring and violent conflicts between rival organizations (left-wing, right-wing and Kurdish nationalist, each of many different shades), alternated by brutal but indecisive clamp-downs by the military. For the inhabitants of those districts it was virtually impossible to remain neutral, because that would make them suspect in the eyes of all parties in the conflict. Many therefore left these districts, for cities elsewhere in Turkey or preferably for western Europe. They were followed by others who had been affiliated with one party or another but were reluctant to go along with further radicalization or feared government reprisals. Economic and political motives are almost inseparable in these migrants – who numbered at least tens of thousands.

The military coup of 12 September 1980 was immediately followed by large-scale military operations throughout Kurdistan and mass arrests. Not only activists and sympathizers, but also many villagers who had never been involved in political activities suffered greatly, and the stream of political and "economic" refugees further swelled. Most of the Kurdish organizations virtually ceased to exist on Turkish soil. The most radical of them, however, the Workers' Party of Kurdistan (PKK), consolidated itself in foreign exile and organized military training (in Lebanon, apparently) for its members.

In 1984 the PKK opened a guerrilla offensive inside Turkey, attacking military targets as well as Kurds whom it regarded as "collaborators" with the military regime. Although their numbers were small, several hundreds at most during the first years, this offensive soon became a severe embarrassment to the Turkish army. Military "search-and-destroy" operations inside Turkey and air raids on supposed PKK base camps in Iran and Iraq failed to paralyse it. The government then recruited "loyal" Kurds into the paramilitary village guards which, it was hoped, would be more effective in fighting the PKK guerrillas. As was mentioned earlier, these village guards soon acted as the local strongman's private armed retinue, in many places terrorizing his rivals and opponents. They and their families also became the prime targets of the PKK's most violent actions. A few spectacular raids in which wives and children of the village guards were brutally slaughtered by the PKK guerrilla units horrified public opinion and created fear among the village guards. A cycle of violence and counter-violence, in which both sides made many innocent victims, again caused an exodus from several Kurdish districts, especially those close to the Iraqi border, where the PKK and the army have been most active.

The PKK has won little popular sympathy with its brutally violent actions, but it gradually came to enjoy the grudging admiration of many Kurds, both for the prowess and recklessness of its guerrilla fighters and for the courage with which its arrested partisans stood up in court and in prison (cf. van Bruinessen 1988a; Heinrich 1988). By the end of 1990, it enjoyed unprecedented popularity in eastern Turkey, although few seemed to actively support it. There were fewer accusations of violence against civilians,[19] and the PKK seemed to be evolving towards less extreme political standpoints, proposing to hold negotiations with the government and speaking of "provisional, partial solutions". The PKK is the only Kurdish organization that has successfully challenged the Turkish army's domination of Kurdistan. It was also the PKK, not the more moderate and democratic organizations, that forced Turkey's political élite to admit that the country has a Kurdish problem which needs to be solved, not denied. But even the first steps in the direction of a peaceful solution, the granting of basic cultural rights and a recognition of Kurdish grievances, still seems far away.

Village society is torn apart between the PKK's guerrilla activities and the military's reprisals. It has become increasingly difficult for villagers to remain neutral; many have therefore fled from their villages to the relative safety of the towns. In strategically important areas, the government has speeded up this exodus by forced expulsions (see below). After Iraq's invasion of Kuwait and Turkey's firm posturing against Iraq, fears that the ensuing war might spill over into Turkish territory has led to another major wave of migration from south-eastern Turkey to the West.

Deportations

The central governments of all three countries have, in their efforts to counter Kurdish nationalism, at times had recourse to massive deportations. After the rebellions of the 1920s and 1930s, Turkey resettled tens, possibly even hundreds of thousands of Kurds in other parts of the country, while in Iran in the same period Reza Shah deported several entire tribes and many influential families. More recently, Turkey has announced the establishment of a *cordon sanitaire* along the Iraqi border as a measure to prevent further guerrilla activities. Severe pressure has been put on villagers in the province of Tunceli (inhabited by Alevi Kurds and long a hotbed of oppositional movements) to leave the region. A reforestation project in the same province is the ostensible reason for the planned dispersal of another twenty villages there (Laber and Whitman 1988, pp. 35–40). Deportations from the regions north of the Iraqi border, especially the provinces Siirt and Hakkari, began on a large scale in 1990. A decree giving the governor of the south-eastern region extraordinary powers to censor the press and to evacuate villages for security reasons provided the legal basis for these deportations and caused them to go on almost unnoticed (cf. Whitman 1990; van Bruinessen 1990). The military build-up in this area after the Iraqi invasion of Kuwait has further limited access, so that the extent of the deportations can only be guessed at. The few press reports published suggest that they were massive. The villagers in this area were allegedly given the choice between signing up as "village guards" or evacuating their villages, with little or no compensation given (van Bruinessen 1990).

The most sweeping recent deportations, however, took place in Iraq. In the early 1970s, tens of thousands of Fayli Kurds, mostly from Baghdad, were deported to Iran, on the pretext that they were not Iraqi citizens (although most had lived there for generations). Smaller numbers of members of the Goyan tribe in northern Iraq were similarly expelled to Turkey. Kurds from the oil-rich districts of Kirkuk and Khaniqin were deported to other parts of the country and Arabs settled in their place. Parts of the Sinjar mountains on the sensitive Syrian border were similarly "arabized". These measures have obviously to be seen in the context of the proposed autonomy for the Kurdish-majority region, that was to become effective in 1974.

After the 1975 defeat of Barzani's movement, the government attempted to prevent the resumption of a new Iranian-supported Kurdish guerrilla war by creating an empty buffer zone along the border. In a strip 10 to 15 km wide, all villages were destroyed, fruit trees cut and wells filled up in order to prevent reoccupation. An even wider zone along the Turkish border was also depopulated. The inhabitants were resettled in camps and large "strategic villages" futher inland, which were more easily controlled by the army. These security measures were, however, combined with large agricultural development schemes; the strategic villages fit in with the mechanization and rationalization of agriculture.[20] Materially, many of those resettled were perhaps better off. People were warned that they entered the empty zones at the risk of their lives. Unexpectedly, however, it was precisely in these zones that the PUK and the KDP established their bases. In the 1980s, they claimed large parts of them as their "liberated areas", and people fleeing government-controlled areas joined the parties there, especially in the far north.

By the mid-1980s, the government embarked upon a new wave of deportations, in an apparent bid to cut off the guerrilla from its social base. Numerous Kurdish villages further inland (thousands, according to Kurdish sources) were razed and their inhabitants allegedly driven off to camps near the cities or to the south of the country. The drive has not slackened since the end of the Iran–Iraq War. The large-scale offensives of 1988 against Kurdistan served the dual aim of destroying the Kurdish guerrilla and of forcing the remaining village population out of the mountains. Chemical weapons provided the necessary persuasive power. The zone along the borders that was to be completely evacuated was enlarged to 30 km, and not only the villages in that zone but even towns such as Rania and what remained of Halabja were completely razed. Recent visitors to the area report that even further from the borders many villages appear to have been destroyed. New settlements constructed in recent years alone accounted for around half a million deportees;[21] many others have been resettled in southern Iraq. According to Kurdish calculations, almost four thousand (out of a total of around eight thousand) villages have been destroyed since the mid-1970s and their inhabitants resettled elsewhere (Rasool 1990; Medico International 1990).

Sectarian conflicts

Numerous members of religious minority groups have also fled Kurdistan, claiming to be victims of religious persecution by the state or the Sunni Kurdish majority. Massacres and mass deportations of Nestorians, Armenians and Suryani in the nineteenth and early twentieth centuries, followed by emigration of many survivors, have greatly reduced the numbers of the Christian communities still living in Kurdistan. This has obviously weakened their ability to resist pressure from their neighbours. In Iraqi and Iranian Kurdistan, the relations between the remaining Chaldaean, Nestorian and Armenian communities and the Kurds have in the past decades generally been cordial. In Iran, the Christians have again since the Islamic revolution become second-class citizens and suffered some harassment but no persecution. The recent problems all took place in Turkish Kurdistan, where especially the Suryani have suffered much oppression.

Officially, the Christian minorities are not discriminated against in Turkey. International treaties signed by Turkey even guarantee them certain cultural rights which are denied to the Kurds and other Muslim ethnic groups. In actual practice, however, the situation is rather different. A distinct anti-Armenian feeling pervades the military and the bureaucracy, and other Christian communities suffer by association. Turkey has always refused to admit that the Armenian massacres ever took place (although the Turks killed by Armenians in retaliation during the "National War of Liberation" have a place of honour in the school books). The care with which every trace of former Armenian habitation (except a few medieval churches) is hidden, destroyed or disguised suggests a collective sense of guilt, which finds further expression in strong anti-Armenian sentiment. Armenian terrorism against Turkish diplomats abroad and increasing international pressure on Turkey to acknowledge the massacres have only strengthened this sentiment. This anti-Armenian (and, by extension, anti-Christian) attitude has only seldom led to direct persecution or oppression by officials, but rather frequently to the withholding of protection or connivance in oppression by local strongmen.

The settlement of former nomads in south-eastern Turkey and the drastic changes in agricultural production of the past four decades led to an acute land hunger and numerous conflicts over land use and ownership. Chiefs and other strongmen among the Kurdish and Arab tribes of Mardin province (where most of Turkey's Suryani used to live) appropriated, often by physical force, land from the peasant holders. Whereas tribesmen could defend themselves against the encroachments of rival tribes, and Muslim peasants could sometimes (though often unsuccessfully) seek redress by having recourse to the state, the Christian communities were virtually helpless. In the 1960s many of the able-bodied men went to western Europe as migrant labourers, leaving only the weaker members of the community behind. The weaker the community became, the more the pressure on it mounted. Land and other property was simply taken by force, daughters were abducted, men beaten up. The Christian towns of Midyat and Idil were invaded by Arab and Kurdish newcomers, who put pressure on the original inhabitants to vacate their houses.

Local government officials were often hand in glove with the chiefs who were responsible for this violence. In this sense one could speak of persecution of the community by the state. The only protection the Suryani ever received came, surprisingly perhaps, from the PKK, which, in the late 1970s, had singled out the "collaborating" chieftains as its major enemies. In a few cases "revolutionary justice" was meted out to such chieftains' thugs who had maltreated Christian peasants. Understandably, this did little to improve the overall position of the Suryani community. The Suryani seem to have decided that they have no future in the region (or elsewhere in Turkey), and all wish to emigrate.

The situation of the Yazidis is similar to that of the Suryani. They too have no protection and are frequently victims of violence and expropriation by local strongmen. They also complain of other, more direct, forms of oppression by the state. There have been cases of Yazidi men being forcibly circumcised when in military service, and all Yazidi conscripts have to shave off their, religiously prescribed, long moustaches. Much more painful, however, is the oppression by their Muslim neighbours, in which religious fanaticism and greed for their possessions go hand in hand. A large proportion of Turkey's Yazidis have already migrated to West Germany, as ordinary migrant workers when this was still possible, and later as applicants for political asylum. Their community leaders believe that their only possible future as Yazidis lies in Europe (cf. Schneider 1984).

The most violent recent sectarian conflicts have been those between Sunnis and Alevis in central and eastern Turkey (Laçiner 1985). As long as the Alevis remained more or less territorially separated from the Sunnis there were few problems, but rural–urban migration brought them into close contact – and fierce economic competition. In the largest cities, with their very hetero-geneous immigrant populations, conflicts remained limited in scope, but the situation was different in minor towns like Sivas, Elazig, Malatya, Kahramanmaraş and Çorum, where Alevis made up a large percentage of the newcomers and where the original Sunni population, especially the traditional middle and lower classes, felt their precarious livelihood threatened by increased competition. Such towns came to be divided along sectarian lines, in Sunni and Alevi quarters. Ethnicity hardly played a role here; both religious communities consisted of Kurds as well as Turks.

Political agitation by rival extremist parties further exacerbated the tension. The Sunnis were courted by the religious and the Turkish-chauvinist right, while the younger Alevis in particular overwhelmingly supported left-wing organizations. (Several radical left-wing organizations drew their membership almost exclusively from the Alevi communities.) The local government authorities in these towns were and are heavily biased against the Alevis (who are quite generally regarded as "communists" by the Sunnis). The "discovery", in the mid-1970s, of a blueprint for carving up Turkey into a Kurdish state in the east, an Alevi state in the centre and a much reduced Turkish state in the west (attributed to a clandestine communist organization but probably an intelligence fabrication) indicates that at least certain military circles saw the Alevi identity as potentially disruptive. This "document" and similar allegations by political agitators served to rally Turkish nationalists and conservative Sunnis against the Alevis.

During the mid and late 1970s several violent clashes between Sunnis and Alevis took place in these towns, in most cases ending in Alevi massacres and the massive flight of surviving Alevis. The most serious of these clashes seem to have been triggered by deliberate provocation. Violent communal riots of the same scale did not recur during the 1980s, when political agitation was strongly proscribed, but the relations remain very tense, and low-level violence continues. Many of the Alevis who fled earlier are afraid to return, aware of continuing Sunni resentment and official distrust. Communal violence may well rise again when the political climate changes, causing more Alevis to flee the region.

CONCLUSION

Iran, Iraq and Turkey all face a Kurdish problem, different in each case but equally serious. Improved communications, nationalist struggle and even government repression have contributed to making the Kurds into more of a nation than they ever were before. Iraq apparently still believes that it may achieve a solution by a combination of radical socio-economic transformation of Kurdish society, coercion and extremely violent repression. The Kurdish policies of Iran's post-Khomeini government are not yet very clear. Assassinations of Kurdish leaders (besides Ghassemlou and his companions, a Komala leader was also recently assassinated abroad) suggest that Iran believes that the Kurdish population may be eased away from nationalist politics and co-opted with limited cultural but not territorial concessions, once the charismatic leaders are gone. It is unlikely to grant the Kurds autonomy, their present chief demand.

Turkey is more sensitive to European pressure on behalf of human rights than its neighbours, but there are strong ideological impediments to recognition of the Kurds as a distinct ethnic group with its own culture, and further concessions are almost unthinkable. The military and civilian élites (which include assimilated Kurds) are deeply committed to the Kemalist dogma that the people of Turkey are one homogeneous nation and they perceive each denial of unity as a vital threat to the state.

Kurdish society itself has drastically changed over the past half century. One of the most significant changes is the movement of large numbers of Kurds away from Kurdistan, as migrant workers, displaced persons (due to warfare), deportees or political refugees. This population movement contributed powerfully to the emergence of Kurdish nationalism as a mass movement. The gradual spreading of Kurdish nationalism was answered with increasing repression by the central governments, leading in turn to further population movement out of Kurdistan. Perhaps a quarter or a third of all Kurds now live outside Kurdistan, and only a minority of them are likely ever to return.

This has important consequences for the Kurdish movement: a purely territorial nationalism, aiming at political independence, has become highly unrealistic. Virtually all Kurdish leaders in fact seek solutions within the framework of the existing states: cultural recognition, a measure of regional autonomy for those living in Kurdistan, and equal rights and proportional representation in the central institutions of the state. So far, however, only Iraq has granted the Kurds a very limited autonomy and the right of education and publishing in their own language, and these have been much curtailed in the past years. Turkey, on the other hand, is the only country where they enjoy equal political rights and access to all institutions – as long as they do not manifest themselves as Kurds. To many Kurdish intellectuals, therefore, the need to maintain and develop Kurdish culture is more urgent than that of territorial rights.

It is in this field that Kurdish political refugees in Europe have set themselves an important task. Since the 1960s, numerous Kurdish immigrants from Turkey have found work in West European countries (hundreds of thousands, by the end of the 1970s). Their numbers were later swelled by "economic" and political refugees. The political activists among the latter set out to organize the Kurdish workers and awaken their nationalism, the intellectuals attempted to educate them and to develop Kurdish literature and scholarship. Press freedom and state subvention of migrants' cultural activities enabled the intellectuals to publish journals and books in Kurdish. Kurmanji, which had remained a relatively backward language (due, at least in part, to its supression in Turkey), was developed into a modern literary language adequate for political and intellectual discourse. A modern Kurmanji literature is rapidly developing in European exile and finds its way back into Turkey. Paradoxically, it is precisely the repression of Kurdish cultural activities and the persecution of those engaged in it, which created the conditions for its present resurgence.

The political refugees and other migrants in Europe have also performed another function. Until a decade ago, hardly anyone abroad, apart from a few romantics, was interested in the Kurds. That has now changed; the Kurds and their plight have become known to European and American public opinion. The beginnings of a Kurdish lobby are there, and as a result there has been some pressure, though still ambiguous and ineffective, on Turkey and Iraq for more humane treatment of the Kurds. This foreign support encourages the Kurds "inside" to continue their struggle for basic rights. Indirectly, those who have voluntarily or involuntarily left Kurdistan have perhaps contributed more to the strengthening of the Kurdish movement than they would have done had they been able to remain there.

Chapter 3

On the Kurdish language

Philip G. Kreyenbroek

ABSTRACT

Language plays a powerful role in the struggle of the Kurds for recognition as a people. In the eyes of many, the Kurdish language is both proof and symbol of the separate identity of the Kurds, and impressive efforts are made to preserve and develop it. Some governments, on the other hand, have also realized the significance of language, and have sought to "assimilate" the Kurds by attempting to suppress Kurdish altogether, or to discourage its development. The problems created by official repression are compounded by the fact that considerable differences exist between the various dialects of Kurdish; this has precluded the development of a unified standard form of Kurdish that could be used as a generally accepted written language. As a result of the partition of Kurdistan after the collapse of the Ottoman Empire, two different standard languages have now emerged, one of which has evolved almost entirely in exile. This paper will give a brief survey of the origin and early history of Kurdish, and go on to examine in greater detail the recent history and present position of the Kurdish language in Turkey, Iraq and Iran, with special reference to the development of written forms of Kurdish. Some developments which took place in Syria will be discussed in the context of the history of Kurdish in Turkey and in exile. The situation in the Soviet Union, including questions of language, is discussed elsewhere in this volume.

INTRODUCTION

It would hardly be possible to give an exact definition of the links between language and national or group identity. Where no problems exist, such links are usually simple and self-evident. When the identity of a people is in question, however, language can become a focus for nationalist sentiments: in some cases, new demands are then made on the language, often leading to unforeseen problems. Kurdish is a case in point. Although there was some literary activity before the late nineteenth century, Kurdish was not normally used as a written language: for administrative, religious, and indeed most literary purposes, the dominant languages of the region, Arabic, Turkish and Persian, were used. While Kurdish remained mainly a spoken language, the differences between regional forms of speech did not present a problem. Towards the end of the nineteenth century, however – probably as a result of a heightened awareness of Kurdish identity prompted by various developments in the internal affairs of the Ottoman Empire – a new interest in the use of Kurdish as a written language began to emerge. In the years immediately preceding and following the collapse of the Ottoman Empire, when the creation of an independent Kurdish state was a real possibility, the need for a standard written language was evidently felt more acutely. When, a few years later, hopes of an independent Kurdistan were dashed, and the partition of Ottoman Kurdistan became a fact, Iraqi and Turkish Kurds continued independently to cultivate their language, fearing no doubt that the loss of Kurdish might result in the disappearance of their identity as Kurds, which was all they had left.

To create and develop a written language is a daunting task: even if, as in the case of Kurdish, two different standard forms emerge (each based on the dominant dialect of the country of origin of those who write it), rivalries between speakers of different regional variants still present problems, and decisions have to be made about linguistic purity (does one, for example, adopt or even coin a Kurdish-sounding word when most native speakers use an Arabic or Turkish one?). Moreover, in writing a language native speakers are often confronted for the first time with problems of grammar which they cannot solve on the basis of their feeling for the spoken language alone.

It would be untrue to say that the future of the Kurdish language depends entirely on the success of its speakers in evolving and cultivating one or more written languages: Kurdish has survived for a long time without a written language and, on the other hand, national states might conceivably succeed in eliminating the language by some means other than the suppression of a written literature. Yet it would seem that the Kurds are right in recognizing the vital importance, in the modern world, of developing their language into an adequate means of written communication and, especially, education.

THE ORIGIN, EARLY HISTORY AND DIALECTOLOGY OF KURDISH

Kurdish is a western Iranian language, a member of the Iranian branch of the Indo-European family of languages. It is therefore almost as different from Turkish and Arabic as English and French, but very similar to *Farsi*, the national language of Iran. The Kurds themselves often claim descent from the Medes, the northern neighbours and imperial predecessors of the ancient Persians. This theory has been convincingly challenged on linguistic grounds (MacKenzie 1961). It seems that the Kurdish tribes originally lived somewhat farther to the south than the Medes. At some stage, Kurdish tribes migrated to the north, and settled in eastern Anatolia. It is possible that their migrations displaced another Iranian people, whose original home may have been near the Caspian sea. One branch of this people, it seems, moved farther into Anatolia, where they became the ancestors of the modern Zaza, or Dimli, who now live in the triangle between Dyarbakir, Sivas and Erzurum. The Zaza language is closely akin to that of the Guran, small groups of whom survive in the area near Bakhtaran (formerly Kermanshah) in Iran. (Both Zaza and Guran are normally identified as Kurds, and regard themselves as such. From a purely historical and linguistic perpective, this is probably incorrect, but such considerations seem insignificant in comparison with the feelings of the people concerned.) We do not know for certain whether these groups originally formed one people, or if the ancestors of the Guran were also displaced by the migrations of the Kurds. It seems probable, however, that at a later stage some of the Kurdish tribes moved back south, where they encountered the Guran. At that time the Gurani language deeply influenced the speech of these "southern" Kurds (i.e. the central and southern dialects), while leaving the northern form of Kurdish unaffected.

Of these three main groups of dialects, only the northern and central ones concern us here: the southern dialects do not play a major role in the development of standard dialects of Kurdish. Although some Kurdish scholars (e.g. Nebez 1975, p. 98, n. 7) have raised objections to the names, the usual terms *Kurmanji* and *Sorani* will be used here for the northern and central dialects respectively, both for the regional and local sub-dialects belonging to these groups, and for the standard written forms (the form of Kurdish written in Iran, based on the Mukri sub-dialect of Sorani, differs only slightly from the standard Sorani used in Iraq).

Kurmanji is spoken in Turkey, Syria, the Soviet Union, and in the northern parts of the Kurdish-speaking areas of Iraq and Iran; groups of Kurmanji-speakers also live in the Iranian province of Khorasan. Since 1932 most Kurds have used Roman script to write Kurmanji; in the Soviet Union Cyrillic is generally used. Sorani is spoken in Iraq, south of the Greater Zab, and in central parts of the Kurdish-speaking area of Iran. It is normally written in an adapted form of the Arabic script.

It may be somewhat misleading to speak of "the main dialects of Kurdish". Firstly, the only obvious reasons for describing Sorani and Kurmanji as "dialects" of one language, are their common origin, and the fact that this usage reflects the sense of ethnic identity and unity of the Kurds. From a linguistic, or at least grammatical point of view, however, Sorani and Kurmanji differ as much from each other as English and German, and it would seem more appropriate to refer to them as "languages": Sorani has neither gender nor case-endings (like English "to the man", "to the woman"), whereas Kurmanji has both (cf. German "dem Manne", "der Frau"); in Sorani pronominal enclitics play a crucial role in verbal constructions, while Kurmanji has no such enclitics, etc. Differences in vocabulary and pronuciation are not as great as between German and English, but they are still considerable. Many Kurmanji-speakers therefore cannot understand Sorani, and vice versa. Furthermore, as mentioned earlier, there are the substantial differences between local and regional sub-dialects of each of these "dialects"; speakers of different sub-dialects can usually understand each other, but tend to disagree as to the proper way of expressing many things.

It has proved impossible, therefore, to evolve one single standard form of Kurdish. In 1934 participants of the Congress of Kurdish

Writers, Poets and Authors of the USSR held in Yerevan, arbitrarily decided that the (Kurmanji) sub-dialect of the Soviet Kurds should be adopted as a standard written language for all Kurds; needless to say this failed to impress most people. Since then, several attempts have been made by Kurdish scholars to bridge the gap between Sorani and Kurmanji (e.g., recently, Nebez 1975), but the results of such academic efforts are too artificial to have much chance of finding wide acceptance. Instead, standard forms of Kurmanji and Sorani have developed separately, as a result of "natural" historical processes.

In the late sixteenth or early seventeenth century, Mulla Jaziri (Melê Cizirî), a Kurmanji-speaking poet from Jazira, on the border between modern Turkey and Syria, began to write poetry in his own sub-dialect. Although at least one poet is known to have written in Kurdish before him, Mulla Jaziri's work apparently served as a model to others, and a number of literary works appeared in the Jiziri sub-dialect in the seventeenth century; perhaps the most important of these was Ahmad Khani's *Mem-û Zîn* (the literary version of a well-known oral epic). After a time, interest in such efforts seems to have waned (as far as we know, no literary works in Kurmanji appeared in the eighteenth and nineteenth centuries), but the Jiziri sub-dialect became the basis of the standard Kurmanji that was to develop later.

In southern Kurdistan, the situation was complicated by the fact that Gurani, the sacred language of the Ahl-e Haqq (a heterodox religious group), which was protected, moreover, by the noble house of Ardalan, already shared the position of a literary language with Persian and Arabic in that region. As the fortunes of the Ardalan princes waned, however, the star of another local dynasty rose: in 1784 the princes of Baban founded the city of Sulaymaniya, and the speech of that city gradually became the language of poetry in the area, thus gaining prestige, and emerging in due course as the basis of standard Sorani.

The early literary efforts of the Kurds, however, were hardly more than a prelude. From the late nineteenth century onwards, Kurdish intellectuals began to write periodicals in Kurmanji (*Kurdistan*, Cairo 1898; *Kurd*, Istanbul 1907; *Kurdistan*, Urumiyeh 1912–14; *Rôzhî Kurd*, Istanbul 1913; *Hêviya Kurd*, Istanbul, 1913; *Zhîn*, Cairo 1916; cf. Jebari 1970), while Sorani continued to develop chiefly as a language of poetry until after the defeat of the Ottoman Empire.

KURMANJI IN THE TURKISH REPUBLIC AND IN EXILE

Kemalist nationalism saw no place in the newly created republic, for anyone but Turks. In 1924 all Kurdish institutions such as schools and religious foundations, and also publications, were officially abolished. The period from 1925 until the early 1930s witnessed a succession of serious Kurdish revolts, which were eventually crushed with great brutality. Many Kurdish intellectuals fled to Syria, which was under French Mandate; there they supported the struggle of the Kurds in Turkey, and worked to develop their language.

Official attitudes towards the Kurds, and thus towards their language, are perhaps best characterized by the following pronouncement by a Turkish cabinet minister: "I believe that the Turk must be the only lord, the only master of this country. Those who are not of pure Turkish stock can have only one right in this country, the right to be servants and slaves" (*Milliyet* no. 1655, 16 September 1930, quoted by Kendal in Chaliand 1980, p. 65). In 1932, a law was passed in Turkey which legalized massive forced resettlements of Kurds. Ironically, in the same year the Kurdish magazine *Hawar*, published in Damascus, began to write Kurmanji in Roman script, in direct imitation of Atatürk's reforms in Turkey (the reason for this, presumably, was a practical one: most Kurmanji-speaking Kurds were citizens of Turkey, and future generations would be taught to read and write Roman rather than Arabic script; to expect them to use the latter for Kurdish was plainly unrealistic). *Hawar*, incidentally, was one of the first of a long series of Kurmanji publications in exile after the creation of the Turkish republic.

In 1938 a further Kurdish revolt in the area of Dersim was suppressed with great difficulty. (Dersim was then razed to the ground and renamed Tunceli.) From this time onwards, the use of Kurdish was banned, and the words "Kurd" and "Kurdistan" disappeared from the official vocabulary: the Kurds had become "mountain Turks". For a long time, Kurds who bargained in the market-place in the only language they knew could be fined a certain sum per word. After this, the Kurds appear to have lost hope, and the period 1938–61 may well have been the most dangerous in recent history as far as the survival of Kurmanji in Turkey is concerned. Most Kurds, of course, continued to speak Kurdish at home; indeed some groups speak little else to this day. However, those who did not speak Turkish inevitably became alienated from the main-stream of public life in Turkey. The lack of educational facilities, publications and broadcasts in Kurdish naturally had its impact, and even now many educated Kurds who are ardent champions of the Kurdish cause, find it easier to express abstract ideas in Turkish. Only the most motivated Kurds in Turkey have learned to read and write their own language, and many periodicals published by Turkish Kurds in the West are bilingual, written in Kurmanji and Turkish, since purely Kurdish editions would not be accessible to many Kurds.

However, as long as Syria continued to be under French Mandate, Kurdish intellectuals found a basis for their literary activities there: *Hawar* continued to appear intermittently until 1943; other publications in Kurmanji included *Roja Nû* (1943–6), *Stêr* (1943), and *Ronahî* (1942–5). Leading figures in Kurdish literary circles in Syria were the brothers Celadet and Kamuran Bedir-Khan. The former was editor in chief of *Hawar*, and author of a Kurmanji grammar and many articles on Kurdish culture. His brother Kamuran was editor of *Stêr* and *Roja Nû*; in 1950 he became Professor of Kurdish Language and Culture at the Sorbonne in Paris. After the end of the French Mandate in Syria in 1945, the centre of literary activities in Kurmanji gradually shifted to western Europe (see further below).

In 1950, with the first free general elections, in which the Democratic Party came to power, life became a little easier for the Kurds. It was not until 1961, however, that there was something of a breakthrough: in that year the new constitution allowed freedom of expression, of association and of the press. Kurdish affairs could once more be discussed, or at least alluded to, in the media, and there appears to have been a surge of renewed interest among the Kurds in their own cultural identity. Perhaps manuscripts came out of drawers where they had long been mouldering, and the years 1962–8 saw a number of publications in Kurmanji, such as the bilingual (Kurdish/Turkish) periodicals *Dicle-Firat* and *Deng* (Istanbul 1962), a play (Anter 1965), a Kurdish Grammar, a Kurdish–Turkish Dictionary, etc. Most of these were banned soon after they appeared, but some copies were usually available, and these were passed from hand to hand. Clandestine literacy courses in Kurmanji were set up. Moreover, the Kurds in Turkey had reports of the struggles and successes of their Iraqi brothers at this time: broadcasts in Kurdish reached them, as did cassettes with songs and stories in various dialects. All this had the effect of strengthening their sense of identity, and their pride in Kurdish. The Turkish authorities reacted: in 1967 it was officially forbidden to bring publications and recordings in Kurdish into Turkey from abroad, and ever since that year there has been a general pattern of official repression, especially of written Kurdish, which has been implemented with varying degrees of success (there were some publications in Kurmanji in the 1970s). The constitution of 1982, promulgated after the military coup of General Evren, leaves no doubt about official attitudes to Kurdish: art. 26 states that "no language prohibited by law can be used in the expression and diffusion of opinions"; art. 28 states "No person may publish in a prohibited language." Kurdish, needless to say, was a prohibited language. In the 1980s some Turkish academics have attempted to prove – apparently in all seriousness – that Kurdish is of Turkic origin, and therefore akin to Turkish (instead of "mountain Turks", the Kurds have become *Kürttürkler*, "Kurd-Turks" in such publications; e.g. Parmaksuzoğlu 1983). The year 1983 witnessed the introduction of new repressive laws aimed against the use of Kurdish (Law no. 2392, art. 3: "The native language of Turkish citizens is Turkish. It is forbidden: a) to use as a native language a language other than Turkish and to participate in any activity aiming to diffuse these languages"). In the same year Mehdi Zana, the former mayor of Diyarbakir, was condemned to 32 years' imprisonment (later reduced to 26 years), for speaking Kurdish with his staff. In general, however, semi-official attitudes towards spoken Kurdish appear to have been relatively relaxed until recently (the severe international criticism of Turkish treatment of the Kurds which met Turkey's application for membership of the EC may have played a role here). In 1989 and the beginning of 1990 repression seems once more to have been severe in some areas. Publications in Kurdish continued to be banned. Early in 1991, however, the Turkish government formally declared its intention of legalizing the use of Kurdish in Turkey; at the time of writing (May 1991), it is too early to speculate on the significance of this announcement.

The real development of written Kurmanji is still taking place almost entirely in exile. After Lebanon and Syria had gained their independence of the French (in 1943 and 1945 respectively), the climate in those countries was no longer as favourable to the Kurds as it had been, and western Europe gradually became the centre of literary activities in Kurmanji. After 1967 many Kurdish intellectuals from Turkey fled from the repressive climate that was once more prevalent there. The 1960s and 1970s, moreover, saw an influx of immigrant workers from Turkey into western Europe. Since Kurdistan is among the poorest areas in Turkey, many of those who were known to the host-countries as Turks were in fact Kurds. In their new environment many of these became more politically aware, and felt freer to express their Kurdish identity. As a result of these factors, there has been a very varied output of written material in Kurmanji published in exile; these include novels and collections of short stories (e.g. Şemo 1983; Uzun 1984), literary and cultural journals (e.g. *Hêvî*), as well as various publications by political groups. In the last ten years or so, there appears to have been a marked improvement in the standard of written Kurmanji: it has become more flexible and authors seem to have a larger Kurdish vocabulary at their disposal for abstract terms. The latter development is partly due to borrowings from Sorani, but Kurmanji-speaking intellectuals are making serious efforts to evolve a vocabulary that is appropriate for their own dialect: since the spring of 1987, Kurds from different Kurmanji-speaking areas meet on a half-yearly basis to discuss proper Kurmanji usage; the results are published in in the journal *Kurmancî*. Kurmanji, in short, is one of the very few languages in the world whose modern standard form has so evolved almost entirely in exile.

KURDISH IN IRAQ

One's first impression when studying the history of the Kurdish language in Iraq since 1918, may well be that the Iraqi Kurds (or at least the Sorani-speakers) faced far fewer obstacles in developing their language than the Kurds of Turkey. Certainly the authorities in Iraq never sought to suppress spoken Kurdish, and the Iraqi Kurds were able to create a standard written Sorani that is entirely adequate for academic and literary purposes. It should not be forgotten, however, that these are the hard-won results of a long struggle against official apathy or indeed hostility, rather than a boon granted by a benevolent government. The very fact that the Iraqi authorities have found it necessary time and time again to recognize publicly, in various forms, that the Kurds have rights, including the right to their own language, gives some indication of the realities of the situation (in Britain, for example, such assurances seldom need to be given about Welsh or Gaelic).

The main reason why the situation in Iraq developed differently from that in Turkey can probably be found in the fact that Mesopotamia was under British Mandate during the period 1920–30. Although the British authorities were plainly baffled by the discovery that there was no such thing as "the" Kurdish language, they insisted that the Kurds were entitled to education and administration in their own language, and urged the Kurds to agree on a standard form of Kurdish. British officials (particularly Major E.B. Soane, who had a deep interest in Kurdish), clearly favoured a form of Sorani, the dialect of the majority of Kurds in Iraq. The efforts of Shaykh Mahmud Barzinji to carve out a Kurdish kingdom for himself also did much to promote Kurdish. Shaykh Mahmud's capital was Sulaimaniya, the city whose sub-dialect already served as a standard language of poetry, and in the years 1922–3 a number of newspapers appeared in this dialect (*Rozhī Kurdistan, Bangī Ḥeqq, Umēdī Istiqlal*; cf. Edmonds 1925). The sub-dialect of Sulaimaniya thus gained a lasting prominence over other dialects of Sorani. Under British Mandate the Iraqi government had undertaken to honour the recommendations of the League of Nations that the Kurds should have the right to use their own language in schools and in local administration, but no such provisions were included in the Anglo-Iraqi treaty of 1930, which accorded Iraq its independence; nor had any serious progress been made as to the production of school textbooks in Kurdish, the training of Kurdish teachers, or indeed the official standardization of Sorani. This led to renewed and serious friction between Kurds and Arabs, and in 1931 the Local Languages Law was passed, which recognized the use of Kurdish in primary schools. After this, the Iraqi Kurds' struggle to preserve and develop their language appears to have continued comparatively uneventfully for over two decades.

A major breakthrough came in 1958, with the coup of General Qasim. The newly created Republic of Iraq recognized the Kurds as "partners" of the Arabs, and for a time Kurdish received official encouragement. In 1959 a Chair of Kurdish Studies was founded in the University of Baghdad, a General Directorate of Kurdish Studies was set up to supervise Kurdish schools, and

there were many newspapers, magazines and radio broadcasts
in Kurdish. Sorani was officially recognized as the basis for a
standard Iraqi Kurdish, (which to some extent alienated the
Kurmanji-speakers in the north). In spite of renewed tensions
between the Kurdish leadership and the Iraqi government,
Kurdish literary life flourished for some years. The tensions
increased, however, and in 1963 there was an 8-month ban
on all Kurdish periodicals. After the Ba'thist coup of 1968
mutual distrust between Kurds and Arabs continued, but in
1970 an agreement was signed providing for the recognition
of Kurdish as the second official language of Iraq, and for
Kurdish to be taught jointly with Arabic in schools; moreover,
it was agreed that all officials in Kurdistan would be required to
speak Kurdish. In the years immediately following the agreement,
institutions were founded or revived (cf. Nebez 1975, p.105):
the Union of Kurdish Writers, the General Directorate for
the Protection of Kurdish Culture and the Kurdish Academy
of Sciences. The latter was to play a very prominent role in
promoting the development of Kurdish. In the early 1970s, for
instance, it proposed a number of reforms in standard written
Sorani, aimed chiefly at eliminating some of the idiosyncrasies of
the sub-dialect of Sulaimaniya (see Nebez 1975, p. 106–7). The
most important of these proposals have been widely accepted.

The year 1970 proved to be a watershed, however. Within two
years there were new major tensions between the Iraqi government
and the Kurdish leader Mulla Mustafa Barzani. These culminated
in an open breach in 1974 (the same year, ironically, that saw a
watered-down version of the 1970 agreement become law). In
1975 the Shah of Iran, who had supported Barzani, signed the
Agreement of Algiers with the Iraqi government and abandoned
the Iraqi Kurds to their fate; as a result the Kurdish resistance
virtually collapsed. In the years that followed, many of the
achievements of 1970 were gradually whittled down by the
Iraqi authorities. In view of the repeated brutal attacks on
Kurdish civilians after the end of the Iran–Iraq war (e.g.
Halabja, March 1988), and the forced resettlements of parts
of the Kurdish population (1989), it seems unlikely that the
atmosphere in Iraq will be conducive to worthwhile literary
activities in the near future. At the time of writing, it is
impossible to predict the effects of the 1991 Gulf War on the
position of the Kurds of Iraq.

The successes of the Iraqi Kurds in the field of language and education have, however, enabled them to create an impressive literature and a fully adequate written language, and have produced a generation of Kurds whose primary and secondary education have been in Kurdish. Such achievements will undoubtedly help the Kurds of Iraq in their future efforts to preserve their cultural and ethnic identity.

KURDISH IN IRAN

In Iran the recent history of the Kurdish language has neither been as tragic as in Turkey, nor as successful as in Iraq. A large percentage of Iranians belong to various ethnic groups whose mother tongue is not Persian (besides the Kurds, e.g. Azeris, Baluchis and Turcomans), and who have coexisted more or less peacefully for centuries under the actual or nominal control of whatever government was in power in the capital. The Iranian authorities therefore appear to be rather more skilful in dealing with such peoples and their languages than those of such younger nations as Turkey and Iraq, where the dominant groups seek to establish absolute control. Official attitudes towards the Kurds in Iran have generally been dictated by the need to keep the Kurdish population reasonably content, while at the same time restraining their aspirations for autonomy and promoting their sense of allegiance to the national state. Thus there have been no serious attempts to suppress spoken Kurdish, but publications in that language have rarely been allowed. Also, most Farsi-speakers regard Kurdish as no more than one of the many dialects of Persian; indeed some believe that Kurdish, which sounds archaic to them, is a "purer" form of that language. Consequently the Kurdish language as such has seldom been regarded as a challenge to national unity in Iran, and perhaps the Iranian Kurds have been less strongly motivated than their brothers in Iraq to cultivate written Kurdish.

Until the mid nineteenth century, Kurdish principalities on both Iranian and Ottoman territory were largely independent of either government, and no useful distinction can be made between cultural developments in Iranian and Ottoman Kurdistan. In the 1860s the Qajars abolished the Kurdish principalities in Iran. The fall of the Kurdish Ardalan dynasty indirectly strengthened the position of the Sulaymani sub-dialect of Sorani (see above), but the loss of Kurdish patrons also appears to have meant a decline in the interest in Kurdish literature and culture. Under Reza Shah (1926–41), efforts were made to promote the use of Persian among the Kurds, and publications in Kurdish were forbidden. During the brief period of the Mahabad Republic (22 January–16 December 1946) and the years leading up to it, publications in Kurdish flourished (for some of these publications see Nebez 1975, p.103). A period of active repression of expressions of Kurdish identity followed the defeat of the Mahabad government (though there is no indication that such measures seriously affected spoken Kurdish), and overt literary activities appear to have ceased altogether. In the later years of the reign of Mohammad Reza Pahlavi (1941–79), there were local broadcasts in Kurdish, and short texts in Kurdish could sometimes be published as part of academic works or as "Iranian folklore", but, generally speaking, written publications in Kurdish were forbidden.

Kurdish groups actively participated in the revolutionary movement that led to the downfall of the Pahlavi dynasty, and many had high hopes that Kurdistan would become an autonomous region of the Islamic Republic, in which Kurdish would have the status of an official language beside Farsi. During the early months of the revolution, plans for the foundation of a Kurdish University were in an advanced stage. This University, which would have branches in both Mahabad and Sanandaj, was to include a Faculty of Kurdish Literature. Before the University could open its doors, however, it was declared illegal by the government. In the areas controlled by Kurdish nationalists Kurdish schools were set up, which continued to function until the authority of the central government was firmly established.

The original draft of the Islamic constitution of Iran stipulated that Farsi should be used for official communications throughout Iran, but permitted the use of local languages in schools and in the local press; the final version of the constitution (approved November 1979), however, stated that local languages could only be used alongside Farsi, and that school textbooks would be in Persian only. As was indicated above, these provisions do not seem to have had any long-lasting effect in the early years of the Islamic Republic: serious tensions erupted between the Kurdish leadership and the government in Tehran almost as soon as the republic was established, and there was heavy fighting. This laid the foundation for deep mutual feelings of resentment and distrust. In spite of the guarantees of the constitution, publications in Kurdish were forbidden. They were legalized, however, in 1984, and this evidently marked a change in official policy as regards Kurdish culture: since that time there have been a number of publications in Kurdish, including a literary magazine (*Sirwe*), and also a steady stream of publications on the history and culture of the Kurds in Farsi; a Kurdish publishing house has been founded in Urumiyeh, and there is (or was until recently) a Kurdish bookshop at a prestigious location in Tehran. Education in Kurdish is now permitted. These developments are still too recent to allow one to claim that a real tradition of writing Kurdish now exists in Iran. Since most Iranian Kurds are Sorani speakers, however, they can draw upon the achievements of their brothers in Iraq.

THE PROSPECTS

A language inevitably dies when the main body of its speakers becomes extinct. This can happen not only through physical extermination, but also when a society disintegrates because of massive voluntary or forced migrations. The reader of this volume will hardly be left in any doubt as to the dangers of this kind that have threatened the Kurds in recent decades in some of the states which embody their country. Sadly, there are no guarantees that the near future will see the end of such phenomena. Yet it is also true that physical attacks, poverty and forced migrations – however tragic – have failed to put an end either to the existence of the Kurdish people (whose number McDowall's conservative estimate in this book puts at 19.7 million), or to its sense of identity.

It seems unlikely, therefore, that the disappearance of the Kurdish people will lead to the death of Kurdish in the foreseeable future. The opposite danger, viz. that the death of Kurdish may result in the loss of Kurdish identity and thus in the gradual extinction of the Kurdish nation, causes serious concern to some Kurds. As no reliable studies are available, all that can be done here is to examine some of the factors that might play a role in such a development. "Language death" is usually due to the strong influence of a dominant language. That language normally has greater prestige than the group's first language, and pressure is often brought to bear on them to speak it; as a result, the dominant language is used so frequently and in so many different spheres of life that it almost comes to replace the first language, and children learn it at an early age. Usually the structures of the dominant language then begin to affect those of the language in question (an abundance of loanwords in itself does not appear to affect the "health" of a language, as the vocabulary of modern English shows), and within a few generations people find it easier to express themselves in the dominant language. To all intents and purposes, this appears to have happened in the case of Gurani, which lost its prestige as a literary language in the nineteenth century, lost ground to Kurdish, and was described in the present century as "the language of old women in the alleys and back-streets of Sanandaj" (Kurdistani in Nebez 1975, p. 101); at present all that is left are "a few speech islands in a sea of Kurdish" (MacKenzie 1961, p. 73). Some or all of the factors that seem to have led to the near-extinction of Gurani, may also affect the situation of Kurdish in Turkey: the Kurds are a minority (albeit a large one), the status of Kurdish in Turkish society is extremely low, official communications and education are exclusively in Turkish, and there is no place for Kurmanji in public life. Undoubtedly such factors have led many Kurds to adopt Turkish as their first language, but it was probably the sheer numbers of Kurmanji-speakers that have prevented this from having a fatal effect on the future of the language. The isolation of many Kurdish communities and, ironically, the low level of education may also have helped to save Kurmanji (and, incidentally, Zaza) in the difficult period 1938–61. In spite of the serious tensions in eastern Turkey in the late 1980s and early 1990s, which have forced large groups of Kurds to leave their villages, it is probably true to say that the situation now is not as bad as it was then. Although, with the spread of education and the greater accessibility of television, the encroachment of Turkish continues, it would seem therefore that there is no immediate cause for alarm.

In Iran, much the same reasoning may apply: as long as a majority of the five million Iranian Kurds continue to live in Kurdish-speaking communities, there seems little likelihood that their language will die out. Moreover, there is no serious social stigma attached to Kurdish in Iran, and there has been no history of systematic efforts to discourage the spoken language.

For reasons discussed above, the situation in Iraq is altogether different. The factors that may lead to a more or less "natural" language death are either absent there, or present to a much lesser extent. However, the Iraqi Kurds are perhaps more directly exposed to outside threats than any of the other communities discussed here; these might conceivably lead to the extinction of Kurdish in Iraq, but at present this seems improbable.

In spite of the many and diverse threats which the Kurds have to face, one may therefore perhaps conclude that it is unlikely that the Kurdish people as a whole will see its language die out in the foreseeable future.

Chapter 4

Humanitarian legal order and the Kurdish question

Jane Connors

> They talk to us of the rules of war, of chivalry, of flags of truce, of mercy to the unfortunate and so on. It's all rubbish . . . war is not courtesy but the most horrible thing in life and we ought to understand that and not play at war . . . The aim of war is murder; the methods of war are spying, treachery and their encouragement, the ruin of a country's inhabitants, robbing them or stealing to provision the army, and fraud and falsehood termed military craft.
>
> (Prince Andrew Bulkhonsky,
> *War and Peace*, Book X, Chapter 25)

INTRODUCTION

The traditional ambit of international law has been conflict between sovereign states. Increased recognition of the international repercussions of internal strife in states, combined with the growth in the acceptance of international human rights norms has led to, at least, minimum regulation of intra-state behaviour in violent situations in international law. Such regulation finds its genesis in two strands of international law – humanitarian law and human rights law – which, although different in historical and doctrinal origin, find their basis in a common concept of humanity and exhibit a parallelism in terms of norms such as the prohibition of torture and cruel, inhumane or degrading punishment which they prescribe. These two strands, theoretically, present a continuum of norms which can be drawn upon to secure the protection of human rights in all situations.

The following purports to be an examination of these two strands of international law and their application to the situation of the Kurds in Iraq, Iran, Turkey and, to a lesser extent, Syria.

The conclusion of this examination – politically rational, but ideologically disappointing – is that while it appears clear that both strands – humanitarian law and human rights law – apply to the situations under consideration and have been violated repeatedly, the mere fact of application or, indeed, violation, provides no remedy in the absence of national and international commitment to the legal norms applicable. Insofar as the Kurdish question is concerned, national and international commitment to the applicable legal norms has been tenuous.

HUMANITARIAN LAW

International legal regulation of the Kurdish situation is to be found in the various sources of international law, which are commonly agreed to be those set out in Article 38(1) of the Statute of the International Court of Justice and comprise:

(a) international conventions, whether general or particular, establishing rules recognized by the contesting states;
(b) international custom as evidence of a general practice accepted as law;
(c) the general principles of law recognized by civilized nations;
(d) . . . judicial decisions and the teachings of the most highly qualified publicists of the various nations, as subsidiary means for the determination of rules of law.

Until 1949, traditional international law relegated the problems of civil violence and even civil war to the state involved, the Hague and Geneva Conventions on the laws of war restricting the protections and privileges of legitimate combatancy to the representatives of states – the armed forces, militia or volunteer corps, resistance movements belonging to a party to the conflict and complying with Article 4(2) of the Geneva Conventions, persons accompanying the armed forces and participants in a *levée en masse*.[1]

Governments could treat rebels or members of national liberation movements as criminals under their own municipal laws, prosecute and punish them as such, subject to any international human rights obligation. Traditional international law did recognize, however, that where the civil conflict fell within the definition of belligerency, which was met when (1) there was widely spread armed conflict within a state, (2) rebels occupied and administered a substantial part of the territory, (3) hostilities were conducted in accordance with the rules of war and through armed forces responsible to an identifiable authority, giving rise to (4) circumstances which made it necessary for third parties to define their attitude by acknowledging the status of belligerency,[2] the belligerent power was a lawful subject of international law, having the right to conduct hostilities and being accorded the protection of the international rules relating to the conduct of hostilities and the use of weapons in war.[3] Theoretically, therefore, were any Kurdish conflict to fall within the definition of belligerency, international law would afford the struggle recognition analogous to that of a state. Given, however, that there has been no recognition of the status of belligerency since the Second World War,[4] exploration of this concept in the modern Kurdish context is unhelpful.[5]

Limited regulation of the conduct of civil disturbance was provided in 1949 by Article 3 common to the four Geneva Conventions which, although not making the Conventions applicable in their entirety, is an attempt to apply the fundamental principles of the Geneva Conventions to non-international armed conflicts. Common Article 3 provides:

> In the case of armed conflict not of an international character occurring in the territory of one of the High Contracting Parties, each Party to the conflict shall be bound to apply, as a mimimum, the following provisions:
>
> (1) Persons taking no active part in the hostilities, including members of armed forces who have laid down their arms and those placed *hors de combat* by sickness, wounds, detention, or any other cause, shall in all circumstances be treated humanely, without any adverse distinction founded on race, colour, religion or faith, sex, birth or wealth, or any other similar criteria.
>
> To this end, the following acts are and shall remain prohibited at any time and in any place whatsoever with regard to the above-mentioned persons:
>
> (a)   violence to life and person, in particular murder of all kinds, mutilation, cruel treatment and torture;
> (b)   taking of hostages;
> (c)   outrages upon personal dignity, in particular humiliating and degrading treatment;
> (d)   the passing of sentences and the carrying out of executions without previous judgement pronounced by a regularly

> constituted court, affording all the judicial guarantees
> which are recognized as indispensable by civilized peoples.
>
> (2) The wounded and sick shall be collected and cared for.
> An impartial humanitarian body, such as the International
> Committee of the Red Cross, may offer its services to the
> parties to the conflict.
>
> The Parties to the conflict should further endeavour to bring
> into force, by means of special agreements, all or part of the
> other provisions of the present Convention. The application of
> the preceding provisions shall not affect the legal status of the
> Parties to the conflict.

This Article, to which Iran, Iraq, Turkey and Syria are States
Parties,[6] although only a shadow of the full Conventions, provides
limited humanitarian protection in internal armed conflict. Only
those "persons taking no active part in the hostilities" are protected
by the Article, thus governments are not prevented from sup-
pressing the rebellion, nor prosecuting rebels under domestic law.
Certainly, any detainees must be treated "humanely" and given a
"judicial" trial, but no government is precluded from punishing
severely. As envisioned by the Article, humane treatment prohibits
four particular categories of conduct: violence to person, the taking
of hostages, humiliating treatment and sentencing without trial.
Torture is prohibited, but not coercion which does not meet
the definition of humiliating treatment, nor is there any specific
limitation on the methods and means of warfare or the conduct
of the combat itself. Thus, while Article 3, arguably, might
prohibit the use of chemical weapons against those who are
regarded as not "active" in the hostilities – a category left
vague in terms of definition – it would not prohibit their
deployment against combatants. If, however, the conflict were
an international one, use of such weapons would be regulated
by, amongst other instruments, the 1925 Geneva Protocol for
the Prohibition of the Use in War of Asphyxiating, Poisonous
or Other Gases, and of Bacteriological Methods of Warfare.[7]
Finally, Article 3 gives a restricted role to the Red Cross or
other aid societies who may offer their services, although parties
to the conflict need not accept it. Even where they do accept
such aid, however, the Article makes no provision for the respect
of such personnel or their facilities, beyond the pithy statement that
"the wounded and sick shall be collected and cared for".

In sum, the protection offered by Article 3 in non-international armed conflict is narrow.[8] Such protection that it does offer is further hampered by the fact that situations of "armed conflict not of international character" which attract its application are undefined and practical enforcement is difficult. Certainly, the level of conflict required falls short of belligerency which, as stated above, brings the entire body of humanitarian law into force, but below that level, civil strife travels a continuum which begins at riots or banditry. G.I.A.D Draper in *The Red Cross Conventions*[9] states:

> Varying criteria were suggested during the lengthy debates on [Article 3]. Examples of these criteria were: (a) that the Party in revolt against the legitimate government has an organized military force, an authority responsible for its acts, acting within a determinate territory and having the means of respecting and ensuring respect for the Conventions; (b) that the legal government is obliged to have recourse to its regular military forces against insurgents operating with a modicum of organization and in possession of part of the national territory.

It is generally accepted that the states present at the conference did not intend low-level violence to be included within the definition of "armed conflicts not of an international character",[10] thus for Kurds to claim even the minimal humanitarian protection offered by Article 3, it would be essential for them to prove that they are involved in an armed conflict which is more organized and intense than generalized rioting or terrorist behaviour. Certainly, up to now, governments have been slow to classify any internal disturbance as armed conflict, the United Kingdom in Malaya and Cyprus, the Portuguese in Angola and Mozambique, the Nigerians in Biafra, being unwilling to admit the applicability of the Article.[11] The French did, however, admit that the Article applied in Algeria in 1956, after the FLN threatened reprisals for the execution of detained rebels.[12] From a practical point of view, thus, notwithstanding the intensity of the Kurdish struggle in any of the states under consideration, the likelihood of such a state admitting that the internal disturbance meets the definition of "armed conflict" for the purposes of Article 3 is remote. Again, despite the fact that each state party to the Conventions is given the right to demand that the provisions of the Conventions are respected by a government engaged in a civil war, thus ensuring that that state carries out its obligations by Article 1,[13] application and implementation of the minimum humanitarian protection offered by Article 3 has been sporadic. Where the Article has been applied, this has been confined to allowing the assistance of the International Committee of the Red Cross, or if it has gone beyond that, this has been due to political expedience.

Wider protection in international law is offered where internal conflict meets the definition of a war of national liberation. Where the conflict can be so classified, it may be possible to argue that the national liberation movement has the authority in international law to achieve liberation[14] and that the entire body of law pertaining to the conduct of war governs the national liberation movement, with the addition of the specific protections to be found in the 1977 Protocols Additional to the Geneva Convention, 1949. In this context, thus, it is critical to explore the meaning of "war of national liberation" and, further, crucial to ascertain whether any of the various Kurdish struggles fall within that meaning.

A war of national liberation arises out of a struggle for self-determination, a right acknowledged in Article 1[15] of the International Convenant on Civil and Political Rights (ICCPR) of 1966 which states: "All peoples have the right of self-determination. By virtue of that right they freely determine their political status and freely pursue their economic, social and cultural development."

This right is echoed in other international instruments and declarations[16] referred to, and in the United Nations Charter itself which, in Articles 1 and 55, adverts to "the principle of equal rights and self-determination of peoples" as the basis for "peaceful and friendly relations among nations".

The principle of self-determination was applied extensively to the situations of mandated and trust territories and non self-governing territories,[17] so that it is now possible to assert that the application of the concept to "colonial" countries and peoples is well established in international law.[18] The application of the principle of self-determination outside the colonial context – as, for example, the case of the Kurdish people – is more controversial. Certainly, the language of Articles 1 and 55 of the Charter is general, leading to the view that the principle is not limited to the colonial context, but there is extensive debate as to whether the principle is so confined.[19] Those who suggest that the principle is not so confined point to the ultimate independence of Bangladesh[20] where self-determination was not based on the colonial status of the territory, but on the denial of human rights in the territory, while those who counter such a view have such examples as the Katangan secession from the Congo (1960–3) and the Biafran secession from Nigeria (1967–70), where self-determination was not supported, to rely on as authority.[21]

The lack of support for the principle of the right to self-determination in Katanga and Biafra contrasts sharply with the situation of Bangladesh, serving to indicate that any struggle for self-determination does not arise in political isolation. Both Katanga and Biafra made African leaders aware of the vulnerability of their own states, most of which are composed of different ethnic and cultural groups and led them to agree that self-determination is not a right of secession from a self-governing state. Both situations make clear that even if the right to self-determination does exist outside the colonial context, not all groups will be able to avail themselves of the right. Bangladesh – originally East Pakistan – occupied a separate geographical territory and was non-self-governing with respect to the remainder of the state. Moreover, Bangladeshis represented a coherent linguistic, religious, cultural and ethnic group.

Kurdistan exhibits a number of problems in the context of self-determination. First, it is questionable whether the region is sufficiently coherent linguistically, culturally and religiously so as to come within the definition of a "people" for the purposes of self-determination.[22] Second, unlike in previous situations, the Kurds find themselves divided among five host countries, a division which renders any struggle for self-determination both practically and legally complex. It may well be that the Kurds of each host state will have to continue the struggle for self-determination independently in order to present a credible "people" for the purposes of the principle.[23]

In the event that any Kurdish movement were to meet the definition of a struggle for self-determination, such would be classifiable as a war of national liberation. United Nations General Assembly Resolutions since 1968 have called on parties to wars of national liberation to apply the Geneva Conventions to such conflicts and in December 1973 Resolution 3103 (XXVIII) classified armed conflicts involving the struggle of peoples against colonial and alien domination and racist regimes as international armed conflicts for the purposes of those Conventions. Further, although states have remained reluctant to confer the status of legitimate combatancy on their insurgent opponents, in some wars of national liberation they have been similarly reluctant to appear inhumane and have, therefore, observed some of the principles of international law, allowing activity by the International Committee of the Red Cross and sometimes treating members of liberation movements as prisoners of war.[24] State practice has, however, been uneven,[25] and it seems doubtful whether Iran, Iraq or Turkey would be generous enough to apply principles of international law to their rebellious Kurds. Finally, Protocol 1, Additional to the 1949 Geneva Conventions, in Article 1 (4) extends the protection of those Conventions to "armed conflicts in which peoples are fighting against colonial domination and alien occupation and against racist regimes in the exercise of their right to self-determination, as enshrined in the Charter of the United Nations and the Declaration on the Principles of International Law Concerning Friendly Relations and Cooperation among States in accordance with the Charter of the United Nations".[26]

Article 1(4) would appear to offer Kurdish groups coverage, but, in practice, such an analysis is optimistic, not least because the only relevant state which has acceded to it is Syria,[27] where the conflict would not meet the requirements of the Article. These requirements are, first, that there be an "armed conflict", which by virtue of Article 1(2) of Protocol 11 does not include "internal disturbances and tensions, riots, isolated and sporadic acts of violence and other acts of a similar nature", thus implying the use of intense force by both sides. The armed conflict by the "people" must be conducted by an authority representing the people,[28] with the armed forces under a command responsible to a party to the conflict and subject to an internal disciplinary system which inter alia, shall enforce compliance with the law of war,[29] clearly suggesting that the Article will apply only where the "people" deploy an army-style force. Further, the Article is limited to situations where "peoples" are fighting, raising again the question of whether Kurds are a "people" for the purposes of a struggle for self-determination. Finally, the Article only applies to extend the humanitarian law of war to the conflict where these peoples are fighting "colonial domination", "alien occupation" and "racist regimes", situations which are highly subjective and difficult to define.[30]

Were Article 1(4) to be satisfied and the conflict waged against a High Contracting Party, the Kurdish combatants and civilians would be covered by extensive international protection, especially as provided by Articles 43 and 44 of the Protocol which govern the conditions under which the individuals shall be combatants and, if captured, entitled to prisoner of war status and therefore immune from prosecution under municipal law.[31] Further, Article 96(3) would give the authority representing the Kurdish armed struggle the right to declare that it intended to apply the Conventions and the Protocols to the conduct of their conflict. Such a declaration would be a politically sound action, conferring legitimacy on the liberation movement.

Nevertheless, given the few High Contracting Parties to the Protocol, a declaration of this kind appears impossible. From a tactical point of view, however, and as a means of gaining political capital, it may serve Kurdish groups well to attempt to accede to the Geneva Conventions and the Protocols,[32] or at least to make it known that they intend to abide by them, such an action serving to promote the idea that the conflicts within the states are more than civil strife.

Protocol 1, as it stands, therefore, provides a hollow solution for the Kurdish people. Moreover, although some writers have suggested that the Protocol is merely a crystallization of extant customary international law,[33] thereby applying irrespective of whether the relevant state is a High Contracting Party, such a suggestion is perhaps premature.[34]

Although boasting even fewer states parties than Protocol 1, Protocol 11, additional to the Geneva Conventions, seeks to extend the protection afforded by common Article 3 to conflict of a non-international nature.[35] A number of preconditions are required to bring the Protocol into operation. First, there must be an armed conflict which goes beyond internal disturbances such as riots, isolated and sporadic acts of violence, which is not covered by Article 1 of Protocol 1. Second, the armed conflict must take place in the territory of a High Contracting Party and involve the armed forces of such a party and dissident armed forces or other organized armed groups, who must act under a responsible command. Finally, the dissident group must have taken over a part of the territory of the High Contracting Party, so as to allow them to carry out sustained and concerted military operations.

Where the Protocol applies it guarantees humane treatment for those who do not take a direct part or who have ceased to take a direct part in the hostilities, children, persons whose liberty has been restricted, those who are prosecuted and punished with criminal offences related to the conflict and extends protection to the wounded, sick and shipwrecked and regulates the conduct of hostilities, insofar as the civilian population is concerned.

Protocol 11 appears to offer more comprehensive humanitarian protection in the context of the Kurdish struggle, in the event that such a struggle fails to meet the definition of a war of national liberation. This protection is, however, more apparent than real. The Protocol applies only where it has been ratified by states, no provision being made, unlike in Protocol 1, for the participation in the Protocol by the rebels. Further, again one might question whether any current Kurdish rebellion goes beyond the definition of internal disturbance and tension so as to meet the definition of armed conflict required for the Protocol, while, finally, even were the Protocol to apply, there is no machinery for supervision or enforcement.[36]

From this survey, it is perhaps safe to conclude that while a significant corpus of international humanitarian law exists to regulate intra-state conflict, its application in the Kurdish context is problematic. Even if it were held to be applicable, resistance by the states concerned would serve to emasculate the protection offered. At most, one might suggest that Kurdish liberation groups organize themselves to represent a viable and recognizable people in search of self-determination, employing tactical strategies, such as attempting to accede to the Geneva Conventions and Protocols, lobbying the International Committee of the Red Cross and seeking recognition in international forums as representatives of the Kurdish people,[37] an undeniably difficult task, but one rendered more difficult in the Kurdish struggle by the plethora of peoples' representatives.

HUMAN RIGHTS LAW

In the event that international humanitarian law proves to be a fruitless avenue of pursuit in the context of the Kurds, it remains possible for the issue to be confronted as one of human rights. Iran, Iraq, Syria and Turkey are states parties to numerous international instruments which guarantee their citizens protection from human rights violations, such as genocide, torture, other cruel, inhumane or degrading treatment and punishment and racial discrimination.[38] Iran, Iraq and Syria have ratified the International Covenant on Civil and Political Rights (ICCPR) and the International Covenant on Economic, Social and Cultural Rights (ICESCR), while Turkey is State Party to the European Convention on Human Rights and its five Protocols, even going so far as to give qualified recognition to the competence of the European Commission to receive petitions under Article 25 of that Convention.[39] These guarantees apply to protect citizens of States Parties even in contexts where international humanitarian law may become relevant.[40]

Strong and undeniable evidence exists which indicates that Kurds in Turkey, Syria, Iraq and Iran are denied, despite the flamboyant commitment of these states to international human rights norms, equitable access to economic resources, access to the power base and civil administration, equal status to that of the ethnic group in power, the right to mobilize politically, the right to use their own language and enjoy their culture and the right to a proper education. Further, there are clear suggestions that all attempts by Kurds to rectify these injustices have been met with imprisonment, execution, persecution, massacre and deportation. While it might be fashionable to suggest that subscription to international human rights norms is mere rhetoric, devoid of any meaning because state sovereignty prevents an adequate enforcement process, limited means of enforcement are provided in most instruments and must be exploited in order to protect the Kurds.

Thus, for example, states must be encouraged to use the enforcement mechanism under the European Convention on Human Rights in contexts where Turkey has been found to be in breach of its provisions with respect to the Kurds,[41] while the United Nations Human Rights Machinery, especially in its monitoring role, can be used more effectively to promote the rights of Kurds.[42]

It is clear that if the responsibility for action is left to states alone, little will be done in the absence of clear political motivation. It must be crudely shown that the international community has a significant stake in ensuring that human rights norms are not cynically ignored, or worse, flagrantly violated. Here stress on the interstate and global consequences of intra-state human rights violation – in terms of refugee movement and environmental degradation because of the use of certain weaponry – may ultimately prove a focus for reaction in a world community which has proved unnaturally silent in the face of the Kurdish issue.

Chapter 5

Political aspects of the Kurdish problem in contemporary Turkey[1]

Hamit Bozarslan

It is not easy to analyse the evolution of Turkish Kurdistan since the foundation of the Kemalist republic within the restricted limits of a chapter. The same is true even of the events since the "Second Republic", when the Turkish constitution was adopted in 1961. A number of questions immediately present themselves. What terms can be used to discuss the Kurdish problem since it is both an integral element of the minority problem within the Middle East and an internal problem for Turkey itself? Is it appropriate to select a historical viewpoint and emphasize the significance of the particularly bloody revolts that shook the Kemalist republic? Or might it not be preferable to refer to economic and demographic factors in order to describe the ways in which the agricultural economy was thrown into crisis and Kurdish towns became vast human conglomerations which only had an insignificant role within the overall national industrial production patterns? Or again, should the socio-political aspect of the issue be highlighted, so that the significance of religious brotherhoods, tribes and new urban social strata within the political life of Kurdish regions and of Turkey itself can be emphasized? Finally, would it not be most convenient to concentrate on geopolitical considerations, as the Kurdish problem extends far further than the confines of Turkey and is a key factor in its foreign policy?

Within the context of this chapter, I shall be obliged to exclude economic considerations as well as the questions of demography[2] and territory.[3] I shall avoid concentration on the period of the formation of the Turkish nation-state, and on the revolts and the repression which succeeded it. I shall, rather, limit the discussion to the principal socio-political characteristics of the Kurdish problem since 1961.

KURDISH NATIONALISM: FROM REBIRTH
TO RADICALIZATION

In its origins, Kurdish nationalism is no different from other types
of Middle Eastern nationalism, particularly that of the Arabs and
the Turks. It was an intellectual creation whose authors aspired to
a level of civilization in which a Kurdish state was justified equally
by the "millenarian" existence of the Kurdish "nation" and by the
need to adhere to Western civilization which was then seen as
"universal". This élitist vision of nationalism was the product of
the experiences of the nineteenth- and twentieth-century Ottoman
world and was inspired by A. Cevdet, who had been a disciple of
G. Le Bon. It sought to initiate "modernization" by rupturing the
socio-economic structures of traditional Kurdish society, without
causing social disorder.[4] It is thus not difficult to identify the
analogy with other forms of regional nationalisms at the time,
both in terms of ideological discourse and in terms of aspirations.

The impossibility of creating a nation-state forced Kurdish
nationalists into a coalition with traditional forces, such as
tribal leaders and the heads of religious orders, for whom the
issue was primarily and primordially opposition to the state –
a sentiment which was translated into rejection of the Turkish
state. The convergence between these two different forms of
opposition resulted in a series of revolts which collapsed
fifteen years after the creation of the republic because its
physical resources were exhausted.[5] Everything seemed to point
towards the extinction of the Kurdish movement in Turkey.[6]
In effect, for twenty years there was not a sign of revolt
or even of Kurdish nationalism. None the less, opposition
continued in the countryside in the form of civil resistance.
Thus, smuggling, the *medrese*, and the rejection of practices
imposed by the "infidel regime" were the signs of the popularity
of this opposition.

The rapid and painful rebirth of Kurdish nationalism only
occurred at the end of the 1950s and at the start of the
1960s. Several factors were behind this revival. First and
foremost was the experiment in political pluralism. It was very
restricted but none the less real, and helped in overcoming
fear and in creating a degree of social mobility, particularly
as far as traditional leaders were concerned. It was no
accident that no *mullas* with nationalist ideas acquired in
their underground *medrese* were to be found at the forefront

of political activities.

The second factor was a relatively little known combination of collective memory and a tradition of rebelliousness. This was particularly concentrated in regions which had suffered the most and where the inculcation of fear had been most effective. It was here, too, that the third factor appeared: the new Kurdish intelligentsia which had been educated, often abroad, during or just after the Kemalist period and who were very strongly influenced by left-wing ideas. This intelligentsia was to play an important role in a Turkey which was undergoing change and which, without wishing to cut the umbilical cord linking it with Kemalism, was by now seeking other paths. The decade of the 1960s was a decade of the development of the social movement in Turkey and of its extremely rapid radicalization. Confused links developed between this social movement (both worker- and student-based), and Kurdish nationalism. Photographs of Atatürk (identified as the symbol of the anti-imperialist struggle), Lenin (showing the road of salvation), and Shaykh Said (symbol of the Kurdish resistance), were ranged side-by-side. This combination, which seems at first sight to be paradoxical, could be explained by the immense impact which the left-wing movement – itself neo-Kemalist at the start – had exercised on Kurdish nationalism in Turkey during the years of its revival.

A final factor which was as important, if not more dominant than those discussed above, was the Barzani revolt in Iraq, echoes and photos of which were quickly spread by the Turkish press. In regions neighbouring those where the revolt was in progress, the population rubbed shoulders with Barzani supporters and tribal links generated support by providing the movement with a rear-guard. The radio station set up by the KDPI (Kurdish Democratic Party of Iraq) not only broadcast in the forbidden Kurdish language, but also spread news of the revolt.

The situation was thus radically different from that during the Kemalist period. The only communality between the two was that the ensemble of the different categories of actors (tribal chiefs, *ulamas* and intellectuals) who had taken part in the Kurdish movement during the Kemalist period were still there. Further, these individuals now had a much larger field of action than previously and the overall system of interaction and interference was more complicated as it related to a Kurdistan far more integrated with the rest of Turkey, and a Kurdish population that was both more mobile and more susceptible to influence from regions to the West. Migratory movements, which were intensified by industrialization, ultra-rapid means of communication and the massive presence of Kurdish students in major Turkish towns, together with a more heterogeneous political environment were crucial in transforming East–West relations in Turkey.

Even though it was never formally acknowledged, "Kurdish representation" in the Turkish political parties, frequently by traditional leaders, increased considerably during these years. The clientalist nature of the political system, which made parties dependent on tribal or religious voting power, encouraged this type of representation. It is true that the majority among the traditional leaders elected to the National Assembly (Kartal, Inan, Bucak, Turk, the grandsons of Shaikh Said himself, Yılmaz and Elçi and many others) played the political game with docility and tried to get the best deal for their clientele. However, some of them began to show signs of nationalist tendencies.[7] An example was S. Azizoglu of the YTP, who was also a member of the 1964 government coalition.[8] The Turkish Workers Party (TIP), which succeeded in making a spectacular entry into the political scene in parliament in 1965, expressed the aspirations of new urban strata and of educated Kurdish youth.

It was also during the first half of the 1960s that the first Kurdish publications appeared in the Turkish Republic – *Yeni Akis* and *Dicle Fırat*, for example. Although they were ephemeral, they did serve to symbolize the first signs of autonomy and specificity for Kurdish nationalism within the social movement. They were followed by other publications; literary, sociological and sometimes educational in character, by persons such as M. Anter, M.E. Bozarslan, Aşik Jhsani, and S. Yastıman.

During this period, probably in 1964, a clandestine political party appeared. This was the Democratic Party of Turkish Kurdistan. It was created under the influence, if not the direct patronage of the KDPI.[9] According to unconfirmed reports, it was led by S. Elçi who was murdered in Iraq in 1971 in circumstances that have never been clarified. This party essentially brought together some urban notables, craftsmen and Kurdish *ulama*.

The creation of this party marked a new stage in the auto-nomization of the Kurdish movement in relation to the worker and student movement in Turkey. It confirmed its position in the sphere occupied by the Kurdish minority in extra-territorial and regional terms. At the same time, however, it also marked the peak of confusion in the "nationalist" camp. One faction refused to accept a Marxist ideology, although it tended quite clearly towards left-wing ideas, while a second faction, consisting essentially of intellectuals, considered that only socialism could resolve the Kurdish problem in Turkey. For the latter, the Kurdish movement, like any other nationalist movement, could only be a natural ally for international socialism. This vision, which also encouraged the predominance of the modernist intellectual élite, obviously did not ensure that future confrontations with actors from traditional society would not occur.

The influences of these different standpoints which, although limited in range, were significant in intensity, were felt particularly strongly during the second half of the 1960s. The effect of these influences was, of course, intensified by the entry of the working-class party into parliament and by the indignation engendered by clearing operations carried out by specialized commandos of the army. Other, basically non-political, factors also played a part, such as the earthquake at Varto in 1967 when the authorities' lack of interest was made quite clear. Between 1967 and 1969 populist demonstrations, often involving more than 10,000 people, occurred in virtually every major Kurdish urban area.[10] The organizers of the demonstrations emphasized that they were making use of a right recognized in the constitution, but the demonstrations themselves showed that the urban environment continued to be a dynamic political arena and that it was being prepared to become the major bastion of Kurdish nationalism.

Quite apart from demands for cultural rights, it is clear that the popular mobilization involved was based on a whole series of demands that could only be identified with nationalism with considerable difficulty. The constant references made to the constitution were also not without significance. Until 1969–70, the demands were primarily concerned with civic and social rights, rather than with the recognition of a specific national identity. They focused around issues such as being recognized as full citizens by the state and being given the same rights as other citizens; an active struggle against under-development; state investment; the construction of schools and dispensaries; road, bridge and factory construction; and the mechanism of agriculture. When formulated in this way, the demands were more concerned with integration than with separation.

Only later on did the demands become more radical and take on a more nationalist character, albeit still without being "separatist". They then involved considerations such as the destruction of "feudalism" – by which they meant the system based on the domination of *shaykhs* and *aghas* who were considered to be as responsible as the Turkish bourgeoisie for problems faced by the community. There were also demands for the removal of under-development, for rights to press, radio and to education in the Kurdish language. This radicalization of the tone of the demands was clearly important because it involved a vocabulary more left than had previously been the case. However, the achievement of these objectives would only, according to those responsible for formulating them, serve to intensify the links between the community and the rest of Turkey.

These demands were often considered to be separatist and contrary to the basic principles of the regime. As a result they were severely repressed. None the less, the 1969–70 period was a turning-point – irreversible in many respects – which only further radicalized the demands of Kurdish nationalists, since they had now gone beyond "developmentist" solutions. It is difficult to explain this turning-point unless account is taken of conditions in the major Turkish metropolitan areas at the time, in which there was a significant component of Kurdish youth. In Turkey, the years 1969 and 1970 prolonged the atmosphere which characterized 1968 in both France and Turkey, thereby witnessing a sudden acceleration in the activities of the working class and student movement. During 1969, hundreds and thousands of workers demonstrated and clashed with the police in Istanbul. The students sought radical solutions in the wake of bloody confrontations with the far right or with Islamists or nationalists. These solutions involved raising the consciousness of the masses by armed struggle and the overthrowing of the regime. In a Turkey which was becoming aware of its harrowing economic and social distortions, it took little time for several illegal organizations aspiring to armed struggle to take root.

This development did not pass Kurdish youth by, even though it was still active within Turkish student organizations. In 1970, intellectuals and youths founded the DDKO (the Eastern Revolutionary Cultural Centres).[11] The centres were soon able to create a network within all the Kurdish towns and in the major Turkish

conurbations. Their members considered that the time for paci-
ficism and conformism had passed and that the 1970s would prepare
Turkey for major upheavals, comparable with those taking place
in certain countries in Asia, Africa and Latin America. Their
understanding of the Kurdish problem had also evolved; it was no
longer an issue of regional underdevelopment. On the contrary, it
was a national (later a "colonial") problem in which a "policeman
of global imperialism" dominated an oppressed nation with the
aid of local collaborators. At a stroke, therefore, the struggle had
become a double-edged one – both of class and of an oppressed
nation. Only "progressive forces" could, therefore, bring such
a situation to an end by liberating Kurdistan – not necessarily
as an independent state – from this double yoke. In addition,
with the emergence of the DDKOs, the Kurdish movement in
Turkey achieved autonomy twice over: firstly from the Kurdish
movement in Iraq in that it became, far more than previously,
a Turkish phenomenon, secondly, from the Turkish student and
working-class movement, in that it became an integral part of the
Kurdish movement in the Middle East.

In 1974, after the "intermediary" military regime, the second
Kurdish revival took place without great difficulty, even though
the DDKOs had not been able to survive militarist pressure.
Within two years, in a Turkey rapidly thrown into fear and terror,
dozens of Kurdish groups and organisations with left-wing and even
Stalinist tendencies were formed, according to the circumstances.
They were in competition amongst themselves and with many
other Turkish groups. They were very active within Kurdish towns
with homogeneous religious affiliations (*Alevi* or *Sunni* but never
mixed), where they made numerous links with Turkish groups and
were able, to the degree that their activities could be described as
pacific, if not pacifist, to involve Kurdish youth overall.

The 1971 *coup d'état* had not been able therefore to destroy
the "new social actor" represented by youth, any more
effectively than it had been able to uproot the traditional
social actors. These forces took their revenge on the generals
in the 1973 elections and, in an even more unanimous
way, in the 1977 elections by a triumphal entry into the
Turkish parliament. Between 1977 and 1979, all these elements
were firmly on the political scene and ready for the next
great turning point for the post-Kemalist Kurdish movement
– the first having been the formation of the DDKOs.

These years were a turning point for many reasons. For the first time in the history of the Turkish Republic independent candidates who were openly nationalist were able to stand for the municipal elections of 1977, or for the municipal by-elections of 1979, and to achieve victory in towns such as Diyarbakir, Lice and Batman. For the first time in the history of the Turkish Republic some traditional Kurdish leaders who were openly nationalist, and some of whom had been found guilty by military tribunals in 1971,[12] were elected and became ministers without having to abandon their opinions. The clientalist nature of the parliamentary system made such a development inevitable.

However, the most dramatic development during this period was the emergence of two political groups which rejected all compromise with the regime and the political system, or with the Turkish left or even with other Kurdish groups. These two groups enjoyed the support of a youth whose economic and social outlook was bleak and which regarded the existing Kurdish organizations as collaborators. These groups were the KUK (the National Liberators of Kurdistan) which was an offshoot of the Turkish KDP, and the PKK (the Kurdish Workers Party) which was founded in 1977 by A. Öcalan.[13]

These organisations, often linked to specific tribes, threw themselves into a merciless combat with other groups, and also indulged in a great deal of infighting. In regions hitherto spared from violence, hundreds of deaths due to these internal struggles were recorded in the sinister statistics of terror.[14] The KUK and the PKK which shared the same social and ideological bases charted a guideline of urban radicalization.

Between 1977 and 1979 Turkey was suffering from terror, fear and economic crisis, and which had also used up all its parliamentary options, from the second National Front coalition in 1977, through the second socialist government in 1978 and the Süleyman Demirel government of 1979. During this time, the massacres at Maraş (a town with a mixed Alevi–Sunni, Turkish–Kurdish population) served to throw oil on the flames of terror,[15] while the 1980 presidential elections which resulted in a crisis, demonstrated the inability of politicians to resolve the crisis and sounded once again the death-knell of Turkish democracy. Along with many other factors, it legitimized the military intervention on 12 September of the same year.

THE TURKISH STATE AND KURDISH NATIONALISM

The Kemalist state aimed to transform Turkey into a country that was 100 per cent Turkish and considered any war waged towards this end as almost a holy war. It was also a state which saw itself as the vehicle of a mission: the civilizing mission of the Turkish nation, and it used this vision to justify its provision of education and civilization to other nations – by force, if necessary. The Kurds thus presented both an obstacle to the objective of homogenizing the national territory and to the Turkish nation's civilizing mission.[16]

One significant aspect of these Kemalist ideas which managed to survive real Kemalism was the concept of the "Party of the State".[17] Its view of the Kurdish problem, however, was to identify it as a purely geopolitical issue. Over time, this vision lost ground, even within the political parties. Yet, with the exception of the Workers Party, these parties supported and developed this idea by theories of regional underdevelopment which they insisted had to be remedied. In Turkey, this geopolitical vision created an almost psychotic fear of the loss of "national unity", particularly amongst the ultra-nationalists and in the army. After all, it was a "revolutionary general", who was also the fourth president of the republic, who declared that:

> The towns in the East are both the doors and the fortresses of our country. If we lose control of the towns in the East, it will not be easy to maintain our position in western Anatolia.[18]

In fact, during 1960 and 1961 while the soldiers were the absolute masters of Turkey, the only bank that had been created by the internal dynamism of the Kurdish regions, the Doğu Bank, was liquidated by military decree, a rare thing to happen to a financial institution. Tribal leaders, with "little loyalty" to the regime, were deported to western Turkey.[19] The body of Said-i Nursi, a great theologian and one of the renovators of Islam who had, in addition, the misfortune to have been a long-standing Kurdish nationalist, was interred by the army.

During succeeding years, while tribunals applied the laws forbidding the Kurdish language and culture, often with considerable zeal, the extreme right and the army came into conflict over plans for negotiation and general strategic questions. The extreme right, led by one of the leaders of the *coup d'état* of 27 May 1960, Colonel Türkeş, did not hesitate openly to threaten Kurds with a "final solution" of the kind that had been adopted by the Unionist government towards the Armenians in 1915:

> If the Kurds run after an illusion of creating a state, their destiny will be wiped off the face of the earth. The Turkish race has shown the way in which it can treat those who covet the homeland which it has obtained at the price of its own blood and untold labours. It has eliminated the Armenians from this land in 1915 and the Greeks in 1922.[20]

There were two dramatic developments during the second half of the 1960s. The first was the clearing operations by specialized army units, known as "kommandos", in villages suspected of involvement in smuggling or of aiding the Barzani movement in Iraq. Hints of what was happening were reported in the Turkish press by Ismail Cem.[21] Later the press also published details of the second development – Army Staff projects for a struggle against guerrilla warfare based on the strategy of "drying up the sea to catch the fish".[22] The 12 March *coup d'état* which had intensified the kommando operations, used as one of its justifications the desire to overcome the "separatist" danger and to guarantee the "unity of the homeland".[23] Certainly, this transitional regime repressed the radical Turkish movement above all, which as a result lost many of its leaders. However, the repression was no less in Kurdish areas where hundreds of peasants, workers and intellectuals were arrested, tortured and sentenced between 1971 and 1973. The fledgling DDKOs could not survive such an offensive by the state.

Between 1974 and 1980, when the third military intervention occurred, Kemalist propagandists, the extreme right and the army never hesitated to express their discontent. State repression was often intensified by the nomination of a large number of rapacious administrators to run Kurdish towns, particularly those with mixed Alevi–Sunni populations.[24] The "Kurdish syndrome" also continued to trouble the generals who were worried about the increasing numbers of young Kurds in the army and who were preparing plans to suppress any possible Kurdish uprising in the barracks.[25] Many military manoeuvres also took place in frontier regions, which were poorly covered by the press, in which some soldiers were dressed up as Kurds.[26]

The events of 12 September 1980, which first caused a great sense of relief throughout the population and then led all of Turkey into a bloody nightmare need not be repeated here. Kurdish towns were particularly affected by this state terror. Arrests, torture, extra-legal executions,[27] several laws forbidding the use of the Kurdish language,[28] major military concentrations in the area and, finally, forced deportations[29] appear in the chronicles of international humanitarian organizations. An idea of the size of these measures is represented in the case of Tunceli, which has a population of 19,000, but still hosts a garrison of 55,000.[30]

On three occasions in 1983, 1984 and 1987, the army also undertook military expeditions in the Kurdish region of Iraq, a country by then weakened by the Iran–Iraq War.[31] These interventions took place within the provisions of a treaty signed with Baghdad. At the same time, the Turkish ministry of foreign affairs tried to persuade the Iraqi leader, Saddam Hussain, to renounce an agreement which he had signed with Talabani, the leader of the PUK, a Kurdish political party in Iraq, in 1984.[32] These attempts were precursors to initiatives to achieve similar treaties with Damascus and Teheran.[33]

However, despite all these drastic measures, the military plan failed. As Artunkal points out, "this last intervention by the army, which was the longest and most brutal of all, has paradoxically been the one which has sounded the death-knell of Kemalism".[34] In effect, the 1980 *coup d'état* showed that the army could certainly take power in Turkey without upsetting civil society, but that it was impossible for it to impose its control *sine die*, both in the Kurdish region and in the Turkish areas. Overall, Kurdish nationalism only increased as a result of the 1980 coup.

Several events mark its development since 12 September 1980. First, the PKK has been forced into armed struggle – organized this time in a professional way – by military violence. This has been encouraged by a degree of tolerance shown by some states and has considerable support in the regions from youth and certain elements of rural society. The struggle, which has lasted since 1984, has cost the lives of over one thousand persons, including soldiers and guerrillas, but mainly civilians. Although it has not taken on the dimensions of a popular uprising, the struggle covers vast stretches of Kurdistan today. The civil population is a pawn in this war, where the state, the army and the PKK consider any means capable of achieving their desired aims justifiable. Secondly, there has also been a kind of revenge by Kurdish society on its oppressors. After the *coup d'état*, it became clear that Kurdish society could not be excluded from political life except under a state of emergency. To the great astonishment of observers, the Kurdish countryside continued to exercise an influence through the sheer size of tribes and religious orders and also created new systems of solidarity with the towns. These had become great human conglomerations which, despite its efforts, survived the military regime and managed to acquire both electoral power and act as centres of resistance at the same time. In addition, the activities of urban Kurds revived, and public opinion in the towns was mobilized by the publication of journals which were openly nationalist.[35] Further, to the great irritation of the military, the political parties had to accept Kurdish candidates, whether tribal or not, on their lists. Once elected, often by large margins, these new politicians further affected public opinion, criticizing the army, reporting numerous cases of torture to the parliament and, in a move which was completely new, explicitly espousing nationalist claims. As a result, the "Septembrist" generals had to draw back when confronted with these events.

Finally, as a result of the influence of the Iran–Iraq War, Turkish public opinion began to take an interest in the "taboo" subject of the Kurdish problem. Certain journalists, such as Mehmet Ali Birand[36] explained that to continue to deny the existence of the Kurds was an "ostrich policy" and, given the great challenges that faced Turkey, Ankara should change its approach. The weekly *Yeni Gündem* published a dossier on the Kurds in which some Kurdish spokesmen, including the president of the Kurdish Institute in Paris, were able to openly express their views.[37] Another weekly, *2000'e Doğru*, published a large number of secret army documents concerning the Kurds.[38] Suddenly all of Turkey that had been aware that there had long been a "problem" in the East of the country could now identify it and give it a name – the Kurdish problem. This engendered a sense of deception which must certainly have been one of the most serious difficulties ever faced by the army and by Turkish nationalism, which has always been the real basis of official ideology.

THE REFUGEE PROBLEM: FROM KEMALIST IDEOLOGY TO POLITICAL PRAGMATISM

The end of the war between Iraq and Iran marked a flood of Iraqi Kurdish refugees into Turkey. It also demonstrated that the army and even the Turkish political class lagged far behind the rest of society. The expulsion of the refugees by Turkey during the first days of the exodus caused massive discontent, particularly amongst the Kurds in Turkey. The government had to change its position under the critical, even aggressive eyes of Turkish nationalists. On the other hand, those in power had taken note of the degree to which Kurdish society itself had taken up the case of the Kurds from Iraq.

The press, particularly journalists close to the army and to the official view, did not hesitate to write numerous articles expressing their anxiety.[39] However, once again the press lowered its tone in order to show Turkey as the "father protector" of these "poor Kurds", the "victims of Ba'thist atrocities". The Minister of the Interior had particularly forbidden any aid going from the civilian population to the refugees. Very quickly, however, this prohibition was lifted in order to dissipate discontent and to legalize the situation that had developed despite the order. The size of the aid provided by the civilian population, particularly the Kurds, was considerably greater than had been estimated. A second mobilization, as significant as the first, occurred when Madame Mitterrand visited the refugee camps. The welcoming ceremonies were transformed into veritable nationalist demonstrations both on behalf of the refugees, as might have been expected, but also by the Kurdish population in Turkey, including some mayors and parliamentary deputies.[40]

The most remarkable change, however, occurred when political leaders such as Ecevit, Demirel and Inönü visited the camps and condemned Iraq formally. Ecevit, who recognized for the first time in his long political career the existence of different ethnic groups in Turkey,[41] even advised the refugees to reject the "deceptive amnesty" offered by Iraq.[42] These initiatives on the part of political leaders affected the conditions under which the visit of Mr Kamali, then the Minister of the Interior, and of the premier, Turgut Özal, to the camps took place. The event was naturally one of considerable importance. The two dignitaries of state talked to the refugees by means of interpreters. The televised transmission of their visit also signified the effective recognition of a language long stated to be non-existent.

The peak of paradox in this surrealistic event was achieved when the local population greeted Mr Özal's gesture with cries of "Long live Özal. Long live Barzani".[43] It was, perhaps, the best expression of an ambivalent political phenomenon, that of a double adhesion to two separate entities; the first the state and the second the minority, itself supra-territorial in nature and extending beyond the limits of Turkish political geography.

Mr Özal's change in attitude was not without ambiguity and, on the face of it, continues to be difficult to interpret in an intelligible way. Some observers, and also certain political leaders, have seen in it a gesture with purely political ends closely linked to a referendum that was being prepared and that would effectively serve as a plebiscite on Mr Özal himself. It is difficult to estimate to what degree this change in attitude limited the decline in the political support Özal received. It is undeniable that his party suffered a stinging setback in the March 1989 municipal elections, even in Kurdish areas. However, quite apart from the results of the referendum and the elections, the fact that his party, the Motherland Party, was able to transform the Kurdish problem into a partisan political factor, is a clear proof of the emergence of political pragmatism in Turkey. The admission to the party of N. Yılmaz, a Kurdish nationalist who had been imprisoned and tortured under the military regime, is another sign of this political pragmatism.[44]

The second reason that may explain this change in attitude seems to be a desire to undermine the PKK and to win the confidence of the civil population. There have been many journalists, after all, who have claimed that a state which aids "the Kurdish brothers" beyond its frontiers cannot be an enemy of its own Kurds.[45] Despite extensive arrests just before the municipal elections in 1989 at Batman and at Siirt, despite the shameful events at Yeşilyurt[46] and despite the fact that many refugees have been sent back to Iran and that those that remain have been subject to repression, it is possible to see in the government's attitude a desire to improve the image of the state, which is at its lowest level in the post-Kemalist era, and to recover for it a degree of legitimacy.

A final reason which could explain the change in attitude seems to be the pressure exerted by the EC and the Reagan administration on Turkey. Brussels and Strasburg have, in effect, since 1980, warned that Ankara's policies over the Kurdish problem would be considered an important criterion to measure the sincerity of "democratization" in Turkey. In addition to US Senate reports, there is other information to suggest that the American position has undergone a considerable degree of change and now considers that peaceful solution of the Kurdish problem would be a guarantee of security in the Middle East.[47]

The change in attitude of the Turkish government has clearly influenced not only the situation in Turkey, where it has permitted new forms of mobilization and political practices, but has also affected the Turkish vision of the region. Immediately after the arrival of the refugees, Kurdish leaders such as Barzani, Osman and Talabani, were able to express themselves in person and without being censored.[48] Even more importantly, according to unconfirmed sources, the authorities in Ankara had direct or indirect contacts with leaders and members of the Iraqi Kurdish political parties.[49] Whatever the truth of this, Ankara has, in effect, recognized the legitimacy of the Iraqi KDP in the refugee camps, even though 30,000 refugees have been expelled to Iran. This recognition is also a de facto acceptance of the minority role of the Kurds in the Middle East and of its participation in "parallel diplomacy" – at least to a limited extent. It is clearly unlikely that Turkey will attempt to use or manipulate a Kurdish political party against another Middle Eastern country in the near future. Nonetheless, as some observers have noted, "the equation has changed".[50] In this era, it is not impossible that Ankara will be forced to make contact with Kurdish political parties in Iraq in order to neutralize the PKK and establish its control over its own Kurdish territories. In fact, even if the refugees have not been able to obtain the status to which they are entitled under the Geneva Convention and although they are held in unenviable conditions,[51] the fact that they were accepted marks the beginning of the recognition by the Turkish government of a Kurdish entity and of a Kurdish problem with which it must deal on a regional level.

THE PLURALIST NATURE OF KURDISH NATIONALISM

Since the 1960s Kurdish nationalism in Turkey has experienced a painful and extremely rapid radicalization. As I have shown, the recognition of this nationalism coincided with the emergence of a Turkish form of Marxism. It was quite natural that this nationalism, which was partially the product of the social movement in Turkey and which had experienced several periods of military rule, should have been impregnated both by an ideology which it opposed, namely Kemalism, and by a Stalinist and Maoist version of Marxism. It is also clear that from a political point of view this nationalism could not have produced an alternative vision which would have differed from those already in operation under single-party regimes world-wide but particularly in the Middle East. It can even be said that the incorporation of a Marxist ideology merely permitted it to provide an expression of a distinct identity. Nonetheless, Kurdish "Marxism" in Turkey, like Turkish Marxism itself, and that throughout the Third World, offered little opportunity for political pluralism. Democratic practices were often rejected in favour of a Leninist–Stalinist concept of the party, a vision in which the ends justified the means.

It is still difficult to talk of political pluralism within the Kurdish nationalist camp in Turkey. Yet, such a plurality seems to exist within Kurdish society itself and has been integrated into the Turkish political system to some degree. It is now possible to identify "Kurdish groups" within the major political parties, which are often quite public in nature.

This is particularly the case in the ANAP, the SHP, the DYP, the RP[52] and throughout the Islamist movement. It would be difficult to deny that this pluralism corresponds to socio-economic structures within a region in which the population is socially heterogeneous, unless a "conspiracy theory" were applied in which it could be described as a "separatist plot" against the "resistance". On the other hand, it is clear that the political clientalist system in Kurdistan, the role of the religious brotherhoods and the religious divides have played a major role in the proliferation of different political tendencies within the Kurdish political arena. The major towns normally vote for the left, even if the religious party (the Refah Party) still continues to register its highest support in these regions. The SHP, which claims to depend on the urban potential of the region, still largely depends in reality, just like the DYP and the ANAP, on the tribal vote or on the solidarity networks created from the tribal base. In the mixed Alevi–Sunni towns, where the MÇP[53] has been able to create the conditions of a civil war, remnants of this party still retain a significant influence because of its hold on the Sunni vote.

Apart from this party (the MÇP), the impact of the other parties seems to be imposed on top of an underlay of expressions of identity. It is not impossible that these "Kurdish factions" within the political parties could in future take over from the groups controlled by the "intellectuals" of the left. The existence of separate Kurdish Islamist groups – a phenomenon which can easily be understood in view of the antecedents of the Kurdish movement – seems to be significant from this point of view.

The importance of a new factor – the factionalization of Kurdish nationalism – must also be emphasized. There are indications that seem to show that certain types of religious or linguistic identity have generated distinctive nationalist demands and visions. As a result, there is today a vision expressing the concept of the "Alevi nation" claiming the "State of Alavistan of Anatolia", and another denouncing the repression carried out by the Turkish and Kurdish "nations" against the "millenarian Zaza nation".[54] The parallelism between these terms and those of Kurdish nationalism is not surprising since it is the latter which has, in large measure, been its cradle. It should also be noted that the "faction of the state" has made a major contribution to this division, particularly through the Institute for Turkish Studies in Ankara. Its aim has been to make the Zaza and the Alevi accept their "Turkish origins". It seems today increasingly difficult for the "sorcerer's apprentice" to control the structure that it has helped to create by its arguments. An explosive – albeit still latent – situation continues to exist and it is quite probable that it will stimulate new confrontations nourished by centuries of linguistic and religious divisions.

THE FUTURE

The future, as ever, is unpredictable. Certainly, the "Eastern Problem", now the "Kurdish Problem", is one of the crucial aspects of Ankara's domestic and foreign policies. Neither the army nor the "faction of the state" will be able to pursue a policy based on fire and blood, even if international humanitarian organizations may have to continue to report sad events. A Turkey which has registered its request to join the EC will be forced, temporarily at least, to project a good image.

Since the 1960s, activists originating from Kurdish society, whether traditional or modern, have shown that it would be impossible to imagine a pluralist political life in Turkey without their participation. Gellner, in discussing Turkey, has underlined how it is impossible for laicism and democracy to coexist there.[55] His view can be paraphrased and extended to establish a correlation between political plurality, or political life itself, and the Kemalist ideology. This ideology involves, of course, accepting Turkish nationalism as the sole legitimate basis for power, but also implies an absolute right for modernist élites in the name of the nation to control sovereignty and authority over the individual, and to condemn all loyalties that are not loyalties to the state, whether they involve tribes, religious orders or ethnic identity. Such a vision of the relations between the individual and the state can succeed, albeit at the heavy price of the suspension of all political life. It is, in fact, possible to consider Turkish military regimes as being primarily a suspension of political life, or its reduction to an absolute minimum. However, once the military can no longer sustain itself in power, loyalties to entities other than the state or the "nation" become inevitable. It thus takes on the appeal of a dominant electoral factor and becomes an essential element in political life.

The same is true for "ethnic loyalty", even though it is rarely sufficiently powerful to be the origin of a social movement. It becomes, however, an uncontrollable mobilizing force once it is combined with other factors. It also militates against "loyalty to the state" and to the realm of the sovereignty of the nation-state. However, for the past three decades it has essentially been confused with urban discontent and dynamism.

The interaction of the town, with its different elements, and peasant society, with its own aspects and its extension into the towns, generates a conglomerate which is simultaneously demographic, economic, social and political in nature. This conglomeration seems to be both one of the keys to the Kurdistan policy and one of the reasons for the radicalization of Kurdish politics and its slide towards nationalism, which may be explained by the phenomenon of traditional leaders who are increasingly nationalist.

The state has sought to combat this conglomerate by the use of various measures: by suspending the political arena, by putting its immense ideological machine into motion, and even, curiously, by a policy of alliance within the conglomerate whether under the cover of tribal or religious loyalties. In doing so, it has revived the role of the tribes, thereby violating the spirit of the constitution which it itself promulgated. It then classifies tribes in different categories, particularly in terms of whether they are pro- or contra-state. Those which it considers loyal it arms.[56] In effect, it acts as a *makhzen* – an experiment introduced by Sultan Abdulhamid almost a century ago and now revived for tactical purposes and never rendered so systematic as it has been today. In its most extreme form, it implies today that the sovereignty of the "nation" has been transferred, for all practical purposes, to the "tribe" allied to the "nation". Thus several decades after the political parties – which realized the electoral potential of the tribes very early on – the state has now also opted for pragmatism to achieve its ends. The same is true of religion in a state which is officially secular. Although the entry of the army into political life has been justified as a defence of secularism, the army itself does not hesitate to bombard Kurdish villages with tracts calling on them to join a "holy war" against the "insurgents" and reminding them of their "religious duty" of "obedience" to the state.[57] Once again, this road has already been trod by the political parties, who have abandoned, little by little, the secularist Kemalist heritage. That heritage fits with political life itself so poorly that the army, the last bastion of such a heritage, has been forced to borrow a similar approach.

None the less, this ultimate bastion of the unionist–Kemalist tradition – in which "revolutions from above" are introduced into a society which is considered immature and on which "cultural cadres" are imposed in order to make it homogeneous – is still a real sword of Damocles hanging over political life and political pluralism. It must be realized that this sword is more than an imaginary spectre. It is nourished by other factors in addition to the Kurdish problem and the army's own Kemalist attitudes. The Kurdish problem is today, more than ever before, a key problem on which the future of political life and political pluralism depends. Even if most of the political forces in the country now tend towards pragmatism and see the Kurdish issue as a political matter requiring a political solution, this is not the case for the "faction of the state", for the army, for the MÇP of Türkeş and for the "sacred coalition" of the ANAP.[58] While accepting that the tribes and the religious arena should be manipulated in order to establish "state control", they consider that the problem directly affects the survival of the "Fatherland" and thus must be confronted with intransigence in which all means are legitimate. The refugee affair clearly revealed the split between these two positions.

There is no doubt that most of Turkey does not support the "intransigent" tendency, as the tragi-comic experience of the Septembrist generals made clear. However, the repeated intervention of the army has equally shown the incapacity of

Turkish society and of the political class to block the road to a victory – ephemeral, no doubt, but none the less costly – by this tendency. This fact, also, does not offer us the luxury of adopting blind optimism and forgetting the precariousness of "Turkish democracy". On the other hand, it would also be an error to deny the importance of the changes that have occurred in the past three or four years.[59]

Chapter 6

The situation of Kurds in Iraq and Turkey: current trends and prospects

Munir Morad

THE KURDS IN THE POST-WAR ERA

The situation in Iraq

The ceasefire in the Iran–Iraq War, Iraq's invasion of Kuwait and the subsequent Iran–Iraq War ushered the Kurdish movement into a new era of uncertainty. By April 1988, it had become apparent that, despite official denials, Iran was preparing for a ceasefire. Indeed by the time the Iraqi army recaptured the Faw peninsula a few months earlier, the Iranians had clearly abandoned major operations. Tehran's sudden announcement of the truce understandably perplexed both friends and foes. One cannot doubt that the ensuing confusion was perhaps precisely what Iran had hoped for.

The ceasefire in the Iran–Iraq War has endured despite initial scepticism by international observers, and a return to comprehensive war in the next few years has become quite improbable. Iran's attitude towards Iraq in the future will inevitably be affected by the outcome of the peace process and the long-term consequences for the Gulf region of Iraq's invasion of Kuwait. In any event, the ill-will between Iran and Iraq is unlikely to subside completely, and will transcend changes in the leadership of either country. This is where the Kurdish dimension may again enter the scene. To the Kurdish insurgents on either side of the fence, the ceasefire between Iraq and Iran marks a brief intermission in their much older dispute with their governments.

Both Iran and Iraq are destined to continue their clandestine support for the Kurds on opposite sides, for potential deployment in a proxy war. So far as one can ascertain from various Kurdish sources, this state of affairs will continue. Most Kurdish leaders argue rather convincingly that, overall, the Kurdish movement has benefited from this geopolitical loophole. Critics both within as well as outside the Kurdish community, however, counter that this irredentism, far from furthering the cause of the Kurdish nation, has exacted a high price. The price has been that the Kurds' fate is inextricably tied to the political transactions between all those countries in the region with sizeable Kurdish minorities – notably Iraq, Iran and Turkey.

Tehran's reliance on Iraqi Kurdish insurgents in settling old scores with Baghdad has been reinforced by the failure of Iraq's Shi'ite opposition to dislodge the Baghdad government. As far as the Kurdish movement is concerned the failure of Shi'ite irredentism has reinforced their argument that Iraq's instability is a function of only two variables: Kurds and Arabs, rather than Shi'is and Sunnis. Iraqi Kurdish leaders therefore regard this as convincing evidence that their struggle will remain viable and will hold the key to any future political settlement inside Iraq. Naturally, the Iranian regime is conscious of this reality, and is likely to continue to use Iraqi Kurdish opposition as a tool for interference in Iraq's internal affairs.

Iraq's entire prospects at present (February 1991) are contingent upon the moves of one individual – President Saddam Hussain. So much so that one is often tempted to confuse the two terms, Iraq and its current president, and use them interchangeably. The president can only be judged as a very special case of leadership in Iraq's modern political history. There is no doubt that he dominates almost all aspects of political, military and economic life in the country. Our analysis of the situation in Iraq will therefore focus on the policies of the current Iraqi regime, assuming that it succeeds in holding on to power for the foreseeable future.

Most Kurdish leaders congratulate themselves on overcoming the temptation to enter into "national conciliation" with the Iraqi government in recent years. There has been one serious attempt by a major Kurdish group (the Patriotic Union of Kurdistan) to negotiate a peace settlement with the central government during the Iran–Iraq War, but disagreements soon brought negotiations to an end. The leaders of Iraq's Kurdish community were particularly concerned that any war-time agreement would probably not survive long, once the concerned parties began to redefine their priorities. Notwithstanding the Iraqi government's official line on the status of the Kurdish opposition, the prospect of future negotiations between the Kurds and the Iraqi regime is real. The unresolved situation in Iraqi Kurdistan is constantly on the Iraqi government's mind, and the regime is particularly frustrated that so few Kurdish citizens appear to take its new election gestures and amnesties seriously.

However, it is not possible to explore any scenario for a Kurdish settlement without examining the issue in the light of the likely direction the Iraqi regime will take in the foreseeable future. Saddam Hussain has pursued a political career styled on all-seasons heroism. During both the Iran–Iraq War and the Gulf War, Iraqi propaganda has relentlessly promoted a wartime image of the president as the country's supreme hero. During the Iran–Iraq War he was dubbed *bal al-Qadisiyya* (literally, the hero of the battle of Qadisiyya, which saw the defeat of a Persian army at the hands of the Arabs in the early years of Islam). Most political observers would perhaps agree that, in view of the recent developments, Hussain's overriding desire would be to recast his image as a dedicated Arab nationalist. However, despite Iraq's obvious success in rallying most of the Arab world behind itself during the Iran–Iraq War, President Hussain has judged (no doubt correctly) that stressing the Iraqi sense of self-reliance was more profitable on the home front. To most Iraqi citizens, Arab solidarity is an abstract concept of no obvious practical value. However, like most other Arab states today, Iraq maintains an indirect role in Palestine and Lebanon as benefactor to a number of nationalist forces.

Of all sections of Iraqi opposition, none are likely to be more crucial in Iraq's future reconstruction than the country's Kurdish community. Not only do they represent a sizeable proportion of Iraqi public opinion, but they also have the capacity to disrupt any national policy that excludes them and will never be short of allies to help them do just that. A peace initiative towards the Kurds to negotiate a political partnership is inevitable, but will the Kurds agree to it?

It is impossible to predict whether the Iraqi government, under President Hussain, will ever be successful in winning the goodwill of the leaders of the Kurdish insurgency. After all, there has been so much mistrust between the central government and its Kurdish opponent, particularly since Hussain's term of office. This does not mean, however, that none of the Kurdish groups would like to open a dialogue, only that all of them have serious doubts which can be summarized as follows:

1 What guarantees, if any, are available for the safe conduct of the talks? The Iraqi regime has gone back on previous commitments and promises in this regard.
2 Is there a prospect of an agreement being underwritten by an international arbiter? There have been many peace agreements and promises of reform, but without a third-party arbiter that both sides could trust it has not been possible to apportion blame when things went wrong.
3 How can the Kurdish movement enter peace talks with President Hussain who, as Kurdish sources would say, has repeatedly lived up to their suspicion of him? This psychological barrier is perhaps the most serious impediment of all.
4 How can the Kurdish movement present itself as a united front and guarantee consistency among all groups. A Kurdish consensus has not yet been achieved despite the many transient and fragile alliances between the major Kurdish opposition groups.
5 How can the major representative Kurdish organizations prevent gatecrashers from marching into the peace process in the name of the Kurdish movement? Kurdish politics has never been short of minor leaders willing to speak on behalf of the rest of the Kurdish nation.

While these problems may not discourage the Kurdish movement from acting positively in pursuit of peace, most Kurdish leaders seem to agree that their movements have paid too high a price in the past for overlooking important safeguards in their peace agreements with the central government. Leaders of some movements, however, while dismissing the chances of a genuine pact under the current regime, believe that restoration of a measure of coexistence may still be possible. They contend that the most important benefits drawn from any future agreement with the present government will be an opportunity to recruit, reorganize and ponder further moves. A marriage of convenience is perhaps an apt phrase to define a future peace in Iraq along these lines, with or without Saddam Hussain at the top. In the event of national reconciliation, however, major obstacles are likely to persist, not least concerning basic definitions: what are the exact borders of the Kurdish areas? How could the Kurds agree to coexist with a government that may still consider its Arab national identity as relevant to the unity of a country so sharply divided along racial lines?

The situation in Turkey

The Gulf War has had a significant, albeit indirect, influence over the situation of the Kurdish community in Turkey. Although the war mainly affected the Kurds of Iraq and Iran, the conflict also had important consequences for Turkey's Kurdish population. Most Kurdish areas saw an escalation in "armed struggle", carried out by militant groups receiving assistance from fellow dissidents operating in Iraq's "liberated" Kurdish enclaves. Training, logistical support and bases were provided in various parts of Iraqi Kurdistan for Turkey's Kurdish activists. The diplomatic confusion, breakdown of border controls and the emergence of new regional alliances, precipitated by the Iran–Iraq conflict, enabled the Kurdish militants for the first time to move relatively freely inside Syria, Iraq, Turkey and Iran. Furthermore, both Syria and Iran saw fit to tolerate (and at times directly assist) various dissident Turkish groups to ensure Turkey's neutrality in the Gulf War. Turkey's membership of NATO and her economic and military cooperation with Iraq were viewed with concern, during the Iran–Iraq War, by both the Iranians and their Syrian allies. Indeed, the sharp increase in militancy in Turkey's Kurdish areas since the outbreak of that war could be attributed, to a great extent, to the political situation created by the Iran–Iraq conflict.

The cumulative impact of the Iran–Iraq conflict on the Kurdish scene in Turkey has scarcely diminished with the end of hostilities between the two warring states. In fact, the Kurdish question was reinforced two years later by Turkey's involvement in the Gulf War, on the side of the Allied forces. The situation has revived the controversy over Turkey's territorial ambitions in northern Iraq (the so-called Mosul Question).

The potency of Kurdish militancy and its significant effect on Turkey's internal security have placed the Turkish government under enormous strain, especially as much of the new insurgency was coordinated from abroad and was therefore very difficult to control. As is often the case in the Middle East, once an insurgency has established itself in one state, it usually attracts benefactors from other rival states willing to extend support in return for an opportunity to settle old scores. The new generation of Kurdish dissidents in Turkey have consequently succeeded in drawing a great deal of sympathy and support, not just from fellow Kurds in the local communities but also externally. As far as diplomatic difficulties persist between Turkey and some of its neighbours, and so long as Turkey's handling of ethnic minorities and human rights continues to draw criticism, the new Kurdish militancy is bound to thrive, and its sense of mission will harden. The Turkish government's denial of a "Kurdish problem" did not last (as indicated by recent legislation unbanning the usage of Kurdish language); but while the wider cultural aspirations of the country's largest ethnic minority remain unfulfilled, few Kurdish activists can be persuaded to abandon the pursuit of strife.

With most Kurdish territories still impoverished and under-developed compared to the rest of the country, it is very difficult to envisage an acceptance of government policies by the increasingly disaffected Kurdish population. Poverty has compounded the crisis in Kurdish areas not only by providing the militants with a cause for revolt, but also through engendering widespread corruption and social discord. A sub-economy is taking hold in many Kurdish areas, based on various shady enterprises such as smuggling, money laundering and drug processing and trafficking. For many Kurdish school leavers with no prospects of a decent job or living, the "black enterprises" are the only available economic opportunity. This relatively new development is already exacting a heavy toll in social terms, with drug abuse, crime and delinquency rapidly on the rise in many Kurdish areas, especially those near the borders with Iran.

Matters of ideology

Ideological questions have preoccupied Kurdish intellectuals for a long time. Although this situation is not uncommon in "liberation" movements, some argue that the search for an ideological identity has been divisive and that many practical considerations have been subordinated to it. Many of the factions within the Kurdish movement today have scarcely any claim to separate identity beyond a vague ideological notion centred on Marxism as an instrument of political arbitration. Much of the theoretical debate raised in the political literature of these groups has an unmistakably meretricious and rhetorical air.

The scramble for ideological rectitude in the ranks of Iraqi Kurdish activists intensified after the 1975 setback. Most new factions were born as breakaway groups from the Kurdistan Democratic Party which had dominated Kurdish politics thus far in Iraq. Not surprisingly, most new organizations attributed the crushing defeat of 1975 to lack of ideological rigour in the previous period. However, the various groups who renounced past political traditions have since failed to justify their break sufficiently on ideological grounds. For the most part, the new Kurdish organizations assert similar political values and claims to popular support. But while the proclaimed ideologies have been more alike than different in most instances, the patterns of public support for these organizations are more discernible. Generally speaking, the post-1975 Kurdish organizations in Iraq can be divided along demographic lines into Bahdini-dominated and Sorani-dominated groups. The divide reflects the two major demographic blocs in Iraq's Kurdish community: the more tribal-orientated Kurmanji-speaking region of Bahdinan in north Iraq; and the more urbanized community in the Sorani-speaking areas of the north east.

In Turkish Kurdistan, similar ideological arguments dominated relations between the various Kurdish organization. However, one major difference between the two ideological identities of Iraq's and Turkey's Kurds is the socio-economic background of Turkey's new generation of Kurdish leaders. While the urban middle class and the landed families provided the Kurdish movement in Iraq with most of its leaders, the leaders of the Kurdish organizations in Turkey have tended to come from impoverished families. An inevitable outcome of this situation has been that Turkey's Kurdish politics has been noticeably dominated by radical leftist ideologies. Furthermore, Kurdish organizations in Turkey have tended to favour uncompromising, often indiscriminately violent tactics against the state, echoing a characteristic tendency of the country's radical left.

Although "armed struggle" is today endorsed by most Kurdish organizations, Kurdish politicians have seldom sponsored outright terrorism. Of course the difference between armed struggle and terrorism is largely academic, depending on one's point of view and the scale and nature of the perpetrated violence. The received explanation for not labelling Kurdish activists as terrorists is the localized nature of Kurdish-related violence, which has seldom spread beyond the boundaries of Kurdish areas. To a large extent, this situation remains unchanged for most Kurdish groups. However, since none of the Kurdish communities of Iraq, Iran and Turkey are as yet satisfied with their status, and in view of the severity of government measures against Kurdish opponents in these countries in recent years, the threat of a drastic change in the current pattern of hostilities is growing. While it is too early to anticipate widespread terrorist activities by Kurdish activists, one must be guarded against over-optimism. Already acts of apparently indiscriminate violence, perpetrated by Kurdish activists, are on the rise in Turkey. In Iraq violent acts of retaliation by Kurdish opponents are now a likely prospect if no political settlement is forthcoming to defuse the situation.

Furthermore, traditional Kurdish organizations are acutely aware that adopting too moderate a stance, in the face of an unmistakeable rise in state repression, may cause a shift in public support in favour of the more radical groups. In the absence of a political breakthrough, particularly in the case of the Kurdish communities in Iraq and Turkey, Kurdish-related terrorism may sadly become the dominant form of violence emanating from the Middle East, now that many Palestinian groups no longer feel the need for further terrorist activities to draw the world's attention to their plight.

THE KURDS IN WORLD POLITICS

Superpower policies

For a long time, the Kurdish question has failed to feature in world affairs. Apart from occasional press attention, world opinion has been given little opportunity to reflect on the plight of the Kurdish nation. Such platforms as have been provided in the wake of extraordinary events like the use of chemical weapons against Kurdish targets, have not succeeded in stealing the limelight from other regional issues. The reason for this state of affairs is not entirely accidental. The blame must largely be laid at the doorstep of inept Kurdish politicians, in both Iraq and Turkey. Their failure has manifested itself particularly in three forms:

1 Confining public relations and alliances to a narrow circle, often delineated by the need to appease long-term "strategic allies".

Traditionally, these allies have mainly been Iran, the Soviet Union and Syria.

2 Pursuing an unquestioning "anti-Imperialist" fellowship with the left. An independent observer viewing the announcements of the various political groupings often suspects a self-censored leftist dogmatism. This is especially perplexing since it is taking place at a time when leftists everywhere are redefining their anti-imperialist policies.

3 Shying from contacts with the West, even where such contacts would have – with the benefit of hindsight – proved advantageous. Kurdish leaders have clearly failed to discern the need for pragmatism in their self-motivated pursuit of non-alliance, a term often reserved to describe their antipathy towards Western policies. The anti-Western stance adopted for so long has undoubtedly cost the Kurdish cause many potential sympathizers.

The anti-Western attitude readily finds protagonists who claim that their sentiments are based on historical experience. Kurdish activists argue that on two historic occasions, the Kurds came very close to gaining self-determination, and that in both cases the West was responsible for quashing their hopes. At the West's behest, the Lausanne Treaty of 1923 revoked a previous agreement (the Treaty of Sèvres, 1920) which had promised self-determination to the Kurds and other minorities previously under Ottoman rule.[1] And in 1975 the United States, which had been encouraging the Kurds of Iraq in their war with the central government, abandoned her erstwhile allies at a time when (by Iraq's own admission at a later date) the situation was heading towards a total defeat for the government.[2] On such grounds, the anti-Western voices in the Kurdish movement argue that while the West has been frequently apathetic towards the Kurds, the Soviet bloc has been consistent in terms of political, and at times military, assistance.

Kurdish pragmatists, however, find little time for recriminations, replying that realistically neither superpower has advanced the cause of the Kurdish people. This, they argue, has largely been the fault of the Kurds themselves, as diplomacy has taken second place to pride. The Kurdish movement has lost precious time in search of "true friends", failing to grasp the futility of this sentimental exercise in an international atmosphere which no longer recognizes such forms of political loyalties. The Kurds have failed to realize, for instance, that the superpowers are unlikely to act humanely against their best interests in either Baghdad or Ankara (or Tehran for that matter). Iraq and Turkey have strong trade links with both the Soviet Union and the West. Also, Turkey's membership of the North Atlantic Treaty Organization, and the substantial backing Iraq received from the superpowers during the dispute with Iran, presented the Kurds with a daunting diplomatic challenge.

How can a nation without a country and without reliable sponsors compete in the complex world of diplomacy, which is slanted to perpetuate the status quo? Kurdish leaders still correspond with the world through communiqués and their mastery of the arts of lobbying and diplomacy is all but non-existent. Incoherence, lack of unity and overstated rhetoric in Kurdish politics have left a damaging impression on world opinion. Indeed one wonders if things have changed much since the First World War when the current territorial set-up came into being. The Kurds' lack of unity and facility with diplomacy have been cited in various international documents as early as the 1920s, and used as pretext by some states to deny the Kurdish people the right to self-determination.[3]

Notwithstanding the anti-imperialist stance of most Kurdish organizations, Britain occupies a special position in Kurdish politics, due to a combination of historical fact and lingering old habits. Because of colonial legacy and the role played by Britain in delineating the frontiers of the modern Middle East and Turkey, Kurdish politicians, particularly traditionalists, still hope to enlist Britain as an advocate of the Kurdish cause. British foreign policy is perceived as the most consistent in the Western Alliance. To date, most Kurdish leaders who appeal to Britain for diplomatic support invite the British government to ponder the past and recall past pledges and obligations. However, this stance could only be interpreted as a reflection on the lack of realism in Kurdish diplomacy. Throughout the Iran–Iraq War Britain pursued a policy of approximation with both Iran and Iraq, albeit with less success in the case of British relations with Tehran.

It is of course too early to decide whether Britain's effort have paid off, but judging by the number of diplomatic incidents between Britain and both Iraq and Iran, it appears that these countries are still very suspicious of British motives. In contrast, Britain's relation with Turkey have improved during this period, especially in view of the former's support for the Turkish bid to join the European Economic Community. However, neither Britain's difficulties with Iran and Iraq, nor her good relations with Turkey have, so far, held any practical promise for the Kurds and their cause.[4]

The Arab scene

Arab disunity has often been perceived as a blessing by Kurdish politicians, particularly in Iraq and Turkey. This statement does not imply, however, that such disunity is of real benefit to the Kurdish cause, because it involves factors impossible to measure and predict. While the Kurdish movements in both Iraq and Turkey have seldom been short of Arab allies (Syria being an obvious example), the balance of interests has frequently been disrupted by sudden changes in Arab political temperament. At best the Arab world has tended to provide the Kurds with useful tactical allies, on whose support they could count from time to time. Despite the pragmatic mood dominating the Arab world nowadays, unity of purpose in the Arab fold is still in doubt, and Kurdish organizations are unlikely to run short of Arab allies opposed to Baghdad or Ankara.

Even where relations between "brother" Arab and Muslim states appear cordial on the surface, mutual suspicion often abounds. For example, long periods of antipathy between Iraq and Syria on the one hand, and between Syria and Turkey on the other, have dominated the nature of Kurdish alliances in the Arab world. For decades, Syria and Iraq have been apparently divided by a common nationalist Ba'th ideology. However, as in most Third World countries, ideology is subordinated to the style of leadership, and where governments are not elected, style of government is all that matters. Syria's rivalry with Turkey is of a historical and economic nature. The Syrians still dispute Turkey's control of Alexandria, a province with sizeable Arab and Kurdish populations. Syria is also worried about Turkey's increased control over the Euphrates river system through the building of dams for hydroelectric purposes and the diversion of water to agricultural projects.

Relations between the Kurdish movement and various Palestinian groups also deserve some mention. Many Kurdish organizations in both Iraq and Turkey maintain working links with Palestinian groups, including exchange of equipment and training facilities. Some of the radical Kurdish factions in Turkey, such as the PKK, have had members trained by Palestinian groups.[5]

Turkey's EC prospects

The future of Turkey's relationship with Europe is likely to take the shape of full membership of the European Economic Community. Turkey's membership of NATO, her small but strategic European enclave and the country's non-socialist economy are points in favour of Turkey's application for EC membership. Nevertheless, there remain significant stumbling blocks in Turkey's path. The country's constitution and system of government do not accord with the European democratic model of government. Freedom of speech, belief, worship and ethnic expression – which are fundamental liberal European values – are severely curtailed under the Turkish system. It is not only the state, however, that could be accused of intolerance towards nonconformism. Many of the country's unofficial opposition groups are committed to violence as a means of achieving political ends. As far as one can gather from demonstrations of public support, various banned fascist, communist and fundamentalist organizations receive sympathy from sizeable sections in Turkey's society. Both the militancy which characterizes the actions of most opposition groups, and the unmasked intolerance of them by the state, epitomize the dilemma of modern Turkish politics. Human rights abuses and various forms of political indiscretion mark the activities of both the state and the unofficial opposition.

The Kurdish question is by no means the only significant ethnic problem in Turkey today, although the Kurds constitute the country's largest ethnic minority. The country's Armenians (and their large exiled community) as well as many other smaller groups can summon wholly plausible arguments in support of their charge of unfair treatment by the Turkish state. Despite the recent relaxation of previous restrictions on the use of Kurdish, Turkey's ethnic communities are still deprived of basic freedoms, such as the right to found or join organizations representing their interests in parliament. Of course, there have been times when the state's vehemently secular, pan-Turkish rules were relaxed to allow ethnic groups to exercise a minimum degree of free expression, such as publishing books, holding public meetings and ceremonies of worship. But in general, Turkey's record of suppression of minorities is unrivalled by any other state in non-communist Europe.

The problem is compounded by an unfortunate tendency on the part of the Turkish state to deny that even the most appalling of past mistakes in dealing with ethnic unrest has ever occurred. This policy is best exemplified by Turkey's outright rejection of a substantial body of historical evidence showing state involvement in the genocide of dissident Armenian communities earlier in the century. Indeed it remains to be seen whether the strength of Turkey's desire to join the European Economic Community will (as now seems more probable) finally compel her to demonstrate greater sensitivity towards the grievances, past and present, of her ethnic communities.

The state's dedication to the cause of building a nation united by common purpose and identity need not, however, be incompatible with the country's European aspirations. The resentment and mistrust that exist between the central government and Kurdish activists owe as much to economics as to cultural causes. The state's inability to summon and inject more funds into the Kurdish areas to temper the growing crisis there accounts for a great deal of the mutual frustration which has, in turn, often accentuated both the government's high-handed policies as well as the militancy of the activists. Unfortunately for both sides, the state does not have sufficient resources to correct the enormous disparities which exist between the Kurdish areas and the other parts of the country, and to improve the quality of life for the impoverished Kurdish population.

Turkey is no doubt aware of the gravity of her economic woes and their political consequences. Indeed the country's current economic and political crisis are significantly interdependent. Liberalizing Turkey's narrow electoral base, without engendering an equitable system of economic opportunity to go with it, may deepen the crisis even further. Turkey's leaders fear that in their highly polarized society, with an impoverished majority, instituting a more liberal electoral system could lead to an endless series of hung parliaments or – worse still – a radical political organization being voted into office. Implementing the western European model in Turkey in its authentic form is therefore deemed unworkable by the ruling elite, without prior establishment of a state of economic welfare comparable to those of the western European countries. But in order for Turkey to achieve parity with the rest of non-communist

Europe, the EC must be directly involved. Only then, it is argued, will Turkey's ruling élite feel safe enough to loosen their tight grip on such matters as human rights, political freedom and ethnic expression. The European fellowship is good news for the Turkish state – not only because it is likely to spearhead greater prosperity, but also because it could soften the political temperament of its critics at home. Turkey's prospective membership of the EC, therefore, holds particular promise for the country's Kurdish community and its representatives.

PROBLEMS OF DISPLACEMENT

Overall picture

It is impossible to give an accurate assessment of the scale of the displacement affecting Kurdish refugees, deportees and exiles. No exact figures are available of the size of the problem. However, there appear to be as many as two and a half million Kurdish refugees distributed over Iraq, Iran, Syria, Turkey, Israel, central and western Europe, the United States and Canada. The estimate is for the period 1960–88 and includes other minorities traditionally based in Kurdish areas such as Assyrians, Yazidis[6] and Kurdish Jews. Approximately half of all Kurdish refugees have originated from Iraq, with the rest from Iran and Turkey (as well as small groups from Lebanon and Syria).

It is impracticable to discuss the problems of all these categories of refugees in this section. The discussion will therefore be confined to the problem of Faili Kurdish refugees, most of whom, since the 1970s, have been stripped of their Iraqi citizenship and deported to Iran. This group of Kurdish refugees deserve particular mention in view of the fact that although they constitute a substantial percentage of the total Iraqi Kurdish refugees (approximately 30–40 per cent), their plight and unique circumstances have received very little attention from the outside world.

Plight of Faili Kurds

Faili Kurds make up about 10 per cent of all Kurds in Iraq. Most of them live in the capital Baghdad and other major cities and towns, including Kut, Mandali, Khanaqin, Badra, as well as smaller communities in Hilla, Imara, Nassiriyya and Basra. Approximately half of these are descendants of Kurdish tribespeople from the central sector on the Iran–Iraq border. Only 60–70 per cent of all Faili Kurds from Iraq speak the Faili Kurdish dialect, which is akin to the Sorani dialect spoken in central Kurdistan, but shows distinct Persian and Arabic influences. In an attempt to escape obligatory service in the Ottoman army, most Failis in Iraq (then Mesopotamia) declined to take up Ottoman citizenship. During the British Mandate after the Second World War and the early years of the State of Iraq, the Faili communities in the Iraq–Iran border area faced restrictions on their freedom of movement because of newly enforced border arrangements. Given the choice between registering as Iraqi or Iranian citizens, most Faili Kurds chose to become Iranian subjects but continued to reside inside Iraq. Their preference for Iranian citizenship was probably prompted by liberal Iranian citizenship arrangements and – once again – in order to avoid conscription. The fact that most Faili Kurds are Shi'is may also have influenced their choice of nationality since the Iraqi government has from the start been dominated by Sunni Arabs. The new borders cut through traditional Faili territory, and while the Failis on the Iraqi side of the border were given the choice of becoming citizens of the newly created Kingdom of Iraq, their relatives across the border (in and around Kermanshah/Bakhtaran and Ilam) were not eligible for Iraqi citizenship. Since tribal loyalties were more important to most Failis than allegiance to the modern state, members of the same tribe often preferred to take up the same nationality, usually on the basis of what the majority had chosen to become at the time. The decision was rarely based on considerations of locality, as people sometimes chose to follow the example of relatives now living on the other side of the newly-drawn border; in any case, location was to the semi-nomadic Failis a less important consideration than family ties. A sizeable section of the Faili community remained unregistered as citizens with either country, and the plight of this particular group was consequently decided by the authorities on the basis of their original tribal affiliations. By the 1940s, however, the majority of Faili Kurds residing in Iraq no longer wished to hold on to Iranian citizenship and had applied to be registered as Iraqis. By this time, however, Iraqi citizenship laws had evolved into a complex jigsaw with no provisions concerning the status of fellow countrymen who had failed to register as citizens in the first instance. As a consequence, most Faili applicants were no longer eligible for automatic citizenship and had to be naturalized instead. Nationality regulations in Iraq have rarely changed since they were first put into effect and have generally adhered to a peculiar premise: only Arab inhabitants or non-Arabs whose forebears were Ottoman citizens are given citizenship; others can only be naturalized, irrespective of how many generations they and their ancestors lived in the country. This tricky aspect of Iraq's citizenship arrangements has been exploited as early as the 1960s by the government to justify the deportation of thousands of Faili Kurdish families to Iran. The fact that for many generations these people and their forebears had lived in Iraq apparently did not make any difference.

More than 130,000 Faili Kurds were deported from Iraq in the period 1969–88. About half of these were sent away after 1980, and although the deportation process has slowed down in the past few years it has by no means stopped. Approximately 5,000 male individuals aged 16 to 40 have been kept back in Iraq in various prisons, presumably as hostages, to prevent them from being drafted into Iran's armed forces, and in order to intimidate their families. Indeed the hostage factor may be responsible for the reluctance of most Faili Kurds to discuss their problems with pressure groups and humanitarian organizations. Most Faili deportees approached by this author were loath to reveal much information about their problems and background, citing the fate of their relatives in Iraq as the reason for their silence. Also, unlike members of other Kurdish communities, most of the Faili Kurds of Iraq combine a curious mixture of Kurdish identity, Shi'i faith and urban culture. This has made it difficult for them to rally around one representative institution in the highly polarized societies in Iraq and Iran.

In addition to the racial and religious factors, the persecution of Faili Kurds in Iraq can be attributed to a number of other causes. In 1932, the Iraqi government legislated a "Land Title Settlement Law" which altered previous land ownership arrangements in the country. One of the effects of the new legislation was that many semi-nomadic tribes lost control over communal agricultural lands and pastures. As a result, there was an influx of Faili migrant workers who descended on the country's major cities in search of alternative economic opportunities. Aided by a reputation for physical endurance and loyalty, many of these found work as porters and assistants in Baghdad's major commercial centre, the

Shorja. In the boom years following the Second World War, the Shorja, then dominated by Jewish merchants, saw Failis starting their own businesses.

The fortunes of many Faili would-be merchants received a dramatic boost when they took over Jewish businesses abandoned hurriedly by their owners, in the wake of the violent anti-Jewish riots which broke out shortly after the proclamation of the State of Israel in 1947. In many instances, Jewish merchants simply handed their businesses over to loyal Faili employees, who became the new class of merchants, dominating the retail sector of the economy for many years to come. By the early 1950s, the traditional resentment by the urban population of the Jewish merchant class, for their domination of the economy, had switched to the new immigrants. Once more, the economy was dominated by a minority whose background was sharply different from the Arab Sunnis who made up the majority of the working class population in the capital.

Political factors also widened the gulf between the new-comers and the host community. Most first-generation Faili immigrants were apolitical, but there was a distinct tendency for their children to sympathize with the left, chiefly the Iraqi Communist Party. This preference by the new generation of educated Failis was perhaps due to the fact that most other political parties at the time were Arab nationalist, hence unattractive to all non-Arabs. In later periods (from the late 1950s onwards), many members of the Faili community began to identify with the Kurdish movement in Iraq, spearheaded by the Kurdistan Democratic Party. During various times in this period members of Faili families became leaders in both the Iraqi Communist Party and the Kurdistan Democratic Party.[7] With neither the Iraqi Communist Party nor the Kurdistan Democratic Party becoming major parties in government (save for insignificant spells), the Faili community was seen as a potential threat by the successive (Arab) nationalist governments that have ruled the country for decades.

CONCLUSION

Developments surrounding the Iran–Iraq conflict, and the ensuing governmental and popular alliances, have ushered the Kurds of Turkey and Iraq into a new era. However, the two communities have adjusted differently to the aftermath of the inconclusive Gulf War. Iraq's Kurds suffered a severe blow to their aspirations as a result of the present no-war-no-peace situation that exists between Baghdad and Tehran. While in Turkey, the prospects of an eventual easing of the state's firm grip on Kurdish affairs are strengthened by Turkey's desire to join the European Community, and the dilution of communist influence in Turkish politics following the recent developments in the Eastern bloc.

The Islamic revolution in Iran has undoubtedly left a significant mark on the Kurdish scene, not so much in the form of ideological induction but as a result of adjustments in the foreign policies of the governments affected by the new development. In spite of Turkey's official neutrality, open feuds and mutual suspicions between Iran and Syria on the one hand, and Iraq and Turkey on the other, have galvanised the Kurdish movements in the area. Kurdish insurgents in each state have readily found sympathy (and at times active support) from one government or another, eager to pressurize a rival neighbouring state. The emergence of a militant and relatively well-armed Kurdish insurgency in Turkey is a direct consequence of this new political era. Equally, Iraq's brutal suppression of its Kurdish population, especially since the truce with Iran, highlights the sheer apprehension shared by the governments of the region about the new developments in Kurdish politics.

Yet, despite the apparent deadlock, the prospects of a new realism *vis-à-vis* the Kurdish population in the region are not too distant. The Kurdish movement is beginning to show some signs of maturity and an understanding of its weaknesses and past shortfalls. For the first time, it appears that Kurdish leaders from the various parts of Kurdistan are talking to each other meaningfully. Notwithstanding occasional rhetorical outbursts, Kurdish politicians are demonstrating a capability to further their cause along clearly defined and seemingly reasonable lines. And although references to self-determination have peppered some recent Kurdish statements, most groups do not appear to dismiss out of hand the possibility of "autonomy talks", within the framework of their countries of abode in the region. Realism must, however, be shared by all sides concerned if it is to secure a tangible result; and it is reasonable to suggest that it is time the central governments of the region addressed the Kurdish issue with greater imagination.

At present, the most unsatisfactory aspect of the Kurdish problem is a confusion on the part of the region's governments between the two issues of Kurdishness and borders. Indeed, so long as the issues of border security and nationality (with respect to local Kurdish populations) dominate the official agenda of the central governments concerned, no real progress is achievable.

For example it is difficult to see how Iraq can hope to solve its Kurdish problem while it absurdly continues to classify a substantial proportion of Iraqi Kurds as being "of Iranian origin", a situation illustrated by the plight of Failis whom we discussed in this paper. Equally, Turkey's continued treatment of the local Kurdish insurgency as primarily an issue of "border security" is very unsatisfactory. The restoration of peace through Kurdish territories is a political task that only politicians may succeed in resolving. And until bureaucrats, generals and guerrilla leaders have cleared the way for politicians to embark on a genuine dialogue, no imaginative, lasting solution can reasonably be anticipated.

Chapter 7

The Kurdish movement in Iraq: 1975–88

A. Sherzad

The collapse of the Kurdish armed movement in Iraqi Kurdistan in 1975 signalled the beginning of a new phase and a new experience in twentieth-century Kurdish policy making. This phase has been further conditioned by the appearance of new social and political variables, and its development has been hastened by the transformation of political structures and alliances in the region, notably the collapse of the Shah's regime in Iran in 1979 and the outbreak of the Iran–Iraq War in 1980.

This chapter, based on the view that the collapse of the Kurdish movement in 1975 represents also the collapse of its traditional social basis, will firstly provide a brief overview of the Kurdish political scene to 1975, and secondly, outline the new variables that have *apparently* shaped the Kurdish movement in Iraq from 1976 through 1988.

HISTORICAL BACKGROUND

Most commentators agree that the emergence, in the late nineteenth century, of modern social and political élites – who had broken away from traditional religious education – signalled the appearance of nationalism among the subject peoples of the Ottoman Empire. Modernity – arising out of the notion of secularism – allowed new elements to play an important role in the formation of new cultural and political entities of these peoples, according significance to their specific ethnic character and historical heritage. The growth of the modernizing elements was of course proportional to the social dynamism of each ethnic group. In this context the appearance of Kurdish nationalism presents no exception to its Middle Eastern homologues. The dissolution of the Ottoman Empire following the First World War gave some of these modern entities their legitimate political structures, in that they found themselves directing newly established states. Modernity, thus, became an important criterion for state and/or national legitimacy and recognition. Indeed, the existence of two antagonistic poles of political outlook – traditional and modern – has, since the beginning of this century, characterized the social and political evolution of the contemporary Middle East. In parallel with the foundation of the new states, conflicts and alliances between the traditional and modern forces were not resolved within groups that had not obtained a state structure, but had been relegated to minority status. This was particularly apparent in the case of the Kurds who, as a result of the Treaty of Lausanne, signed in 1923, found themselves minorities in Iraq, Iran, Turkey and Syria, without having a juridic status.

Thus, despite the violent resistance of the Kurds in the years from 1922 to 1938, all Kurdish social networks of self-expression were suppressed in Turkey, justification being offered in the form of the Kemalist nation/state ideology, while in Iran campaigns for state centralization justified the assimilation policies.

THE KURDS IN IRAQ: UP TO 1975

In Iraq, however, the situation was quite different. The weak and newly founded State of Iraq was obliged, under the influence of growing Kurdish nationalism on the one hand, and pressures from the British on the other, to accept the League of Nation's resolution of 1925, recognizing an official status for Kurdistan within the State of Iraq. This official recognition gave Kurdish political and cultural modernity the opportunity to develop. Two kinds of leaders appeared, to occupy this restricted political space: the traditionalists (tribal chiefs and/or leaders of the religious brotherhoods) and modernists (urban dwellers who had a high status in the traditional society, but who had received a secular education). These two kinds of political actors formed the pillars of an autonomous Kurdish political sphere, relatively independent of the state ideology. In the long term, they were able, albeit often by violence in the form of guerrilla warfare, to create conditions which would allow the social, political and cultural expression of Kurdishness.

Paradoxically, the modernists – for whom modernity is a

fundamental criterion of "national recognition" – were able to pursue their nationalistic goals only through collaboration with the traditionalists. Indeed, the modernists exploited the grievances voiced by the traditionalists – which arose out of the declaration of the current post-1925 frontiers which divided tribal zones and thereby diminished the power of the traditional religious scholars. The role of the modernists in "nationalizing" and kurdifying the tribal movements, based mainly on the economic interests of each tribe, succeeded in developing nationalist feelings in the urban centres. The modernists took advantage of the influence of the tribal chiefs and the charisma of the religious leaders as a social mobilizing force. This can be seen particularly in the context of the creation of the Kurdish Democratic Party in 1946 by the urban political actors. Mustafa Barzani, an influential tribal chief with a religious education, was chosen as party leader. He was later to become the representative figure of Kurdish nationalism. The modernists' ability to exercise a certain influence on the traditionalists allowed them to put pressure on the Iraqi state to satisfy some Kurdish social and cultural claims, with significant long-term consequences. Although their realization was entirely conditioned by the vicissitudes of Baghdad/Kurdish political relations, the results were nevertheless impressive. For example, three generations received their schooling in Kurdish, while since 1920, various Kurdish periodicals have served as a forum for literary renewal, and permitted the birth of a Kurdish historiography, which could create, for the coming generations, a real national myth. Further, the gradual creation of urban-bred generations, who gave a Kurdish dimension to their cultural, social and political actions, has progressively transformed the basis of forces of social mobilization, which some decades ago were mainly dependent on the tribal and/or religious mass mobilization. The increase and gradual dominance of urban elements within the body and the upper echelons of the Kurdish movement can already be observed in the late 1950s. Thus, the Kurdish movement in Iraq consisted of an interaction between the traditional, rurally based political actors and modern urban educated ones.[1]

Iraq has been the scene of a confrontation between two unequal, hierarchically structured entities: an Arab entity, endowed with a state structure, and a semi-independent Kurdish entity, lacking a state structure but possessing its own political sphere, albeit in a minority capacity. The creation and institutionalization of this

Kurdish entity in Iraq, directed from the late 1940s to 1975 by the KDP, was of course a gradual process. There have been many periods of armed resistance, and other, peaceful ones.[2] As far as Baghdad's strategy is concerned, it has aimed, and still aims to integrate the Kurdish entity within its own state structure and ideology, thus destroying its autonomy, reducing the Kurdish question to one of mere cultural recognition. This recognition could be progressively eliminated through long-term strategies, such as the intensification of campaigns aimed at promoting the arabization of the Kurdish regions.

IRAQI KURDISTAN: 1976-88

From 1976, a new movement began, marked by the resumption of guerrilla warfare. The collapse of the Shah's regime in Iran in 1979 permitted the intensification of this guerrilla warfare, which transformed itself, during the Iran–Iraq War, into a real front war, leading the Iraqi army to lose control of some main Kurdish regions. Here, the systematic use of chemical weapons from April 1987 to November 1988 allowed Iraq to regain control of almost all the Kurdish territories, inflicting a severe setback upon the Kurds.

Two main developments differentiate the Kurdish movement in the post 1975 period from earlier movements. From a social perspective, urban-bred elements provided most of the new leadership. Similarly, the upper levels of the military hierarchy within the movement mainly consisted of urban elements, such as school teachers, students, medical personnel. Compromises with religious and tribal elements were made only at relatively low levels in the political, military and social organization of the movement. Therefore, the break with the earlier social structure is clear: the political leadership is no longer characterized by the key role attributed to a traditional, charismatic figure.

From the political standpoint, the Kurdish movement ceased to be a one-party movement. Numerous political parties arose to oppose the Iraqi regime. For the post-1976 period three kinds of political parties may be discerned:

1 *Older political formations*: the KDP, led by the sons of Mustafa Barzani.
2 *New political formations*: founded by former members of the KDP, such as the Kurdistan Socialist Party, or former dissidents

from the KDP, like the Patriotic Union of Kurdistan led by Jalal Talabani. The PUK is, along with the KDP, a major political formation.

3 *Marginal or secondary formations*: this category comprises the political parties formed as a result of the Iran–Iraq War. They have no profound roots, no "natural" social base, no historical depth. They include the three Kurdish Islamic parties, created with the help of the Iranians, and virtually ignored by the other Kurdish parties. There are also two small Kurdish Christian formations, who depend upon other Kurdish parties, especially the KDP, in their politico-military actions.[3] Moreover, the dissemination of leftist ideas after 1975 led to the formation of many small Kurdish parties.

Each party dominated different geographical areas, which are regarded as "liberated land". Each party has a certain number of fighters, called *peshmerges*, the number of fighters being proportional to the influence of the party. It is estimated that the PUK and KDP, the two main political parties, have about 10,000 *peshmerges* each, while the smaller parties are estimated to have about 5,000 fighters each. Less important parties, like the Islamic ones, have 800 to 1,000 armed men. The rapid increase in the number of fighters has several causes.

First, following the Kurdish defeat in 1975, the Iraqi government undertook the mass deportation of the population inhabiting the frontier zones, creating a "no-man's land" 15 kilometres deep, along a line running from the Iranian to the Syrian frontiers. This provoked enormous social discontent, leading a significant part of the population to join the guerrilla movement launched by the political parties in 1976.

Second, the outbreak of the Iran–Iraq War led to a large-scale draft, especially after 1982 when Iranian forces advanced to positions near Basra. The Iraqi Kurds proved to be more responsive to the Kurdish cause, than to the Iran–Iraq War "officially" aimed at defending arabism. This led several thousands of young men to volunteer their services to the *peshmerge* groups in Kurdish-controlled territory.

In most areas of the liberated lands, the social life of the inhabitants of the villages and small towns was organized on the basis of administrative units known as *komelayeti*, which entrusts a representative of one of the political parties with the administration of some twenty villages or small towns. This representative is elected and each party may present its candidate. For the fighters, the villages form a vital communication as well as an economic network. The villagers were also considered to be *peshmerge*, for the purpose of defending their areas in the event of major Iraqi offensives, and were armed by the political parties.

It is currently true that the post-1975 Kurdish leadership is no longer characterized by the central presence of a tribal or religious leader, but two issues are significant here.

First, Mas'ud Barzani, the son of Mustafa Barzani, remains the only leader of tribal origin in the post-1975 Kurdish leadership. Support for Mas'ud within the KDP from non-urban elements is based primarily on nostalgic affiliation to his father. However, Mas'ud, whose leading associates are mostly urban, no longer has the solidarity and the full support of the Barzani tribe.[4]

Second, the emergence of counter-powers within the Kurdish political movement, following the appearance of new parties after 1976, has resulted in armed confrontations between the different Kurdish parties. These inter-party conflicts are reminiscent of inter-tribal confrontations of past centuries. The difference, today, is that the Persian and Ottoman Empires are replaced by centralized states, surrounding the Kurds, which attempt to manipulate the Kurdish parties against one another.

Perhaps the conflict between the political parties has been inevitable, but it indicates that the Kurdish leadership, despite its modern composition, has not entirely broken away from the political concepts of traditional Kurdish society. The 1975–88 experience, however, seems to suggest that the influence of tradition is breaking down and may result in the formulation of a new political concept for the coming generations.

Only in May 1988 did the various Kurdish parties succeed in forming a unified political and military direction in a coalition known as the "Kurdistan Front", hardly welcomed by governments having a Kurdish minority.

THE REGIONAL PERSPECTIVE

It has not been the purpose of this paper to analyse the regional dimension of the Kurdish problem, but as political developments in one part of Kurdistan directly affect four other states, it is necessary to touch on some regional perspectives.

The Kurdish movement – especially in Iraq and in Iran – has been an important factor, influencing political and military manoeuvres in the Iran–Iraq War. The Kurds constitute a national, territorially based minority which can, in case of conflict, imperil the integrity of existing states. This factor is more important for Iraq and Turkey because they are relatively new states than for Iran, which has a state tradition of a millennium.

During the Iran–Iraq War, manipulation of the political opposition within the enemy country became a second battleground. At the beginning of the war, Iran concentrated on developing the Iraqi Islamic opposition, especially Shi'ite. Thus, Iran had a big hand in forming the Supreme Council of the Islamic Revolution in Iraq, with its largely Shi'ite membership. In 1984, however, Iran began courting Sunnite and nationalist groups in Iraq. At the same time, Iran was faced with an armed resistance movement supported by Iraq in its Kurdish region. In consequence, Iran legalized, for the first time since 1920, Kurdish language publications, even permitting the operation of Kurdish publishing houses, whose activities are, of course, strictly controlled. Further, in 1985 the Iranians increased their aid to the Iraqi Kurds. Meanwhile, a second country, Syria, entered the game. Syrian help to Iraqi Kurds had preceded that of the Iranians, going back to the resumption of guerrilla warfare in 1976, and was a result of tensions between Iraq and Syria preceding the Iran–Iraq War, deep enough to lead to a military confrontation. The manipulation and financing of each other's opposition groups constitute, even now, the other front of conflict between the two countries. At the same time, the alliance between Iran and Syria, who share a common enemy in Iraq, seems rather contradictory, since the final objectives sought by both countries are quite different. In addition to the Lebanese situation, the differences between Iran and Syria during the Iran–Iraq War revolved around the nature of the government that would replace the current Iraqi regime: Islamist or arabist?

In the shadow of these inter-state conflicts the Kurdish longing for independence – a political constant in the Middle East – has been exploited as a destabilizing force.

The ceasefire in the Iran–Iraq War in 1988, and the setback inflicted upon the Kurds, has put an end to a stage in the post-1975 Kurdish movement, and another one is introduced due to the appearance of new variables, different from those of 1976. Actually, several factors are likely to influence future developments in Kurdish movement.

In so far as Iraq is concerned, both during and after the Iran–Iraq War, Iraq has pursued a radical solution to its Kurdish problem: mass deportation (over 800,000 Kurds have been deported to camps near the Saudi and Jordanian borders), systematic destruction of villages and small towns (over 4,000 villages have been destroyed since the ceasefire between Iran and Iraq), and the establishment of a "no man's land" 30 kilometres deep along its northern borders. These developments may have three major consequences.

First, the resulting destruction of the countryside – symbol and traditional basis of Kurdish armed resistance – has made guerrilla warfare extremely difficult. The break with traditional forms of Kurdish armed resistance is already clear, since all its social networks are destroyed.

Second, the rapid growth of the urban Kurdish population, has led to a radical transformation of urban structure. For example, Arbil, which four years ago had 400,000 inhabitants, now has 900,000. The four biggest Kurdish cities in Iraq have significant concentrations of Kurds in shanty towns and internment camps for the deported. This may result in a repetition of events following the creation of the 15 km deep "no man's land" after the collapse of Barzani's movement in 1975, where great social discontent among the population resulted in large-scale commitment of rural Kurds to the resistance movement. The essential difference is that now the deported, discontented population is concentrated in big cities; this may lead to speculation as to whether the Kurdish movement might turn to civil protest or armed resistance in other areas. In other words, can armed resistance, or civil protest, in urban centres become the new strategy of the Kurdish movement?

Finally, the use of chemical weapons has led to an exodus of Kurdish refugees from Iraq to Turkey and Iran. In the context of Turkey the issue of the impact of the presence of over 60,000 Iraqi Kurds is raised. Officially, the Iraqi Kurds are not considered as refugees, but rather as "northern Iraqi combatants", since Turkey, who signed the Geneva Convention of 1951, introduced a reserve, according to which only persons of European countries can have refugee status in Turkey. Currently, the debate revolves around the issue of whether these "northern Iraqi combatants", should be granted refugee status. If so, this would have serious consequences for Turkey, not the least of which would be the acknowledgement of the Kurdish language, since international law requires that refugees be schooled in the language of their country of origin, and Kurdish is the official language of Iraqi Kurdistan. Further, the emergence, since 1920, of an autonomous political entity in Iraqi Kurdistan, has represented a continuous danger for other states in the region with a sizeable Kurdish minority. This is especially the case for Turkey, where the influence of the Iraqi Kurdish movement may have contributed to the failure of the assimilation policies of Kemalist Turkey. Here, the unguarded nature of the frontiers, as well as the informal communication networks linking the various parts of Kurdistan, have helped preserve the collective memory of Turkish Kurds and increased their national sentiment.

Chapter 8

The Kurds in Syria and Lebanon

Ismet Chériff Vanly

HISTORICAL AND GEOGRAPHICAL DATA

There are few publications and little information on the Kurds in Syria[1] who have seldom occupied a place in the world press. This is probably because they are less numerous than those of Turkey, Iran, or Iraq, and hence less prone to uprisings against the government in demand of their rights. Most of them live on the plains just south of the foothills of western Kurdistan in Turkey, a terrain which is not suited to guerrilla warfare. Furthermore, their regions are isolated from the main communication routes and have little appeal for the foreign visitor.

Under the Abbasids, Syria was called "al-Sham", a name still in current use, and administratively it was an "*iqlīm*", that is, a country or province, like "Misr" (Egypt) or "Iraq" (which was limited to Arab Iraq or Lower Mesopotamia). The Arab geographers referred to Kurdistan as "Bilad al-Akrad" (Country of the Kurds)[2] and, since the eleventh century,[3] as "Kurdistan".

The territory of present-day Syria and that of the former province of al-Sham do not altogether coincide. The latter included the entire eastern coast of the Mediterranean and its hinterland, from Cilicia and Marash down to the Arabian Desert and Aqaba on the Red Sea. To the east, al-Sham was bordered by the Middle Euphrates, with Palmyra in the Syrian desert. Beyond the Middle Euphrates, there began another "*iqlīm*" or province, "al-Jazira" (the "Island" or Upper Mesopotamia).[4]

Under the Ottomans, Syria was divided into four *vilayets* or *paşalıks*; Damascus (with Palestine and Jordan), Aleppo, Tripoli and Saida. The Allied Powers conference held in San Remo on 19–26 April 1920, acting on the secret Anglo-French Sykes–Picot agreement of May 1916, separated Palestine and Jordan from Syria, bringing them under British Mandate, while the rest of the country passed under French Mandate. In 1920 the French carved a new state, the Lebanon, out of Syria and in 1939 transferred the Sanjak of Alexandretta to Kemalist Turkey. While Syria was thus reduced in the west, a significant part of the former Jazira province, a region which had never hitherto been considered "Shami" (Syrian) was added in the east. The new Syria achieved its independence in 1946.

According to the Treaty of Sèvres of 10 August 1920 (arts 62–4), Ottoman Kurdistan, which would normally have included the Kurdish areas in present-day Syria, was to be given autonomy within the new Republic of Turkey, with the choice of full independence within a year of the treaty's coming into force if such was the will of the Kurdish population. The text of art. 64, para. 1, of the treaty reads:

> If within one year from the coming into force of the present treaty the Kurdish people within the areas defined in Art. 62 shall address themselves to the Council of the League of Nations in such a manner as to show that a majority of the population of these areas desires independence from Turkey, and if the Council then considers that these people are capable of such independence and recommends that it should be granted to them, Turkey hereby agrees to execute such a recommendation, and to renounce all rights and title over these areas.

The third paragraph of the same article adds:

> If and when such renunciation takes place, no objection will be raised by the Principal Allied Powers to the voluntary adhesion to such an independent Kurdish State of the Kurds inhabiting that part of Kurdistan which has hitherto been included in the Mosul Vilayet.

As is well known, after the Kemalist victory in Turkey, the Treaty of Sèvres was superseded by that of Lausanne of 24 July 1923, which totally ignored the Kurdish question,[5] except in so far as the unrepresented Kurds were the object of an interesting exchange between the British and Turkish delegations.[6]

In ethnic terms, the Arabs living in Syria and Iraq have as immediate neighbours to the north no other ethnic group but the

Kurds, with the exception of the Sanjak of Alexandretta where several nationalities coexist, including a Kurdish minority.

The Syrian–Turkish border was fixed by the Franco–Turkish agreement drawn up in London on 9 March 1921 and was twice modified, first by the Ankara agreement of October of the same year, and then by the Jouvenal agreement of 1926. This border does not follow the line of ethnic demarcation between Arabs and Kurds; it assigns to northern Syria three regions inhabited by Kurds or by a Kurdish majority, that is, Kurdh-Dagh, Arab-Pinar and Jazira. These regions, while separate from each other in Syrian territory, are all contiguous with western Kurdistan in Turkey, of which they are, indeed, merely a southward extension across the border. The same border leaves two regions with an Arab majority within Turkey: Harran and Gaziantep. As both Kurdistan and Syria were under foreign rule for centuries, the demarcation line between Arab and Kurdish territory was never clear-cut. This is true also for the Jazira, where both ethnic groups have lived side by side from pre-Islamic times to the present.

In an earlier study[7] I have given extensive references documenting the antiquity of the Kurdish presence in Syria. It may be relevant here merely to recall that the Kurd-Dagh had already long been inhabited by the Kurds when the wars of the crusades began at the end of the eleventh century. A number of Kurdish military or feudal settlements were found in inner Syria, for example in the Alawite and the north Lebanese mountains, and in the town of Hama and its surroundings. The huge fortress "Krak des Chevaliers", still known in Arabic as "Hisn al-Akrad" (Castle of the Kurds),[8] located in the Alawite mountains between Homs and Tartous, had been built as a Kurdish military settlement before being conquered and enlarged by the French crusaders. Indeed, the word "krak" has no meaning in French and is simply a deformation of the word "Akrad", which is the plural of "Kurd" in Arabic.[9] The Kurdish quarter in Damascus, where several Kurdish Ayyubid princes are buried, dates back at least to the Ayyubid epoch. As to the Jazira, the Danish writer Carsten Niebuhr, who visited the area in 1764, published a map showing his itinerary there and mentioning five Kurdish tribes (the Dukurie, Kikie, Schechchanie, Mullie and Aschetie) and one Arab tribe (the Tai).[10] His map is thus valuable historical evidence against the claim that the Kurds are newcomers to the Jazira. The same tribes are to be found in present-day Syrian Jazira with this difference, that while the Kurds have become settled peasants and city dwellers, the Arabs have remained nomadic camel breeders.

In his monumental work on the life of Nureddin, the Zangid Turkish prince of Mosul who preceded the advent of Saladin, Professor Nikita Elisséeff notes that the Zangid state, which included Syria, was governed by a joint "Turkish and Kurdish military aristocracy,"[11] and that its army, which fought against the crusaders, was "essentially a Turco-Kurdish army".[12] Under the Ayyubid Kurds the governing class was predominantly Kurdish.

THE KURDISH POPULATION IN SYRIA

The Kurds constitute the largest national minority in Syria and the only one with a territorial base, which may to some extent explain their difficulties. There are no official statistics as to their numbers since Syrian law denies their existence. The Syrian constitution calls the country "the Syrian Arab Republic", implying thereby that all its citizens are to be considered Arabs, their ethnic origins notwithstanding. Yet the Syrian authorities have shown notable tolerance towards the Armenians who are indeed relative newcomers, comprising some 200,000 individuals living in the large Arab cities of Aleppo and Damascus. They are permitted to organize themselves as a community and engage in cultural activities such as the teaching of Armenian in recognized private clubs and societies, elementary rights strictly denied to the Muslim Kurds whose numbers are much greater and whose presence in the country is as old as that of the Arabs. According to Michel Seurat, writing in *La Syrie d'aujourd'hui*:[13] "The Kurds in Syria represent at least 7 per cent of the total population or 600,000 people." In the same work, the total Syrian population is estimated to have been 7,845,000 people in 1977.[14] In 1988, when the population as a whole was estimated at 11.5 million, it seems probable that the Kurds, including those living in the large Arab cities, numbered at least a million, or 9–10 per cent of the whole.

In the province of Jazira, also called Hasaka, the Kurds represent an overwhelming majority in the northern half along the Turkish and Iraqi borders. In this area, which is well irrigated by natural rainfall and the Khabour river and its tributaries, there are about 700 Kurdish villages as well as five Kurdish towns: from west to east, Ras al-Ain, Derbasiye, Amouda, Qamishli and Derik. Qamishli is predominantly Kurdish and the largest, with about 15,000 inhabitants, including a few Arab and Armenian families and a Christian Assyro-Chaldean community.[15] Derik, upon which the government bestowed the Arab name of al-Malikiyya's is, situated in the north-easternmost part of the Jazira, a hilly area stretching between Turkish and Iraqi Kurdistan and as far as the Tigris and the outskirts of the town of Cizre (on the "Turkish" bank of the river). The oilfields exploited by Syria are in this area, in the hills of Qarachok and Remilan.

The Kurds of the Jazira are estimated at around 400,000, taking into account young people who have migrated to the towns of inner Syria but kept their links with home. As Philippe Rondot wrote, "The Kurdish peasants have made the Jazira the granary of Syria",[16] with the cultivation of wheat, barley, rice and cotton. Some of these Kurds, possibly about 10 per cent, settled in the Jazira in the 1920s, having fled Turkish Kurdistan after the revolt of Shaikh Said and the ensuing repression. The newcomers were well received by the French mandatory powers who both recognized their need and saw that they brought agricultural skills. All were granted Syrian citizenship by the responsible authorities.

General Pierre Rondot, a French officer serving in Syria at the time of the mandate, wrote of the Jazira in 1936:

> It is a borderland between two worlds: while the Arabs, inveterate nomads whose existence depends on the camel, are not drawn to the rocky mountains, the Kurds covet the steppe border country which is relatively well irrigated and easier to farm than the mountains, and where they could bring their sheep and begin cultivating. As soon as security allows it, that is, as soon as the government – or the armed sedentary populace – is strong enough to impose on the Bedouin a respect for agriculture, the Kurds will descend from the mountain on to the plain.[17]

Since the time of the Mandate such peaceful conditions have been assured in the Jazira, which no doubt helps to explain the progress of agriculture in the area, largely thanks to the labour of the Kurdish peasantry. It is interesting to note in this connection that Captain W.R. Hay, the British administrative officer responsible for the district of Arbil, in Iraqi Kurdistan, in 1918–20, had observed a similar phenomenon on the plains of the south-western parts of his district.[18]

The southern or lower half of the Jazira province is almost desert. Barely cultivated and more sparsely populated than the rest of the province, it is inhabited chiefly by Arab nomads today especially by the Shammar and Jubour tribes. Its centre, Hasaka, is an Arab town with a growing Kurdish community. Arabs are also found to the north of Hasaka, among the Kurds. In this area relations between Kurds and Arabs have traditionally been friendly.

The second, and smallest, Kurdish region in Syria, separated from the other two but bordering on Turkish Kurdistan, is Arab-Pinar or Ain-al-Arab, to the east of the point where the Euphrates enters the country. This is an undulating plain, slightly hilly, and inhabited by about 60,000 Kurds, mostly villagers subsisting on cereal cultivation. The chief town of the area, Ain-al-Arab, is little more than a large village.

The Kurd-Dagh is a mountainous area linked to the rest of Kurdistan. The mountains which continue northwards and north-eastwards into Turkish territory, like the Barakat massif, are also inhabited by Kurds. This is the westernmost edge of the Kurdish homeland which stretches to within 20 kilometres of the Mediterranean if one includes the Kurds of Hatay, close to the district of Kurd-Dagh. To the east of Kurd-Dagh and separated from it by the Afrin valley lies the western and mountainous part of the Syrian district of A'zaz which is also inhabited by Kurds, and a Kurdish minority lives in the northern counties of Idlib and Jerablos.

There is reason to believe that the establishment of the Kurds in these areas, a defensive site commanding the path to Antioch, goes back to the Seleucid era. In the early period, Kurdish tribesmen served as professional mercenaries, mounted archers or catapultiers.

Well irrigated by the river Afrin and numerous mountain springs, and with an abundant rainfall, Kurd-Dagh is one of the most densely populated rural areas in Syria, with flourishing villages in their hundreds, olive groves, vineyards and orchards. Its industrious and wholly Kurdish population of about 300,000 people[19] exports olives, charcoal, wool, kilims (carpets), milk products, meat and market-garden produce to Aleppo. Its main town of Afrin lies on the river of that name, and numbers some 40,000 inhabitants.

Contrary to what might be believed, no less than 90 per cent of the Kurds in Syria use Kurdish alone in everyday life, and their peasantry has practically no knowledge of Arabic. Those who have lost the use of the language are the Kurds who inhabit isolated villages in the interior, city-dwellers in Hama and parts of its surrounding countryside, and the younger generations of the Kurdish quarter in Damascus. In this quarter, the Kurds number perhaps around 50,000, while for the capital as a whole their numbers reach 70,000 or 80,000 (out of a population of 1.5 million), and they are fully integrated into the life of the city, having been there for generations. The newer arrivals coming from the north to the Damascus district or to Aleppo differ in that they maintain their links with their areas of origin and speak mainly Kurdish, though they have become virtually bilingual.

While the French and the Syrian authorities tolerated private cultural activity among the Kurds, no state-funded Kurdish school was established in the country. The French discouraged any political or military action against Turkey on the part of the Kurds in Syria, especially those who had emigrated to the country from Turkish Kurdistan after the failure of Shaikh Said's revolt. Nevertheless, the anti-Turkish Kurdish independence organization, Khoyboun, was constituted in 1927 at a congress held in Bhamdoun, Lebanon. Several of its leaders used the Jazira as a rear base and enlisted supporters from among its Kurdish inhabitants. Kurds, moreover, played a part in the Syrian movement for independence against the French Mandate.

From 1932 to 1935, and then from 1941 to 1943, Prince Celadet A. Bedir-Khan, heir to the ancient Bohtan principality of central Kurdistan, published in Damascus a respected literary and patriotic journal, *Hawar* (Appeal), in Kurmanji Kurdish – the northern and most widely-spoken dialect. For the first time too, he used the Roman script which is so much better suited to an Indo-European language like Kurdish. He also published an illustrated bilingual Franco-Kurdish supplement to *Hawar* called *Ronahî* (Light). His adoption and adaptation of the Roman alphabet has parallels with the language reforms of Atatürk in Turkey, and played a large part in raising the literacy level in Kurdish of large sectors of the Kurds in Syria, a development which spread without any official help to the Kurds in Turkey where it remained underground – and later to the Kurdish diaspora in Europe. Equally importantly, the late Prince Celadet standardized the rules of Kurdish grammar,[20] thereby providing the impetus for a Kurdish cultural movement in Syria, promoted by writers like Cegerxwin, Qedri Can, Osman Sabri and Nureddin Zaza. Cegerxwin, who died in Swedish exile became a popular poet nationwide. Prince Celadet's younger brother, Dr Kamuran Bedir-Khan,[21] a fine poet in his own right, was also instrumental in publishing an illustrated French–Kurdish periodical, *Roja Nû* (New Day), based in Beirut and again using the Roman script.

THE TIME OF NATIONAL OPPRESSION

A few years ago, Mundhir al-Musalli published a lengthy work entitled *Arabs and Kurds: An Arab View on the Kurdish Question*.[22] A former Ba'thist army officer and chief of political police in Syria, the author has today turned dissident, but is nevertheless tolerated by the regime. Despite numerous errors and an often slanted representation of Kurdish history, past and present, his work presents a generally positive, albeit condescending attempt at understanding this question. As a Ba'thist believing in the value of nationalism, the author concedes the reality of Kurdistan as the homeland of the Kurdish people and of the latter as a nation with its own culture and history, living on its own territory, but politically divided between the states of Turkey, Iran and Iraq. Colonel Musalli occasionally showers praises on the Kurds, but when he comes to speak of "the noble" Kurds in Syria, "our brothers and fellow-citizens", whose numbers he estimates at "half a million, possibly more, excluding those of Damascus" (*'Arab wa-Akrad*, p. 453), he classes them with the Kurds of the diaspora and claims that they are "completely cut off from Kurdistan". Yet he does not deny "the great antiquity" (p. 463) of the Kurdish presence in the areas of Syria where they are concentrated though he makes an exception for the Jazira.

Musalli says that "a Kurd" is "a person who believes himself to be a Kurd", in the same way that "an Arab" is someone "who believes himself to be an Arab", even if they are ignorant of their respective national languages or live outside their respective homelands (pp. 119–20). He notes that "all Kurds in Syria are proud to be Kurds" (p. 110); however, he believes that they should not have, "and are careful not to have, a double (i.e., Kurdish and Syrian) allegiance . . . at Syria's expense" (p. 293), although "they are quite naturally and legitimately liable to have a sense of solidarity with the Kurdish national movement in Kurdistan". Rejecting the multinational reality of the country, Musalli asserts that these Kurds are integrated or integrating into the civil life of

"Arab Syria" (p. 465). Deliberately equating the civil rights of a Syrian Kurd with those of a national and cultural minority, he cites an impressive list of Kurds who have been ministers, prime ministers and chiefs of state in modern Syria.[23] Significantly, he fails to address the question of why the Kurds, who are so "proud to be Kurds", should be deprived of their basic right to state-funded, or even privately funded schools, Kurdish programmes on state radio and television, or the right to publish books and newspapers in their own language.

In 1957, a group of Kurdish intellectuals, including Dr Nureddin Zaza, Osman Sabri and Daham Miro, with considerable support from peasants and workers, founded the Kurdish Democratic Party of Syria (KDPS), the objectives of which are limited to securing Kurdish linguistic and cultural rights, economic development, and the democratization of Syrian political life. However, the KDPS was never legally recognized and had to remain an underground movement. In 1960 some twenty of its leaders were arrested, charged with separatism and sentenced to six months' or a year's imprisonment, during which time they were physically maltreated. That same year 250 Kurdish schoolboys died when a cinema in Amouda was set on fire, clearly deliberately, while a film was being shown.

In the provisional constitution of 1961, adopted after the failure of union with Nasser's Egypt, Syria was for the first time proclaimed "the Syrian Arab Republic". On 23 August 1962, the government promulgated a special decree (no. 93), authorizing a population census, solely for the province of Jazira. This was carried out in November of that year. As a result, some 120,000 Kurds in Jazira were arbitrarily categorized as "foreigners, illegally infiltrated into the area".[24] The inhabitants had in fact been told to hand over their identity cards to the administration on the understanding that they would be renewed, but those Kurds who did surrender their cards received nothing in return. And for the first time, a mass media campaign was launched against the Kurds.[25] The slogans were: "Save Arabism in Jazira!"; "Fight the Kurdish threat!". The reasons for this policy are obvious: on the one hand, the beginning of the Kurdish autonomous uprising in Iraqi Kurdistan under General Mustafa Barzani and the KDP, and on the other, the discovery of oilfields in Qarachok and Remilan, in the heart of the north-eastern Kurdish region.[26] Twenty-four years later, Musalli was still able to write:

The instigators of the Kurdish movement encouraged Kurdish emigration in order to make the Kurds the majority population in northern Syria, so to fulfil their invidious and unjustified plans for the future. But in so doing they roused the suspicions of the Syrian authorities and damaged the cause of Kurdish citizens as a whole: indeed, they provoked the fears of the entire Arab nation which then took counter measures against the Kurdish movement itself.[27]

Musalli is cited here because he is one of the best-disposed – or least ill-disposed – non-communist Arab authors with regard to the Kurds. In short, for Musalli a Kurdish nation and a Kurdish country are a reality, but the Kurds of Syria should have no truck with it, except in the sense of abstract solidarity. He numbers the Kurds among the best of Syrian citizens, always providing they agree to be gently arabized.

The Ba'th party took power in Iraq in February 1963 and in Syria a month later. In June of that year Baghdad resumed the war in Kurdistan. Taking part in the campaign were Syrian aircraft and a Syrian armoured corps, a force of 6,000 men[28] under the command of Colonel Fahd al-Sha'er. They moved against the guerrilla fighters of Mustafa Barzani, crossing the border into the Kurdish country of Zakho from the direction of Jazira.[29]

In military terms, the Syrian campaign was a failure and its troops suffered heavy casualties. The expeditionary corps was withdrawn by January 1964 having achieved very little, but at a military parade in Damascus on 10 January, described as "The most glorious day in the life of the Syrian Arab people",[30] Colonel al-Sha'er was hailed as a hero by the chief of state, General Amin al-Hafi. The war in Iraqi Kurdistan, the fruitless Syrian intervention and the measures taken against the Kurds in the Jazira greatly damaged relations between the Kurdish population and their Arab rulers.

The anti-Kurdish attitude of the Syrian Ba'thists of this period is well exemplified by the activities of Lieutenant Mohamed Talab Hilal, a native of Hauran, who had served for six months as head of the secret services in Hasaka when he produced his Study of the Province of Jazira in its National, Social and Political Aspects (*Dirasah 'an Mohafazat al-Jazira min al-Nawahi al-Qawmiyya wa-l-Ijtima'iyya wa-l-Siyasiyya*) in November 1963.

This report was not of course generally available. Rather, it was a top-secret document emanating from either the Ba'thist government itself or from the Syrian regional leadership of the Ba'th party. A copy fell into the hands of the KDPS and was sent to the present writer in 1968. I edited and published the Arabic version in Europe and also published large extracts, with commentary and annotations, in English and French.[31] When Kurds and Arabs put angry questions to the government as a result, the embarrassed response was that "this book is solely its author's concern", and that "it does not represent Ba'th policy". The zealous author was, however, rewarded for his work: he soon became Governor of Hama, then Minister of Supplies from 1964 until General Hafiz al-Asad came to power in 1970.

Hilal's book comprises 160 pages entirely devoted to "the Kurdish threat" and how to deal with it. It is undeniably racist, and indeed, an outright call for genocide.

The following excerpts, reproduced without comment, give references to the pages of the Arabic text:

> I believe that the time is now right for a definitive plan to be launched for this province, to purify it of foreign elements, so as to prevent such elements, aided by imperialism, from spreading evil throughout this cherished land which is so rich in resources and so important to our national revenue, particularly since oil is now being found in the fields of Remilan and Qarachok, which adds a further complexity to the problem.
>
> (from the Preface)

> The bells of Jazira sound the alarm and call on the Arab conscience to save this region, to purify it of all this scum, these dregs of history, until, as befits its geographical situation, it can offer up its revenues and riches, along with those of the other provinces of this Arab territory.
>
> (p. 2)

> Such then is the Kurdish people, a people with neither history nor civilisation, neither language nor ethnic origin, with nothing but the qualities of force, destructive power and violence, qualities which are moreover inherent in all mountain peoples.
>
> (pp. 4–5)

> The Kurdish question, now that the Kurds are organizing themselves, is simply a malignant tumour which has developed and been developed in a part of the body of the Arab nation.

The only remedy which we can properly apply thereto is excision (*al-batr*).

(p. 6)

Yes, imperialism recognizes the outlaws and highwaymen of the Middle East. From the moment it was asserted their cause fell in with the aims of the imperialist states. This period in the history of imperialism and of the Kurds is characterized by the efforts of the imperialist states, each acting in its own self-interest, to win the favour of these brigands.

(p. 12)

Since then imperialism has been trying to confront the Arabs with a *fait accompli*, as they did on the subject of Israel. The Arabs say: there was in the past no Kurdish nation but a Muslim religion. That religion has been driven out and Islam has been transformed into a Kurdish communist creed.

(p. 14)

Moreover the Kurdish movement is in every sense of the term a Russian, i.e. communist, movement, particularly since the creation of the Kurdish Democratic Party, born in the lap of the Soviet Union and delivered into the world by Mustafa Barzani, who had spent some time in that country. This party, like Khoyboun before it, crystallizes the activities of all the Kurds, with the difference that the Kurdish movement today has a greater faith in its destiny and wages a more sustained battle.

(p. 18)

Such is the broad outline of the history of the Kurdish question, from its beginnings to the present day. This question, sustained by all the elements hostile to Arabism, old and new, abroad and at home, threatens the Arab entity. It is therefore essential to take every appropriate measure to put a definitive end to it ... The prime and most far-reaching threat to Jazira and the north of Iraq is the Kurdish danger. All other dangers are as nothing compared to this, for the Kurdish situation has developed in the same way as the Jewish situation in Palestine ... The Kurds in Jazira are even prepared to try to prevent the Syrian army from intervening in favour of the Arabs in Iraq against the movement led by Barzani.

(p. 24)

In the north of the Kurdish belt live the Kurds of Turkey. The Kurds in these regions are thus blood brothers and many of the tribes are spread over Syria and Turkey, and also, of course, Iraq. They are brothers and cousins, waiting mounted on horseback at the frontiers for the realization of their golden dream of a Kurdish homeland, Kurdistan. They are bound by close ties across the frontiers, which they cross easily, and this has consolidated their sense of unity and cemented their links. It is therefore extremely difficult to keep track of them and you will rarely find a Kurd willing to collaborate. The non-Kurd understands nothing of what they say, for they speak Kurdish among themselves in the presence of others and so reveal nothing. If you ask a Kurdicized Arab – Kurdicized by virtue of contact with them – or an Arabicized Kurd – if one may use the expression – to translate what they say, you arouse their native suspicion. In addition, the highly organized Kurdish Democratic Party has deliberately alienated them, making it impossible to discover their plans and projects, all of which works in their favour. These factors have all contributed to the Kurds' powerful organizational presence. They are also harsh, crude and unyielding, and they pretend loyalty to dissimulate their guile.

The Kurdish tribes of Jazira, despite their quarrels amongst themselves, are all united and inspired by one idea, that of "the Kurdish race". They have this one desire which gives them their strength: the dream of a Kurdish homeland which is today deeply rooted in the mind of every Kurd, largely thanks to the education we have so generously lavished upon them, and which is being turned as a weapon against us. The idea of Arabizing them through education is misguided, for the results are the opposite of what we expected.

(p. 26–8)

The Kurds are utterly different from the Arabs in ethnic terms. No resemblance, no relationship exists between them, whether on the psychological, physiological or anthropological levels.

As for religion, it has become the protective screen for conspiracy and treachery . . . Moreover, the majority of the *ulama* of Islam in Jazira are Kurds, and do not even speak an acceptable form of Arabic.

(p. 38–9)

We must regard the Kurds as a people putting all their efforts and everything they possess into creating their imaginary homeland. They are therefore our enemies, and religious ties notwith- standing, there is no difference between them and Israel, for "Judastan" and "Kurdistan", so to speak, are of the same species.

(p. 40)

In conclusion, Muhamed Talab Hilan proposed (pp. 45–8), a "systematic and radical" twelve-point plan which was to be imple- mented "at once" against the Kurds of Jazira, in co-operation with Turkey and Iraq and if possible Iran, because, he said, "The whole of the Kurdish area is one, cohesive and continuous, regardless of frontiers". These twelve points, some of which overlap each other, were listed as follows:

1 *tahjir*, or the displacement of Kurds from their lands to the interior;
2 *tahjil*, or the denial of education;
3 "extradition", or the handing over of "wanted" Kurds to Turkey;
4 the denial of employment possibilities;
5 a large-scale anti-Kurdish propaganda campaign;
6 the deportation of Kurdish religious *ulama* who would be replaced by "pure Arabs";
7 the implementation of a "divide-and-rule" policy against the Kurds;
8 *iskan*, or the colonization of Kurdish lands by "pure, nationalist Arabs";
9 the militarization of the "northern Arab cordon" and the deportation of Kurds from this cordon (*sharit* or *hizam*) area, replacing them with Arabs;
10 the creation of "collective farms" (*mazari' jama'iyya*) for the new Arab settlers who were to be armed and given military training "exactly as in the Israeli border colonies";
11 the denial of the right to vote or hold office to anyone lacking a knowledge of Arabic;
12 the denial of Syrian citizenship to any non-Arab wishing to live in the area.

Hilal reproduces "documents" by way of evidence of "Kurdish treason", including private correspondence between Kurds and experts from an interview which the present writer gave to a Greek journalist.[32] He also discloses the names of Kurds held under surveillance as suspicious persons. In 1965, the government and the Ba'th Syrian Regional Leadership adopted Hilal's plan, focusing chiefly on the creation of an "Arab cordon" (*hizam 'Arabi*) in the Jazira along the Turkish border, a strip of land 300 kilometres in length, stretching from the Iraqi border in the east to a point beyond Ras al-Ain westward, and 10–15 kilometres wide. The plan involved the mass deportation of the Kurdish rural population of around 140,000 men, women and children, living in 332 villages inside the strip, most of whom had already been declared "foreign infiltrators", and who were to be replaced by Arabs. It should be noted that according to the 1962 "census", it was not rare for some members of the same family to be citizens and others "aliens". The Kurdish city-dwellers within the cordon were to be spared for the time being. The plan was not announced in these terms but was promoted as a way of dealing with an important social question which aimed to limit the ownership of land and to distribute it to peasants, who were to be resettled in new "model villages" or on state-owned farms. It is true that there were in the Jazira several landlords, both Kurdish and Arab – former tribal chiefs each owning a whole village and sometimes more. But the true objectives of the plan were the denationalization and arabization of the Kurds. The great majority of the 140,000 Kurds to be deported were simple peasants. The government's proposal was to resettle them much further to the south, in the steppe region of al-Radd, but they refused to be moved or to live "in a desert without water". Police harassment, including house searches, and arrests, made life difficult and unpleasant for the Kurds, even in the towns. In many coffee-shops records of Kurdish music were smashed, and any publication in Kurdish or on the subject of the Kurds was confiscated.

In July 1965, the present author was condemned to death in his absence by a military court which ordered the sequestration of his property in Syria, without even the formality of a summons to appear before the court. The charge was "activities in international circles against Arab interests".[33] (The Syrian government did not try to have the sentence carried out, which was rather civilized of them by comparison with the Iraqi secret service's attempt at a summary execution without the preliminaries of a trial in Lausanne in October 1976, which I survived with two bullets in the head.)

The implementation of the "Arab Cordon" policy finally began in 1973, curiously enough at the same time as the Arab–Israeli war. Bedouin Arabs were brought from the Euphrates area, around Raqqa, and resettled in Kurdish territory, on the pretext that their own land had been submerged under the artifical lake of the Tabqa dam. But the Kurdish villagers, although dispossessed of their lands, clung stubbornly to their houses and refused to move. The government did not resort to force to evict them. However, it tried to arabize the Kurdish, in some cases old Aramean, toponymy of the area. For instance, the village of Chav-Shin (Green Eye) became 'Ain al-Khadreh; the localities or towns of Tirbe-Spi (White Grave), Tel-Kochek, Amouda, Derbasiye and Chagher-Bazar (the latter an archaeological site) were respectively renamed Qahtaniyya, Ya'rubiyya, 'Adnaniyya, Ghassaniyya and Hattin, while Derik, as was said above, was made al-Malikiyya. But this endeavour failed. Saladin even became an Arab hero in the school textbooks.

Under President Hafiz al-Asad's rule, Syria apparently supplied limited aid to the autonomous parties of Iraqi Kurdistan after Saddam Hussain became president in Iraq in 1979, no doubt because of the political dispute between the two Arab leaders. Aid apparently also went to the PKK (Kurdistan Workers' Party), in this case because of the Syrian–Turkish dispute over the waters of the Euphrates,[34] not to mention Alexandretta. A visit to Damascus became *de rigueur* for the leaders of several Kurdish parties. But while there are frequent attacks on Saddam Hussain's regime in the Syrian mass media in connection with the "events of North Iraq", Kurdistan does not get much mention.

Despite these developments the Syrian government did not modify its position towards its own Kurds. Because of the measures taken against them, the Kurds suffer far more than other Syrians from the effects of the economic crisis the country has known since the early 1980s. Many of their young people have left the Kurdish areas in the north in search of work in Damascus or Aleppo, and some have pressed on to Europe for political as well as economic reasons. In the city of Bonn and its surroundings, for example, there are some 3,000 young Kurds originating from the Kurd-Dagh alone, nearly all of them little more than boys. But this may be a special case.

There is, however, a certain ambivalence about the situation of the Kurds in Syria. President Asad, as is well known, is an Alawite. The Alawite community, a Shi'ite religious minority, lives in the coastal mountains of Latakiya and Tartus, between Lebanon and the ancient Sanjak of Alexandretta, and numbers some 800,000–1,000,000 inhabitants. Long considered "second-class citizens" by the large Sunni majority, especially in the cities of Damascus, Homs, Hama and Aleppo, the Alawites are today "the President's people", occupying the highest ranks of the establishment. They probably represent a majority at officer level in the army and police force, a fact which causes some frustration among the Arab Sunnis.[35] Meanwhile, the Kurds, who are known throughout the Middle East as excellent, loyal and disciplined fighters, had many of their young people recruited into the military. Together with the Alawites, they went not into the ordinary ranks of the Syrian army, which are largely composed of Sunni Arabs, but into the élite divisions, which might be regarded as the regime's praetorian guard, that is, the Special Units (*al-Wahdat al-Khassah*) attached to the Ministry of Defence, and the Defence Brigades (*Saraya al-Difa'a*), which are directly dependent on the presidency and were commanded by the president's younger brother, General Rif'at al-Asad. Within these divisions whole units are sometimes composed of Kurds alone, openly speaking Kurdish, but always under the command of Alawite officers. Kurdish officers in the army, the gendarmerie and the police force were dismissed in the 1960s, as were Kurdish teachers. Kurds may be promoted to the rank of sergeant, sometimes to warrant officer, but no higher, unless they have been arabized for generations.

In 1980, the Alawite, Kurdish and other "minorities" Defence Brigades and Special Units were used to brutally repress the troubles in Aleppo, and again to crush the Sunni Islamic revolt of Hama in February–March 1982, in the course of which a large portion of the city was destroyed with a high loss of civilian lives.[36] As a result the Arab Sunni majority regards the Kurds as the partners of the Alawites in repression, and occasionally graffiti appear threatening the Kurds with direct vengeance. At the same time, the regime has conceded absolutely nothing to the Kurds as a cultural and national minority, though it has used some of their impoverished youth as an instrument of force. It is impossible to believe that Hafiz al-Asad is unaware of the pressure exerted on the Kurds by the police and the Ba'thists,[37] though it must be said that living conditions have improved for skilled workers and craftsmen.

It now seems that during the health troubles which President Asad suffered around the end of 1983, some of his close collaborators including, and perhaps especially, his brother Rif'at, looked ahead to the question of his succession with a view to serving their own interests. In any case, in 1984 the Defence Brigades were disbanded and apparently integrated with the Special Units, while Rif'at al-Asad was persuaded to take a European holiday, though the family ties have not been severed.

THE SITUATION TODAY

In conclusion it may be of value to look at some of the experiences and accounts of the Kurds themselves for the light they throw on the present situation.

Syria

In October and November of 1989 I had occasion to meet with a number of Syrian Kurds living in Europe, with a view to exchanging information and examining the facts. They were "for the most part" young people – students and workers, some with refugee status, and some holding Syrian papers. A number of them had completed their university studies but could not return home for political reasons. However, one had gone back to the Jazira in 1987 and again in the summer of 1989. With the help of a tape-recorder and camera he had carried out a survey in several villages there (his material can be made available for study). A brief account of some of his findings follows.

Not one of the people he spoke to had the slightest doubt that the cinema fire of Amouda in October 1960, mentioned briefly above, was a case of arson. The screening had been specially organized for the schoolboys of the town (the girls had seen the film separately). Tickets cost three Syrian pounds and the money was to go to the Algerian Liberation Movement, the FLN. The audience consisted of 500 schoolboys, all of them Kurds, aged between 7 and 13. When the fire broke out it was discovered that the projectionist and other cinema staff had left the building and the exits had been padlocked. The police prevented people from outside from attempting to rescue the victims because it would have been "dangerous". A great many boys died in the conflagration and many of the survivors were badly burnt. One man, Muhamad Said Agha Dakori (a descendant of the

Dukuri tribe mentioned by Niebuhr), did manage to force an entry and saved fourteen boys from death before himself perishing under burning rubble. One of those he saved has since completed his PhD in the USSR and now lives as a refugee in Sweden. He was one of the Kurds I met at this period.

As to the 120,000 Kurds classified as "aliens" after the 1962 census in Jazira, their numbers are difficult to ascertain, and estimates varied from 80,000 to 100,000 (Mas'ud Barzani put the figure at 300,000). Their numbers would have increased in the normal way because their children inherited the same status. However, many managed to recover their Syrian citizenship either by bribing the local officials or by recourse to law on the evidence of birth or domicile certificates and other documentation (such as evidence of tax returns). The remainder were obliged to carry the special red card identifying them as "aliens" and *maktumin* (not registered). They are not liable for military duty, but nor do they have any legal or, to all intents and purposes, civil rights. They are not admitted to state hospitals and their children are not accepted by the state schools; they cannot hold posts in the civil service, the police force, or in state, or even private companies. They cannot even marry and die as Syrian citizens. They do not benefit from any form of social welfare and are therefore ineligible for the ration cards which entitle holders to food at cheaper prices. In other words they live wretched lives, as porters, bootblacks or low-paid labourers.

Since the late 1960s, natural increase and the rural exodus has swollen the population of the Kurdish towns in the Jazira. In Qamishli it has risen from 40,000 to 150,000 (my Kurdish friends thought 200,000); in Amouda from 15,000 to 40,000; in Derbasiye from 15,000 to 25,000; in Ras al-Ain from 5,000 to 30,000; and in Derik from 10,000 to 40,000.

Most of the so-called foreigners in the Arab Cordon of Jazira are former peasants and still live in their old villages, preferring to eat *nan u pivaz* ("bread and onion" in Kurdish), rather than leave. Since their ancient lands were either confiscated by the state or given to Arab settlers, they eke out their incomes by keeping chickens and a few sheep, while in some cases help comes from children who have moved to the towns. These people are not allowed to own property, to repair a crumbling house or to build a new one. Within the cordon this is also true of the Kurdish villagers who do have citizenship. All that is open to them is seasonal labour for the Arab settlers or on the state farms during harvest time. Their villages have no schools, no health centres and often no electricity. In the local government offices there are notices in Arabic which carry the warning: "Speaking Kurdish is strictly forbidden".

By contrast, the state farms in the vicinity of the old Kurdish villages are all well-equipped with electricity, tractors and other machinery. But according to the Kurdish informants they are nevertheless an agricultural failure because of bureaucracy, lack of skills, indifference or corruption. The "model villages", which have schools, dispensaries, running water, reservoirs and artesian wells, yield no better result, "because the Arabs brought in to them have no agricultural tradition and they leave most of the land they have been given fallow, while the Kurdish villagers nearby yearn to have it back".

The questioner was told that the model villages numbered "around sixty, all near the highway, with an average of fifty families to each", and that "between Qamishli and Derbasiye, a distance of 58 km, there are seven such villages". This would mean that some 15–17,000 Arabs had been resettled among the Kurds. Could one therefore assume that the "Arab Cordon" policy had not been fully implemented? "Yes", he was told, "but it is still going on".

One example given involved three Kurdish villages. The first was Girkind, 10 km to the south of Derbasiye and still called by its Kurdish name by its inhabitants. Of its fifty Kurdish families, forty are classified as "aliens" while the rest have retained Syrian citizenship. In 1973 all these families had been dispossessed of their land, citizenship notwithstanding. In 1986 they organized a demonstration and sent petitions to the government requesting the return of their lands. There were clashes with the resettled Arabs who arrived in their tractors to face people demonstrating on foot, and in the ensuing confrontation a Kurdish youth and a small girl were killed. When the police arrived at the scene they arrested all the inhabitants of Girkind, keeping the women in custody for 48 hours and the men for 24 days. The latter were physically assaulted while in prison and were told by the governor of Hasaka: "The land question is over." Further petitions and then a delegation were sent to Damascus, to no avail. The Kurds tried to plough the land left idle by their Arab neighbours, but were forbidden to continue. The houses some of them had repaired in the village were bulldozed. Misto, who was the questioner on this occasion, concluded: "Now all that is left for the villagers of Girkind is to work as farm labourers, harvesting cotton for the Arabs on land that was once theirs."

In the second village, Tirbe, which is also situated in the locality of Derbasiye, a small number of former landlords are allowed to cultivate a portion of their old possessions by agreement with the authorities. The majority of the families living there are, however, landless and this includes those who hold Syrian citizenship. In the nearby village of Tel-Kember, the third example given, the majority of the sixty families living there are classed as "aliens" and their situation is the same.

Among the fellow-Kurds I met in Europe was 30-year-old Fawzi, a member of a family of *aghas* (landlords, chiefs) living in a village in the Jazira. He said, "The land reform left my family with only 1,800 *donams* of land in an unirrigated area dependent on rainfall. We managed to live on this until 1986. Then life became hard and the yield insufficient. We are obliged to sell our wheat to the Mira (the government cereal agency) at a price four times lower than that on the free market, but we are not permitted to sink an artesian well and we have to buy our food, including vegetables, at prohibitive prices". (This man has just been refused political asylum and lives in fear of being forced to return to Syria.)

During this period of repression, the Kurdish Democratic Party in Syria, which was once so feared and respected by the secret police as the activities of Muhamed Talab Hilal, discussed above, clearly showed, has disintegrated into seven opposing factions. Two of these are based in Damascus, and while they do not have official recognition, they are said to work hand-in-glove with the government. The other five are based in the north and have been holding secret talks with a view to possible union. In Syria, as in Iraq, the secret police weigh heavily on everyday life. Police informants have been recruited in their thousands from all communities, including the Kurds.

When people were asked if it would be possible for a Western journalist to visit the Jazira or any other region inhabited by a Kurdish majority, the answer was that it would be possible, "but such a visitor would be kept under constant surveillance by the secret police".

Newroz (New Year's Day) is a popular Kurdish festival celebrated on 21 March each year by Kurds everywhere, dressed in their national dress. In 1986, this traditional feast was the occasion of bloodshed. In the Kurdish quarter of Damascus a few thousand Kurds, most of them young, had gathered to celebrate New Year in a peaceful and orderly fashion when police arrived on the scene and told them that the wearing of Kurdish costume was forbidden. The police fired on the crowd and one young Kurd was killed. His body was transported to his family in Qamishli where 40,000 Kurds gathered to march at his funeral. In Afrin, Kurd-Dagh, the celebration of *Newroz* cost the Kurds three dead and eighty arrests. Now the festival of *Newroz* is once again tolerated. President Asad seems to have moderated the zeal of the political police, but people ask – for how long?

From the varying but on the whole confirmatory reports reaching Europe, the Kurds in Syria appear to be doomed, by reason of revenge and chauvinism, to even more brutal repression and perhaps mass deportation, as has happened in Iraq. One cannot know whether their darkest hours are behind them, or whether they are still to come.

The Kurds in Lebanon

In the Islamic early middle ages, there were several Kurdish feudal and military settlements in the Lebanese mountains, like those found among the Alawites, for example in the Akkar, near Tripoli, and in the Shouf, south-east of Beirut.[38] These seigneurial families have long since been fully arabized and integrated into Lebanese society, but in some instances they have retained a sense of their Kurdish origins. This is true of the Jumblat, the leading family of the Lebanese Druze community in the Shouf, whose name is the arabized form of the Kurdish "*Jan-Polad*" meaning "Steel body". Their ancestors, originally from the Hakkari, in central Kurdistan, served in the armies of the Kurdish Ayyubid kings against the crusaders and were rewarded with strongholds and fiefs in the mountains of Kilis to the north-east of Kurd-Dagh, where they settled. In 1607, the Emir Said Jan-Polad in Kilis rebelled against the Ottomans and for a time occupied Aleppo, but was finally defeated. In 1630 he went with his family to Beirut where he was generously received by the Lebanese Emir Fakhr al-Din al-Ma'ani, who granted him the district of Shouf. His son, Rabah Jan-Polad, became chief of the Druze.

The Kurdish community in present-day Lebanon is of quite different origin. It is essentially composed of immigrants, former wine-growers and peasants who left the areas of Mardin and Bohtan in Turkish Kurdistan after the failure of the Kurdish uprisings in the early part of this century and settled in Beirut in the 1920s and

1930s. Some came from the Jazira in Syria and almost all have relatives in Kurdistan.

Apart from one or two articles,[39] the only study on this community known to me is an MA thesis completed in 1983 by A. Ahmed, a Kurd from Beirut, entitled "The Kurds in Lebanon: Social and Political Organization".[40] Mr Ahmed and his wife Adla have for the last few years lived in Uppsala with their four children and Mrs Ahmed's mother. The Ahmeds speak only Kurdish at home and the mother-in-law and the two younger children do not know Arabic.

I was a guest of the Ahmeds in Uppsala in October 1989. In the course of our conversation Mr Ahmed estimated the number of Kurds living in Lebanon in 1983 to be about 90,000. Almost all were domiciled in Beirut (in the western, Muslim half of the city) while a few lived in Tripoli and in the Beka'a valley. All are Sunni Muslims and all speak Kurdish, including the younger generation, although most also know Arabic. This could only be a rough estimate. Because of inter-religious conflicts there has not been a census in Lebanon since 1932: the Christian Maronites are concerned by the growth of the Muslim population, while among the Muslims, the Sunnis have similar fears about the increase in numbers of the Shi'is. The Ahmeds gave this distrust as the reason why 70 per cent of Kurds in Lebanon do not have Lebanese citizenship while among the Christian Armenian and Syriac communities, which are also made up of early immigrants to the Lebanon, the percentage is only 20 per cent.

Kurds without citizenship must carry identity cards which state "domicile under review", and which have to be renewed annually. On renewal these cards are sometimes stamped with a further condition of stay, and the status of the parents is passed on to their children.

This situation has far-reaching social and legal consequences for the non-Lebanese Kurds who are the country's only Muslim national minority. Deprived of legal and civil rights, most of them occupy the lowest end of the social and economic scale, working as porters, small shopkeepers or unskilled labourers, even when they have the necessary qualifications to do otherwise. They are forbidden to join a union, with the exception of the union of the fruit and vegetable market-traders of Beirut, most of whom are Kurds.

On the other hand, in Lebanon there is no nationalist anti-Kurdish feeling as there is in Syria, Turkey and Iraq. Before the

Lebanese civil war began, the Kurds of Beirut openly established a Kurdish Democratic Party and a Kurdish charitable organization, and a Kurdish folklore company appeared on state television. During the civil war they shared the hardships of the Lebanese population and a few of them left for Europe.

The Ahmeds' case provides a concrete example of the present situation of Kurds in Lebanon. Although born in the country, Adla Khanum Ahmed did not have Lebanese nationality, nor did her parents, who were both Kurds. When she married, her husband's citizenship rights did not extend to her automatically. For a non-Lebanese Kurdish woman marrying a Lebanese Kurd the question of citizenship will depend on the resources available to her. Bribes may be offered, for example, and it helps to have influential connections, especially in the legal professions. The first child of such a couple will have Lebanese citizenship like its father, and possibly also the second, but it is seldom granted to a third child, for this would be seen as swelling the number of the country's Sunni Muslims.

Mrs Ahmed's father was a respected figure in Beirut's fruit and vegetable trade, who "worked hard in the market for 42 years without ever taking a holiday". He was a member of the union and during all these years regularly paid his dues through the union. On his death, "my mother was unable to draw her widow's pension". Her only resource was to try to get redress through the law, but in 1972, "the Beirut court refused to grant her the money due to her because my father was not Lebanese".[41]

Another revealing case is that of Dr B.N., a Kurd born in Beirut who qualified as a doctor of medicine from a Lebanese university. He cannot, however, practise medicine in Lebanon because he cannot join the medical association with the status of "foreign immigrant" which passed to him from his father, and with his "domicile under review". The situation is the same for graduates in law, chemistry and engineering, and I am told there are several such cases in Beirut of graduates prevented from practising their professions.

Unlike the more numerous and wealthier Armenian community, which remained neutral in the civil war, the Kurds of Beirut took part in the fighting as a community, though not always a united one, and they suffered along with the other Lebanese. For them, as for many other communities, fighting was in the end a means of earning one's daily bread. Politically the Kurds leaned towards the Socialist Progressive Party of Walid Jumblat, partly because of his distant Kurdish origins, but for ideological reasons too. The Sunni Murabitun militia of Beirut often called on the Kurds for help and it was willingly given. But when it came to sharing out relief supplies from Europe and the United Nations, the Kurds lost out. The Ahmeds explained: "Supplies were usually divided into four parts and handed over to the Maronites, the Druze, the Shi'is and the Sunnis." As Christians, the Armenians received a share from the Maronites and the Kurds, as Sunnis, ought in the normal way to have had a similar share from their co-religionists. But then, "For the Murabitun, the Kurds are just Kurds, while for the Maronites they are Sunni Muslims." Such examples of discrimination against Kurds should not obscure the fact that in the popular mind of the Lebanese the Kurds are fully accepted as one of the country's minority communities. What the Kurdish community in Lebanon needs above all is the formalization of this acceptance, namely, Lebanese citizenship, which would give them equal rights with other Lebanese while allowing them to remain ethnic Kurds who preserve their own culture and language.

The Kurds, as it happens, share the same opponents as the Alawites: the most determined partisans of the plan for the "Arab Cordon" were the Deirites, the Hauranites and the Druzes. On the regional level Alawites and Kurds have, for different reasons, also had common enemies: Saddam Hussain and the right-wing Turkish government. In objective terms, an Alawite–Kurdish "alliance" was thus made almost inevitable. The Kurds and the Alawites are both mountain people. In the Alawite mountains there are still a few Kurdish villages dating from pre-Ayyubid times and the two communities have intermarried. Moreover, before their accession to power the Alawites were socially repressed and therefore have a fellow-feeling for the Kurds.

The new factor in all this, far more than the creation of the autonomist parties of Iraqi Kurdistan, was the realization of this bond in what has the appearance of a strategic alliance between Syria and the Kurdish national liberation movement. This factor has its roots in the presence in Syria from the beginning of the 1980s of Kurdish partisan units of the PKK – Partiya Karkerên Kurdistan (Kurdistan Workers' Party) – which constitutes the hard core of the ERNK or National Liberation Front of Kurdistan. The ERNK was proclaimed in August 1984 when it engaged in a guerrilla war against the Turkish government in north-western

Kurdistan, but its liberation programme is a nationist programme to embrace the Kurdish nation as a whole. The architect of this transformation is Abdullah Öcalan, secretary-general of the PKK and head of the ERNK.

POSTSCRIPT

There have been new developments in the situation of the Kurds in Syria since May 1990 which were more or less foreseeable in the light of the foregoing discussion. They do, however, constitute what seems to be a turning point, in a positive sense, for the Kurds concerned, and perhaps even more so for the Kurdish movement as a whole. These developments can only be understood by taking account of first, the general political situation in the Near East, and second, within Syria itself, the regional, ethnic and to some extent religious identity of the various communities struggling for power.[42]

As has already been said, President Asad's main power base is the Alawite sect (numbering something over 1 million in a total population of 12 million) in addition to the army and a significant section of the working classes. The political opponents, not to say sworn enemies, of Alawite power in the largely Sunni population are, in particular, the Deirites (i.e. inhabitants of Deir-ez-Zor and Abu Kamal, on the Euphrates), whose bourgeoisie is receptive to Iraqi propaganda because of social and commercial relations with Iraq. Also among the anti-Alawites are the Druze of Djebel-Druze in the south, and the neighbouring Hauranites (to whom Talab Hilal belonged). According to the information being received, one may add to their numbers several Syriac chiefs in the Jazira who cooperated closely with the previous regime but have since lost their political power and abandoned Syria.

To begin with, the PKK was allocated a small area among the Palestinians in the Beka'a valley of Lebanon, under Syrian military administration. Some PKK Kurds fought alongside the Palestinians. After the Israeli invasion of Lebanon in 1982 and with the withdrawal of the Palestinian forces, the Beka'a camps became virtually the domain of the PKK and later, of the ERNK, whose units were increasing in number. In 1988, the Turkish MIT (military intelligence) secretly landed a military force in Lebanon in order to attack a meeting of the PKK, but it was annihilated by an ERNK unit with the participation of the Kurdish

Lebanese militia. That same year the PKK supplied the Syrian authorities with information exposing several members of their intelligence as Syrian/Turkish double agents, a service which was much appreciated in Damascus.

While this particular episode was a covert action, what may justifiably be called a strategic alliance between the Syrian presidency and the ERNK is now a public issue commented upon almost daily in the Turkish press. The link is of mutual interest to the parties concerned: the ERNK has a rear base in Syria for its military activities against the Turkish government; the presidency has in the Kurds of Syria a shield against its internal and external enemies. As was said above, President Asad's personal guard is composed of Kurdish elements. In a gesture of solidarity President Asad's brother, Jamil al-Asad, went to Germany to attend the trial of some twenty Kurdish PKK sympathizers unjustly accused of illegal activities in an action brought under diplomatic pressure from Ankara.

In another instance of cooperation, the PKK was allowed to engage in "unofficial" but quite open political activity in those Kurdish areas where it has now become firmly rooted, especially in Kurd-Dagh and Aleppo. The tight internal discipline of the ERNK coupled with its close links with the Kurdish peasants and workers and its clear political objective, is bringing increasing numbers of supporters into its ranks from among the Kurds of Syria and Lebanon, often at the expense of the various splinter groups of the KDPS and other parties. The latter are, superficially at least, less revolutionary by comparison, especially in their declared objective of achieving autonomy and cultural rights within the framework of the existing states.

This new atmosphere of cooperation also works to the benefit of the various political groups that emerged from the old KDPS. In Syria's last legislative elections in May 1990, six Kurds in Kurd-Dagh openly representing themselves as supporters of the PKK/ERNK were elected to parliament, while in the Jazira a further three Kurds, known to be secretaries of various groups connected to the KDPS, were also elected, so making the quota of representatives for the district entirely Kurdish.[43] In the new Syrian parliament of 450 members, 38 are Kurds of whom 21 are openly militant.

However, it remains true that no legal concessions have been made so far in the direction of allowing Kurds to have their own

schools, newspapers and publications and officially authorized
Kurdish associations. President Asad clearly has to strike a balance
between the different political tendencies that make up Syrian
society and it is evident that there are many elements within
the Ba'th apparatus still opposed to any recognition of Kurdish
nationality as a component of Syrian society.

Nevertheless many Kurds are hopeful that some concessions
will eventually be made; for instance, that a television programme
in Kurdish, and perhaps a Kurdish-language journal will be
allowed. There is also the unresolved question of the so-called
"non-registered" Kurds in the Jazira, nearly one thousand people
in all, who were unjustly deprived of their Syrian citizenship and
their lands. If they are to be reintegrated as citizens in the present
legal situation they will have the status of "Syrian Arab citizens"
since no non-Arab is recognized as a citizen by the Republic.

This raises the question of whether such a solution would be
accepted by the Kurds and whether they would be allowed to
recover their confiscated lands. A further question then is whether
Arab public opinion in Syria and abroad would accept a recognition
by Syria of its Kurds as a distinct and non-Arab cultural and ethnic
group – in other words, a nationality? If one disregards for the
moment the policy of genocide against the Kurds pursued by
Saddam Hussain, the fact is that the Iraqi constitution states
that Iraqi society is composed of two peoples – the Arabs and
the Kurds.

Rural migration to greater Damascus is now said to account
for more than two and a half million inhabitants. Besides the
historical Kurdish quarter which, though the population is now
mixed, nevertheless remains mainly Kurdish, several of the city's
new suburbs are also inhabited by Kurds. In Aleppo where the
Kurdish population must have risen to possibly 200–250,000, we
are told that there are "ten Kurdish quarters" of the city of which
six are entirely Kurdish.

The 1991 Gulf War following on Saddam Hussain's occupation of
Kuwait on 2 August 1990 ought to have the effect of consolidating
the alliance between Syria and the Kurdish movement. Looking
to the future, the Kurds in northern Syria are well aware that
their question is closely linked to that of Turkish Kurdistan where
more than 13 million Kurds are living. In the event of the creation
of a Kurdish state in Kurdistan, Syria would have little to lose
and much to win.

Chapter 9

The development of nationalism in Iranian Kurdistan

Fereshteh Koohi-Kamali

Soon after the revolution, Iranian Kurdistan became the centre of opposition to the Islamic government. In an attempt to find out why the Kurds are amongst the most militant and persistent in their demands for ethnic and political recognition, this chapter discusses the historical, social and economic background of Kurdish society, and seeks to show that the political outlook of the Kurds was shaped to a large extent by changes in their lifestyle and social organization which, in many cases, were forced upon them by government policies

The zenith of the Kurdish national movement in Iran was reached with the establishment of the Kurdish republic in Mahabad in 1946. The republic is a major symbol of Kurdish nationalism. The Kurdish movement was not fully conscious of its nationalist aspirations, however, until the Iranian revolution of 1978–9. This chapter goes on to discuss the period after the Iranian revolution, and the relations between the Kurdish leadership and the Islamic regime. Despite their early hopes, the Kurds have not achieved autonomy since the "revolutionary" government came to power in Tehran. Nevertheless, the Kurdish nationalists are destined to remain a significant political and military force in Iranian Kurdistan.

DETRIBALIZATION AND THE RISE OF NATIONALISM: THE KURDS UP TO 1979

Until the mid-nineteenth century, a large part of the Kurdish region was divided into principalities with a mixed population of tribal Kurds and non-tribal townspeople. These principalities, which had enjoyed considerable autonomy, were abolished under the centralization policy of the Qajar shahs, and the last of the princes was deposed in 1865. As a result, Kurdish princes – or chieftains, as they later became – lost some of their freedom of manoeuvre. None the less, because they continued to retain substantial armed forces they could still exert power and influence, which they used sometimes in support of the ruler, and sometimes to press their own demands. However, the disintegration of the large tribal confederations brought the focus of tribal power down to the level of the smaller tribal chiefs who were in constant conflict with each other. A weak central government meant that local rulers were obliged to choose sides in these conflicts to maintain their positions, and this situation was exploited by tribal leaders to increase their influence.

Until 1920, the Kurdish economy in the mountains was almost entirely based on grazing herds and illegal trading across the borders between Persia and the Ottoman Empire. In these areas, land was traditionally controlled by the tribe as a whole, and the *agha* (tribal leader) was given responsibility for the distribution of pastoral rights. In the plains, on the other hand, economic activity has always been a combination of pastoralism and cultivation of wheat, barley, tobacco and rice. The introduction of land registration under Reza Shah (1926–41), led to a situation where land titles were held by individuals, notably the *aghas*. This had the effect of strenghening the power of the *aghas*, in their new role as landholders. Gradually, many tribesmen became tenants on the *agha*'s land, and then labourers, either on other people's land or in the towns. This process increased the stratification within the tribe. Moreover, the new position of the large landholders led them to settle in towns, which further weakened their tribal affiliations, and made them seek support from the central government.

The reign of Reza Shah Pahlavi caused great difficulties for tribes throughout Iran. In order to assert his authority over the country, he felt it necessary to weaken the power of the tribe both as a political–military and as an economic institution. The key to the political–military function was traditional leadership, and the key to its economic role was migration.

Traditionally, chiefs functioned as protectors and spokesmen of their tribes. Their power largely derived from the support of their followers, and it was in their interest to look after these, lest they should transfer their allegiance to a rival leader. However, as the tribes became sedentary and tribal chiefs turned into medium and large landowners, this relationship became one-sided. A sedentary tribesman, who was tied to land held by one chief, no longer had the option of seeking protection from a rival. On the other hand, the tribe's sense of obligation to support the chief also diminished. Under these novel circumstances, the landlords needed the support of the government rather than that of their peasants (who were share-croppers or tenants), since it was with the assistance of government institutions – notably the gendarmerie – that the payment of dues and rents could be enforced. The government favoured such an arrangement, because it gave the authorities some control over the landlords (Pelletiere 1984). For the peasants, however, this cooperation between landlord and government made life more difficult.

Migration – the other key to tribal power – had always been the way the tribe adapted itself to its natural environment; it had provided economic self-sufficiency and mobility, and also ensured political protection for the tribe. The policies followed in Iranian Kurdistan included confiscation of tribal land, forced resettlement of entire communities away from their traditional territories, imprisonment or internal exile of tribal leaders, and prevention of migration by closing borders and prohibiting tribal flocks from passing through certain regions (Lambton 1953, p. 285).

As a result of these developments, some of which were already in train in the late nineteenth and early twentieth century, more and more Kurdish tribes became sedentary without entirely losing the features of Kurdish tribal life. This is demonstrated, for example, by the sharp increase in the number of villages in the tribal regions (Firuzan 1983). The tribal relationships were weakened by the changes, but did not disappear. The great tribal confederations, where the paramount chief did not necessarily share kinship with his followers, disintegrated into small tribes, where the chiefs were relatives of the tribespeople. The traditional power of the *agha* came to be replaced by the power of the landlord. Despite attempts to change the pastoral economy of the Kurdish tribes, herding remained the main economic activity. The Kurdish tribes adapted themselves to a semi-migratory, semi-sedentary life. This meant that they travelled short distances to search for water and pasture, but went no farther than the borders of the province or the neighbouring village.

In addition to the social stratification arising from the new pattern of individual ownership of land, nomadic societies based on a herding economy show some internal dynamics which, at a certain stage, can push it towards fragmentation. "It is a characteristic feature of wealth in herds that its net productivity rate for the owner declines as the size of the herd increases" (Barth 1961, p. 103). As the livestock of the rich herder grows, it becomes increasingly difficult for him to safeguard it and he is often inclined to transfer part of his capital into another form of wealth. In such cases, investment in land is a much-favoured alternative. Furthermore, becoming a herdowner–landowner offers the opportunity of becoming part of the sedentary élites who have close links with power centres in the government. Nor does the process stop there, for the initial, temporary experience of sedentary life often leads such people to prefer a permanently settled existence.

Poor herders, on the other hand, were often forced to abandon pastoralism by the insufficiency of their herds. The policy of transforming nomadic tribes into settled communities left many of the modest herdowners in Kurdistan (who only had goats), without flocks of any market value. Furthermore, in order to survive, the poorer sections of the community were often forced further and further into debt – a process which, once begun, is very difficult to stop. This section of the Kurdish community, therefore, rapidly became marginalized and its members tended to become agricultural or urban labourers.

Thus, two groups at opposite extremes of society were the first to become settled – the top level becoming landowners and the bottom level landless peasants working for others. This economic transformation had an important impact on the social and political outlook of the community. It disturbed the strong sense of belonging and loyalty which had existed until then. Earlier tribal society had been characterized by personal relationships of kinship and obligation. After the transformations described here, these societies lost their cohesiveness. The function of the chiefs changed radically. While nomadic, tribal society generally has a limited outlook, and limited political demands, the disintegration of self-sufficient tribal units led to a feeling of dislocation, but also to an awareness of belonging to a larger, wider community. This larger community, however, was predominantly defined by an urban, detribalized intelligentsia, and appealed chiefly to a detribalized urban community. It is arguable, therefore, that nationalism, as a political movement and an expression of cultural identity, could not have emerged from a functioning nomadic–tribal society. Its carriers, moreover, could only have been precisely those individuals at the extreme ends of society who had been exposed to new ways of life.

It would be untrue to say that any nomadic community which becomes sedentary necessarily pursues ideals of national identity. In the case of the Kurds of Iran, however, Kurdish nationalism did develop largely as a result of the government's repressive policies. The emergence, at this time, of a Kurdish intelligentsia which was exposed to nationalist ideas also played a key role.

The two major Kurdish movements in Iran in the twentieth century, the uprising of Simko in 1918–22, and the Kurdish republic of 1946, invite comparison. Both movements took place approximately in the same geographical district, namely the Mahabad region. The first movement was an attempt by a powerful tribal chief to establish his personal authority *vis-à-vis* the central government throughout the region. Although elements of nationalism were present in this movement, these were hardly articulate enough to justify a claim that recognition of Kurdish identity was a major issue in Simko's movement. In the movement of 1946, on the other hand, the question of nationalism was uppermost in the minds of the Kurdish leaders, many of whom were urban intellectuals.

As the First World War progressed, the government of Iran was ineffective and had very little control over events in the country. Kurdish tribal chiefs gained power and even established large confederations. This increase in tribal influence encouraged banditry, a feature of tribal life. The non-tribal, non-Kurdish inhabitants of the region suffered most from the tribal raids. Under the influence of the wave of nationalism among the different ethnic communities of the disintegrating Ottoman Empire, many Kurdish chiefs posed as Kurdish nationalist leaders. A number of these had some genuine nationalist aspirations, but these were generally combined with the traditional phenomenon of rebellion against the central government.

The most outstanding of these Kurdish chiefs was Isma'il Agha Simko, who established an autonomous Kurdish government in the area west and south of Lake Urumiyeh from the summer of 1918 until 1922. Simko became the head of Shakak, the second biggest tribal confederation in the country. He managed to organize a strong army of his own which was far superior to government forces and defeated them on several ocasions. The government had no means of controlling Simko, and he continued to expand his territory around Lake Urumiyeh, and to raid villages in order to feed his army. In 1922, the area from the west of Lake Urumiyeh to the south, as far as Baneh and Sardasht, was under Simko's control. His position was so strong that he appointed governors from among his men for the regions under his control. He published a journal called *Independent Kurdistan*. Meanwhile, in 1921 Reza Khan began to organize a modern army which finally defeated Simko in August 1922. Simko was forced to escape to Turkey and later to Iraq. In 1924 Reza Khan pardoned him and he returned to Iran, only to flee the country again in 1926, after a failed attempt to re-establish his independence in Kurdistan. Upon his next return to Iran – after a second pardon, and lured by a false offer by the government of the governorship of Ushnaviyeh – he was killed in an ambush by Reza Shah's agents.

Simko's uprising was typical: a tribal chief with the privilege of official recognition, who used it to gain personal power at a time when the government was vulnerable. He had a combination of personal and national grievances, and his aim was to establish an independent state: nationalist in so far as such a state would nominally be a Kurdish state. However, Simko's uprising was based on tribal support and power, and had to rely heavily on conventional tribal motives. Fighting for the sake of "Kurdish identity" was not strong enough as a motive. The main reason for Simko's success is to be sought in his military achievements: the more government troops he defeated, the more his support grew both among tribal and non-tribal Kurds. The concept of Kurdish independence, or unity, played only a very limited role, as is shown by the following ancedote. In October 1921, with the support of a large number of major tribes, Simko attacked Suj Bulagh (Mahabad), and massacred the gendarmerie garrisoned there. However, government forces and non-Kurds were not the only ones to suffer in the attack: the Kurdish population was also robbed and assaulted. Simko's men do not appear to have felt any sense of unity or solidarity with fellow Kurds (van Bruinessen 1983, p. 388).

Simko's weakness was that he neither had clear ideological goals, nor an organizational base. There was no party or political institution to provide systematic support for the movement. Nevertheless, it should be noted that while his military strength was increasing, his influence also expanded across the borders to the north-western districts of Iraq and north-eastern Turkey. Many Kurdish tribal chiefs from those areas expressed their support. It is also thought that Kurdish nationalists from Turkey joined him in his territory (van Bruinessen 1983, p. 390). However, it was some time before a Kurdish leader emerged who sought to achieve independence or autonomy by enlisting the participation of the Kurdish people with an explicitly formulated nationalist programme.

Reza Shah, in his attempts to establish a strong central government, took a harsh line against the tribal chiefs in Iran. Throughout the 1920s and 1930s, any attempt at rebellion against the central government – which usually ran parallel with the tribal leader's personal aggrandizement – met with a severe response. Tribal leaders were forced to live away from their tribal domains. Their lands were confiscated and military positions were established at strategic points in the Kurdish areas. The Persian language was imposed. As has been mentioned before, efforts were also made to control nomadic movements in those areas. The rule of Reza Shah left the Kurds with bitter memories of killing and looting by the regime.

This state of affairs continued until August 1941, when the Allied armies entered Iran. The British ocupied the south of the country, and the Soviet forces the north. Reza Shah, suspected of having German sympathies, was forced by the British to abdicate. The collapse of the government provided a fresh opportunity for the Kurds. The imprisoned or internally exiled chiefs returned to their tribes and re-established local independence. The Iranian army collapsed in these areas. The Kurds, freed from government control, equipped themselves not only with their own hidden arms but also with weapons acquired after the Persian troops fled the area.

Taking advantage of the internal and international situation, the Kurds were able to establish the Kurdish Republic in Mahabad in 1946. The republic, which was established under the influence of the Soviet Union (though it was by no means under Soviet control), lasted only eleven months. Once the Soviet troops withdrew from the north of Iran, the Iranian army, with the backing of the West, took over the area, destroyed the republic and hanged its leaders.

The unusual internal and international circumstances – the weakness of the Iranian government in controlling the country, the presence of Allied forces in Iran, and the strength of anti-fascist feelings in the international community – created an atmosphere which stimulated democratic demands and activities. The establishment of the independent republic of Azerbaijan, and promises of support from the Soviet Union encouraged the Kurdish leaders, who were mainly affiliated with the Democratic Party of Kurdistan, to announce the formation of a Kurdish Republic. The spontaneous formation of the republic created enormous problems: the backwardness (economic, social, cultural and political) of Kurdistan was probably the main internal cause of its failure. Despite changes, Kurdistan remained largely isolated from the rest of the country by its mountainous geography.

A crucial characteristic of Kurdish society, which both encouraged the development of resistance to central authority leading to the formation of the Kurdish Republic, and also contributed to its downfall, is the fact that it is riven by tribal divisions. It is this, more than any other factor, which explains the lack of real unity in Kurdistan. The conflicts and rivalries between the different tribes – or rather between the leaders of these tribes – have always put obstacles in the path of any national movement. An important feature of tribal relations is the influence of tribal chiefs on the tribes' decisions to support one power or another. Appeals to an outside power by one or more tribes in order to safeguard their own interests have been a common occurrence in Kurdish history. Central governments often bribed tribal chiefs and gained their loyalty by offering them the state's support against their traditional rivals. It was essentially the chief's attitude towards a movement, therefore, which decided whether a tribe would lend its support, remain neutral, or become actively hostile. The Kurdish Republic suffered greatly from this drawback. Even though most of the leadership of the national movement was in the hands of intellectuals, the influence of tribal chiefs remained decisive, since it was the armed men of the tribes who constituted the military backbone of the republic.[1] Another internal weakness of the republic was its lack of well-organized and strong leadership. Politically, the leadership was inexperienced. The KDPI (Kurdish Democratic Party of Iran) at that time was not a mature organization. It lacked discipline, as well as trained cadres to lead the movement forward.

The fate of the republic, however, was not determined solely by such internal factors. External factors were also at work. The defeat of the government of Azerbaijan and the hasty flight of its leaders while leaving behind thousands of ordinary cadres, had a demoralizing effect on the Kurdish leadership. The Soviet Union's change of heart *vis-à-vis* the republic, and its decisison to leave the Kurds to face the Iranian army alone, was decisive in the republic's collapse. The Soviet Union was accused of being a half-hearted friend, not because it failed to intervene militarily when the Kurdish Republic was under threat of occupation by the Shah's army, but because it agreed to drop its support for the fledgling republic in return for an oil concession from the Iranian Prime Minister. The Kurdish Republic in Mahabad was short-lived but highly significant. For the first time in the history of Iranian Kurdistan purely nationalistic consciousness and aspirations emerged as a major force. The main leadership of the republic was not in the hands of traditional tribal chiefs (though the republic could not do without their help) but in the hands of a new elite of urban intellectuals and notables.

The collapse of the republic ushered in a period of terror and political quietism. The Kurdish movement went underground, and any challenge to the Shah's regime was harshly dealt with. Further damage to the movement was done by the deal between Mohammad Reza Shah Pahlavi and Mustafa Barzani, who received aid from the Shah and actively hindered Kurdish activists in Iran. In addition to money, arms and ammunition, Mustafa Barzani received secret information about the location and movements of Iraqi army units. In return for the Shah's generosity, Barzani had to offer his services too. Some forty Iranian Kurds who had escaped to Iraq were arrested by Barzani and handed over to the Iranian government. The Shah, while supporting Barzani's movement against Baghdad, oppressed Kurdish activities in Iran. In March 1975, at the OPEC summit, the Algiers agreement was signed between Iran and Iraq; the Shah suddenly ended his support for Barzani, who by then was heavily dependent on it. Throughout this period, the Kurdish movement in Iran was strongly affected by Barzani's movement in Iraq. However, it kept its distance from Barzani's traditional form of leadership in favour of an urban intellectual leadership with a nationalist–socialist ideology.

In spite of the official hostility of the government, there are strong ties between the Kurds and the Persians. The Kurdish language is related to Farsi, and the Kurds share much of their history with the rest of Iran. This may explain at least partly why Kurdish leaders in Iran do not want a separate Kurdish state.

Also, there have been attempts to assimilate the Kurds into the ruling apparatus. Some Kurdish chiefs held important positions in the government, and received many favours from the authorities: they were allowed, for instance, to keep their land after the land reforms of 1962. During the reign of the Shah some members of parliament and high army officers were Kurds, and there was even a Kurdish Cabinet Minister. Yet, this process did not go far enough. The number of Kurdish high-ranking government officials was small, and the Kurds remained isolated. By way of contrast, it is interesting to note that despite the strong presence of a distinct linguistic identity in Azerbaijan, Azari nationalism has been conspicuously absent in Iran. The reasons for this are complex, and fall beyond the scope of this discussion, but there is no doubt that part of the explanation is to be sought in the fact that the Azaris have always constituted an important part of the élites in the army, politics, business and landownership in Iran. The Kurdish élites in Iran, on the other hand, have largely been barred from high positions and circles of power and wealth. Modern studies of similar phenomena elsewhere suggest that such factors are to be counted among the major causes of the emergence and spread of nationalism.[2]

THE IMPACT OF THE ISLAMIC REVOLUTION AND THE IRAN–IRAQ WAR

The Islamic revolution provided a golden opportunity for Kurdish nationalism, which by 1979 had become far more politically organized than it had been in 1946. Kurdistan became the geographic and political centre of the opposition to the Shah's regime. The following is an outline of the political organizations and personalities fighting for the Kurdish cause on the eve of the revolution.

The Kurdish Democratic Party of Iran (KDPI), which was founded in 1945 and was the leading party during the period of the republic, remains the major force in Iranian Kurdistan. Its leader from 1973 until his assassination on 13 June 1989, was the former university lecturer Abd al-Rahman Ghassemlou. It is interesting to note Ghassemlou's past, for the light it sheds on the political orientation of the non-tribal urban component of Kurdish nationalism. Ghassemlou was born in 1930 into a landowning family. After the collapse of the Kurdish Republic in 1947, he left Iran for France, and soon after went to Prague, where he came into contact with communist ideas. Upon his return to Iran in the 1950s, and after the CIA coup against the nationalist government of Mosaddeq, he was arrested and imprisoned for two years by the Shah. He went back to Prague for the second time in 1957, obtained his PhD in economics and later taught that subject at the university there. He was in contact with the "Prague Spring" movement, but left the city after the Soviet occupation. In 1973, he was elected as leader of the Kurdish Democratic Party. Shortly before the revolution of 1978–9, he returned to Iran to lead the KDPI, which was rapidly being transformed from a relatively small underground organization into a mass party with a sizeable membership and a reasonably clear programme for Kurdish autonomy. In 1981 he joined the Mojahedin-e Khalq in the National Resistance Council in Paris, but he left it in 1984 after a disagreement with Mas'ud Rajavi, the leader of the Mojahedin. The principal slogan of the Kurdish Democratic Party of Iran since its establishment was "Democracy for Iran, Autonomy for Kurdistan". The KDPI received its main support from urban middle-class intellectuals (teachers, students), merchants and government employees, and from the tribal elites.

The other major Kurdish organization is the Revolutionary Organization of the Toilers of Kurdistan (Komala), which became active during the revolution. Its leaders state that it was first founded as an underground organization in 1969. The Komala, which is far more radical than the KDPI, considers itself a Marxist organization. In 1981, it went through a period of self-criticism about its extremist past, and stressed the need for strong links with the proletariat. The Komala, far more than the KDPI, has confronted the landowners and tribal chiefs in Kurdistan, and it has been involved in some peasant uprisings. The Komala is the Kurdish branch of the Communist Party of Iran established in 1983 by the Union of Communist Fighters. It is part of the political category known in Iran as the "third line", and has been strongly opposed to the Tudeh Party and to the Soviet Union. Despite many disagreements with the KDPI, it has supported the idea of democracy for Iran and autonomy for Kurdistan.

Apart from these two main Kurdish organizations, most other opposition forces also had a foothold in Kurdistan; this may be due to the fact that the region is relatively inaccessible to government forces. Many political groups and organizations had a

Kurdish branch. Among the more active ones were the Feda'iyan-e Khalq and the Mojahedin-e Khalq. In the early months of 1979, the more radical groups, the Komala and the Feda'is, initiated peasant organizations. Peasants' Councils were established, and some attempts were made to distribute land among peasants around the Sanandaj and Marivan areas.

A few of the royalist generals, such as Palizban and Oveisi, also set up headquarters in Kurdistan with the claim of building a "liberation army" there. This group was not concerned with the Kurdish cause, but merely used Kurdistan as a base for their anti-government activities, because, soon after the revolution, Kurdistan became a centre of political or military activities directed against the Islamic regime. Some young officers joined them but their unity did not last long and – due to corruption among the generals themselves – the initiative collapsed, and the "liberation army" was abandoned before the government began its heavy offensive against Kurdistan.

The Kurdish chiefs reacted in various ways to the revolution. Those who had been favoured under the Shah, actively opposed it; some, taking advantage of the situation and wanting to gain personal influence, participated in attacks on government posts along with the KDPI and the other organizations, but soon withdrew from an alliance with nationalist forces who were demanding Kurdish autonomy. This group also, on occasion, acted against the nationalist movement. Some individuals with strong tribal ties united with the non-traditional leadership to demonstrate their support for the demands for Kurdish autonomy. Furthermore, some of these people confronted the tribal leaders when these attempted to collect the traditional dues from the peasants. A further consolidation of the non-traditional, non-tribal leadership emerged with the organization of the *peshmerges*, the Kurdish fighters, which gradually became a credible military force. This force was organized without reference to tribal affiliations. Expansion of such a force, with increasing loyalty to the KDPI, may in future help to free the leadership of the Kurdish movement from the influence of traditional élites, and of the need to rely on the military strength of the tribal chiefs.

Amongst the individual personalities, one of the most significant for the Kurdish movement in Iran after the revolution was the unconventional Sunni cleric Shaykh Izzeddin Hosseini. Hosseini joined the KDPI and other leftist organizations in their struggle against the Islamic Republic, and enjoyed a great deal of support – not only from political organizations and the tribal leadership but also, perhaps more importantly, from the Kurdish people generally. Some claim that his popularity exceeded that of Ghassemlou. Izzeddin Hosseini opposed Khomeini for interfering in government affairs while his duty as a cleric was only to guide the Muslim community in religious affairs. Soon after the revolution, despite differences of opinion among political personalities and organizations in Kurdistan, the "Council of Kurdish People" was established, with Hosseini at its head and Ghassemlou as its spokesman. For a period, the council acted as the representative of the Kurds in negotiations with the Islamic government.

In January 1979, the Kurds captured military garrisons and gendarmerie outposts, and seized a considerable quantity of weapons. The revolutionary government in Tehran, which came to power in February, gave promises of support to, and respect for, the rights of minorities, which was naturally encouraging for the Kurds. In March 1979 – after thirty years of underground activities – the KDPI presented the party's programme for Kurdish autonomy in Iran at a press conference. The eight points of the plan presented by the KDPI were as follows:

1 The boundaries of Kurdistan would be determined by the Kurdish people and would take into consideration historical, economic, and geographical conditions.
2 On matters of defence, foreign affairs and long-term economic planning, Kurdistan would abide by the decisions of the central government. The Central Bank of Iran would control the currency.
3 There would be a Kurdish parliament, whose members would be popularly elected. This would be the highest legislative power in the province.
4 All government departments in the province would be run locally rather than from the capital.
5 There would be a people's army, but the police and gendarmerie would be abolished and replaced by a national guard.
6 Kurdish would be the official language of the provincial government and would be taught in all schools. Persian would also continue to be an official language.
7 All ethnic minorities in Kurdistan would enjoy equal rights and

would be allowed to use their own languages and observe their own traditions.

8 Freedom of speech and of the press, rights of association, and trade-union activities would be guaranteed. The Kurdish people would have the right to travel freely and choose their own occupation.

(*The Times*, 4 March 1979)

From the start, the Kurdish issue was met with uneasiness by the government. Kurdish leaders repeatedly denied the accusation that the Kurds were seeking independence, and stressed the concept of "democracy for Iran and autonomy for Kurdistan". It was agreed that the central government would keep control over foreign policy, finance, defence, and the army. The argument with the government was over control of domestic policies and regional administration, which the Kurds felt should be left to them. However, the situation did not develop as many who had fought for the revolution had hoped. The political atmosphere was changing rapidly, and the regime curtailed democratic activities every day. It soon became clear that the government had no intention of granting autonomy to any ethnic group, and least of all to the Kurds.

Throughout the spring and summer of 1979 there were frequent clashes between the Kurds and the government forces. In August 1979 the Ayatollah Khomeini declared a holy war against the Kurds, banned all the Kurdish political organizations, cancelled Ghassemlou's membership of the Assembly of Experts and denounced Ghassemlou and Sheikh Izzeddin Hosseini as enemies of the Islamic Republic. The KDPI was called the "party of Satan". In addition to the army, a large number of *pasdars* (revolutionary guards) and armed *hezbollahis* were despatched to the area. Helicopter gunships, Phantom jets, tanks and artillery were used to attack the towns and villages of Kurdistan. The Kurds entered the war with the weapons they had confiscated at the beginning of the revolution. The crushing of the Kurdish rebellion caused bloody scenes in many of the towns and villages of Kurdistan (Sanandaj, Naghadeh, Paveh, Marivan and Saqqiz). The revolutionary trials were held by Khalkhali – the notorious "Chief Justice" – and scores of people were executed at the same time. It is generally believed that most of the trials did not last more than a few minutes, and that the majority of those executed were ordinary Kurds rather than *peshmerges*. Kurdish towns fell into the hands of the government forces, but Kurdish fighters managed to keep control of the countryside. To this day, Kurdish forces still enjoy the same degree of control and mobility.

After bitter fighting, the government in Tehran called for a ceasefire on 2 November 1979, and a group of delegates was sent to Kurdistan for negotiations. The call for talks was welcomed by Kurdish leaders. Shaykh Izzeddin Hosseini represented the programme for Kurdish autonomy. But the Islamic government was not prepared to allow more than a limited cultural autonomy,[3] and it refused in principle to regard the Kurds as anything other than a religious minority. Further, it demanded full disarmament of the Kurdish region as a first condition for any solution. This alone was enough for the Kurds to abandon any hopes of an agreement, since it would have meant giving up the crucial and sole instrument of self-defence. The ceasefire failed and another round of fighting began. The cycle of calls for negotiations and resumption of fighting became a feature of this period, and continued to be so for two years.

In November 1979, the Assembly of Experts approved the Islamic constitution. For the minorities in Iran, the new constitution was disappointing. In the original draft, there had been articles guaranteeing certain rights to the minorities. Article 5 of the draft constitution stated that "All people in the Islamic Republic of Iran, such as Persians, Turks, Kurds, Arabs, Baluchis, Turcomans, and others, will enjoy completely equal rights." Article 21 provided for the use of local languages: "The common language and script of Iran is Persian. All official texts and correspondence must be in this language and script. However, the use of local languages in local schools and press is permitted" (MacDonald 1988). Also, in article 13 of the draft constitution, it was stated concerning the religion of Islam, that: "The official religion of the country is Islam and the Ja'fari school of thought . . . With respect to matters of personal status and religious education, every Muslim acts in accordance with his own school of thought, in whatever area of the country he may be." But in the final, approved, version of the constitution, there was none of this limited concern for minority rights. All mention of the equality of the ethnic peoples was dropped; there was no guarantee of the religious rights of the Sunni and as for the use of local languages, the constitution stated that local languages could be used in the press, the mass media, and schools, but only alongside Persian, and that school textbooks had to be in Persian. The constitution clearly had no intention of accommodating the ethnic aspirations of the minority peoples.

Throughout the negotiations, a major point of disagreement was the difference in interpretation by the two opposing sides of the word "autonomy". At the end of November 1979, Hosseini, the head of the Kurdish Council, presented a plan for autonomy to the government representatives. The government rejected this, and instead offered a plan for Kurdish "self-administration". This suggestion was vehemently rejected by the Kurdish leaders, who argued that the government was treating the Kurdish issue merely as an administrative question, whereas for the Kurds it was a truly national one. They argued that the plan did not even consider cultural, let alone political autonomy. They stated that there was much confusion and many contradictions in different sections of the plan. For instance in section 1, article 4, it was stated that the security of the area would be the responsibility of the self-administered areas, but further on in the same article it was stressed that the heads of police and gendarmerie and their subordinates would be selected by the government and approved by the self-administered area, and that they would be responsible to the Interior Ministry. In other words, the Kurdish leaders argued that the plan for self-administration was incompatible with their programme for autonomy. Furthermore, as far as language was concerned, the plan allowed Kurdish to be taught. In the eyes of the Kurdish leaders, however, this was very different from having Kurdish as the official language of the area. Despite their rejection of the plan, the Kurdish leaders still expressed their willingness for further negotiations. However, while the Kurdish leaders were insisting on autonomy and rejecting the idea of self-administration, they entered another round of fighting with the government. The heavy fighting lasted for several months, and the government accused the Kurds of seeking an independent state.

Another area of disagreement was the question of who would represent the Kurdish people. The government insisted that it would consider the KDPI as the sole legitimate representative of the Kurds, and refused to acknowledge the other parties in the Revolutionary Council of the Kurdish People. Tehran presumably realized that the others (the Komala, etc.), who adhered to Marxist ideologies, would insist on more radical demands.

In May, the power of the radical clerics rapidly increased. The occupation of the US Embassy in Tehran in November 1979 resulted in the resignation of the Prime Minister, Mehdi Bazargan, and the clerics took full control. They announced that there would be no more room for negotiations with the Kurds, and that the only option was a war to wipe out the rebels. The Kurdish fighters fled into the mountains with great losses and continued the struggle. Rebellious Kurdistan became the symbol of opposition to the Islamic regime. Many political organizations supported the Kurdish cause and opposed the regime for its treatment of the Kurds. A notable exception was the pro-Soviet, leftist Tudeh Party, which at the time was collaborating with the regime and did not support the Kurdish movement.

In January 1980, yet another ceasefire was called and Khomeini promised to add an amendment to the constitution, guaranteeing the rights of the Sunnis in the regions where they are in the majority. The amendment never materialized, and the ceasefire was short-lived.

In the winter of 1981 the KDPI joined the National Resistance Council based in Paris. The council, which was to be a united front against the Islamic government, soon appeared to be a predominantly Mojahedin organization. The Komala criticized the KDPI for joining the council and refused to join it on ideological grounds, and also because of the membership of certain individuals such as Bani-Sadr. But the KDPI continued to be a member of the council and, in late 1983, even reached agreement with the council on a plan for autonomy in Kurdistan: while the central government was to retain control over planning, finance, national security, defence, trading and foreign affairs, the Kurds would have a legislative council to draw up regional laws, and they would establish forces to guarantee the security of the territory. However, the concord between the KDPI and the council did not last long. In the summer of 1984 the KDPI showed its interest in negotiation with the Islamic government; the negotiations, however, did not progress and the government once more refused to discuss a separate Kurdish national identity. This move by the KDPI angered the Mojahedin, and resulted in the KDPI withdrawing from the council.

The Iran–Iraq war seemed to hold opportunities for the Kurds in both countries, but, in fact, their situation worsened. It became clear that both the Iranian and the Iraqi governments were using the war as a means of dealing with their internal Kurdish problem. Each country began massive attacks on its own Kurdish population, while at the same time accommodating Kurdish dissidents and deserters from the other side. Both countries were aware of the significance, militarily and politically, of keeping the Kurdish problem alive in each other's territory. After the outbreak of war between Iran and Iraq in September 1980, there were several shifts of alliances. At an early stage, when the Iraqis first attacked Iranian territory, the KDPI, along with many political opposition forces, expressed its willingness to enter the war against the Iraqi aggression in return for a limited autonomy in Kurdistan. The Iranian authorities rejected the offer, and expanded the war zone further north to the Kurdish areas. Their intention was to block the Iraqi forces on the northern borders, and at the same time gradually to get full control of the Kurdish regions. By 1983 all the border areas which had previously been controlled by the *peshmerges* of the KDPI, were in the hands of the Iranian army and the revolutionary guards. In these operations, the Iranians were assisted by the leaders of the KDP of Iraq, Mas'ud and Idris Barzani. It is worth mentioning that, on the northern borders between Iraqi and Iranian Kurdistan, although most tribes in Iran remained independent, some of the influential chiefs supported the Barzanis against the KDPI. The Kurdish political organizations reacted in diverse ways. While Idris and Mas'ud Barzani, at least for the first two years, collaborated with the Islamic regime, Talabani's party, the PUK, supported the KDPI. As the war proceeded, however, Talebani was forced to withdraw to the interior of Iraq. In November 1983 the PUK started negotiations with the Iraqi authorities with Ghassemlou as their representative. Unlike the Iraqi KDP, their Iranian counterparts, despite receiving some limited financial assistance from Iraq, tried to maintain their distance from the Baghdad government.

In any case, towns and villages in Iranian Kurdistan came under heavy artillery attack from both sides; they were attacked by Iraqi artillery on the war front, and by the Iranians on the Kurdish front. Confrontations took place in and around all the major cities of Kurdistan, with Kurdish fighters under great pressure but still firm in their demands for autonomy. The Islamic government also sought to manipulate the different groups in Kurdish society, such as traditional groups and urban intellectuals, and managed to organize the "Islamic *peshmerges*" – as opposed to ordinary, anti-government *peshmerges* – by recruiting Kurds with tribal affiliations (mainly from the region of Kermanshah, where there are Shi'i Kurds), to fight the Kurdish nationalist elements.

While fighting the regime, Kurds also had to deal with internal conflicts. In 1980, a group of pro-Tudeh leaders of the KDPI left the party. Those who followed the Tudeh party's policy of collaboration with the regime failed to gain sufficient support in the party, and were left isolated. The year 1985 witnessed confrontations between the two main Kurdish organizations in Iran, the KDPI and the Komala. This conflict has deepened since, and, continues to undermine the activities of both organizations. A further development of major importance was the split within the KDPI itself. After the eighth congress of the party in April 1988, Ghassemlou was challenged by fifteen leading figures in the KDPI. This new faction, calling itself "KDPI-Revolutionary Leadership", published a ten-point statement which criticized Ghassemlou personally for taking the party to the right by uniting with "Western liberal–democratic elements", distancing himself from the socialist camp, and being ready to enter negotiations with the government in Tehran. Membership of the new faction (KDPI-Revolutionary Leadership) includes the following: 1 member of the KDPI politburo, 8 members of the Central Committee, 4 deputy members, and 2 councillors. The group does not appear to be a unified force, and each member had different motives for leaving the party. The consequences of this split have yet to be seen.

FUTURE OUTLOOK

The Iranian revolution, which was welcomed as the harbinger of democracy in Iran by those opposed to the Shah, failed to live up to the expectations of the people. Despite promises, the Kurds were treated very harshly. Later, the war between Iran and Iraq was thought to provide a golden opportunity for the Kurds of both countries. However, what followed was a period of repression. A report by the Minority Rights Group on the Kurds states that: "by early 1984 a Kurdish-controlled region of Iran had been virtually eliminated. At least 27,500 Kurds were reckoned to have died by this stage, of whom only 2,500 were fighters" (McDowall 1989).

If there was any misunderstanding at the beginning of the revolution in Iran about the intentions of the regime, this should no longer be the case. As long as the Islamic regime retains its present political attitudes and structure, the possibility of any accommodation for the Kurds and their national demands is remote. The idea of an autonomous Kurdistan – or any autonomous minority in Iran – does not accord with the idea of the universality and expansion of Islam as outlined by Khomeini and his followers. Khomeini's attitude to the nationalist aspirations of minorities was that:

> There is no difference between Muslims who speak different languages . . . It is very probable that such problems have been created by those who do not wish the Muslim countries to be united . . . They create the issues of nationalism, of pan-Iranianism, pan-Turkism, and such isms, which are contrary to Islamic doctrines.

As he has repeatedly stated, there is no room in Islam and Islamic countries for such divisive ideas, which aim at weakening the unity of the Islamic community.

History shows that an opposition can grab power and gain success in a political challenge only when the established power is weak and vulnerable. The success of the Iranian revolution is an illustration of this. The Islamic regime in Tehran is no more vulnerable now than when it first seized power. If there are no changes in the political leadership of Iran – and, in particular, if the existing divisions do not deepen and lead to paralysis and self-doubt as to the ability of its leaders to lead – the Kurds will not easily gain further leverage. The consolidation of the Islamic government has increased frustration among its opposition, and the recent split in the KDPI is partly a result of this.

In addition to the theoretical incompatibility of ideologies between the Islamic republic and the nationalist movement, there are other, even stronger divisions. The root of the conflict between the Islamic government and Kurdish nationalism is not the supposed "universalism" of Islam, but rather the Islamic republic's continued attachment – which it shares with the government of the late Shah – to the boundaries of the nation-state called "Iran", and its fear of threats to the sovereignty and integrity of that state. It is this conflict which led to the assassination of Ghassemlou in Vienna. On the evening of 13 July 1989, he and two other Kurds were shot and killed. Ghassemlou was in the process of negotiating with Iranian government representatives.

The meeting was the second session of the negotiations. The first took place on 12 July. As announced by the party, the meeting of 12–13 July was the third of a new round of talks with the Tehran regime. The two previous rounds took place in December 1988 and January 1989, with the knowledge of the party's politburo (*Le Monde*, 21 July 1989). But the third one, which ended with the assassination of Ghassemlou and his colleagues, was kept secret even from the party. At this stage it cannot be definitely shown who was behind the assassination, but the Austrian police have announced that, based on their evidence, they are convinced that the mission was carried out by agents from Tehran during the meeting between the Iranian delegates and Kurdish leaders including Ghassemlou.

It was reported that one of the three government delegates (who was accidentally injured), was a high-ranking revolutionary guard said to be very close to the then Speaker of Parliament, Rafsanjani, who later became president. The Iranian Embassy refused the request of the Austrian police to interview those allegedly involved in the assassination, and the case was closed when the Austrian police announced that the issue was a matter of diplomatic concern between the countries.

Ghassemlou never concealed his readiness for negotiation over Kurdish autonomy with the Iranian authorities, a willingness which created many enemies. Whoever the assassin, and whatever the motive for his killing, one thing is clear: Ghassemlou's assassination is a sharp blow to the prospects of Kurdish nationalist aspirations, and to democracy in Iran. He was by far the most experienced and pragmatic politician in Iranian Kurdistan. In spite of his democratic beliefs, his pragmatic instincts resulted in attempts to explore non-military solutions to the Kurdish problem in Iran. On the national level, Ghassemlou, with his moderate, democratic political orientation, and as the leader of the KDPI, which holds the unique position of being a serious military and political opposition organization inside Iran, would have been an important partner in any future opposition alliance which included the forces inside and outside Iran. The future of the Kurdish movement in Iran will be very much determined by the future leadership of the KDPI. So far, the new leadership has emphasized that the party does not believe in a military solution for Iranian Kurdistan, and will continue to explore political avenues.[4] Nevertheless, the party has also announced that in the present climate it is not possible to sit at the negotiating table with the Iranians. In any case, it seems inevitable that in order to be taken seriously at all, the Kurds are bound to continue some military operations, which in practice means traditional guerrilla warfare.

Nevertheless, the KDPI of 1989 is a very different organization from that of 1947, when the Kurdish republic collapsed. It seems very probable therefore that the party will survive, no matter how hard it has been hit by the assassination of Ghassemlou. The KDPI now has the experience of the revolution of 1978–9 behind it. Militarily and politically it is better organized. It has thousands of members and supporters who have been involved in the national identity struggle for some time. Surviving the years of the revolution and its aftermath has transformed the KDPI from an inexperienced underground party, highly dependent on the Kurds in Iraq, into a relatively independent political force which could not only determine the destiny of Iranian Kurdistan, but may also have a significant influence on the future of the country as a whole.

Chapter 10

The Kurds in the Soviet Union

Ismet Chériff Vanly

THE KURDS UNDER IMPERIAL RUSSIA

At the beginning of the nineteenth century, Georgia, eastern Armenia and northern Azerbaijan were conquered by the Russians. These territories, previously under Persian rule, all contained sizeable Kurdish minorities. Whether these Kurds were the descendants of the Transcaucasian Kurds of earlier centuries was, except possibly in the case of the Azerbaijani Kurds, not clear in the light of the complexity of the historical changes that had taken place since the reign of the Shaddadids, let alone those of the earlier periods of the Khoren and the Medians. All that can be stated with certainty is that the original inhabitants of Kurdistan had always overspilled its boundaries into neighbouring territories, including Transcaucasia, for reasons which ranged from economic pressures and internecine conflicts to semi-nomadism. According to the census of 1897, the first to be based on mother tongue, the Russian empire had a total population of 125,640,200 including 100,000 Kurds approximately as shown in Table 10.1.

The figures in Table 10.1 are unreliable (as are later Soviet statistics) and there are strong grounds for believing that the total of 99,900 refers solely to the Kurdish population of Transcaucasia and does not include Turkmenia, which at that period was the only Central Asian territory with a Kurdish minority.

These, according to A. Bennigsen (1960, pp. 513–30) the least known of the USSR's minority peoples, were in fact a part of the initially small settlement in Khorasan of Kurmanji-speaking Kurds who had been moved there from Azerbaijan in the eighteenth century by Shah Abbas to defend Persia's north-east frontier against the Uzbeks. By the end of the nineteenth century the

Table 10.1 The ethnic population of Russia according to the census of 1897

Ethnic Groups	Numbers
Russians, Ukrainians and Byelorussians	89,933,600
Armenians (total for all Russia)	1,173,100
Georgians	824,000
Tajiks	350,400
Turcomans	281,400
Ossetians	171,700
Kurds	99,900
Kabardins (Caucasian-speaking)	98,600
Tats (Iranian-speaking)	95,100
Abkhaz (Caucasian-speaking)	72,100
Circassians (Caucasian-speaking)	46,300
Persians	31,700
Afghans	500
Jews	5,063,200
Others	27,398,600
Total	125,640,200

Source: *Processus ethniques en URSS*. French version translated by Emery, Larionova and Rygalov, Moscow, 1982, p. 35.

Kurds of Turkmenia were probably as numerous and as thriving as those of Transcaucasia.

As far as the origins of the Kurdish population of present-day Soviet Armenia are concerned, few are descended from those included in the 1897 census because most of the latter were massacred during the First World War or under the Tashnak Armenian Republic in 1918–20. They were largely replaced by Yazidi Kurdish emigrants from northern Kurdistan during the Second World War as was confirmed to the author by Armenian Kurds in 1990.

During the second half of the nineteenth century the Armenian nationalist movement laid claim to six vilayets in Eastern Turkey: Erzurum, Van, Bitlis, Diyarbakir, Mamuret Aziz and Sivas. Despite their being represented to public opinion in Europe as "Armenian vilayets", only 17 per cent of their population was in fact Armenian according to contemporary Ottoman statistics (Fany 1933, p. 159). These exaggerated claims caused considerable damage to the relatively good relations that had hitherto existed between the Ottoman government, the Kurds and the Armenians, for while the population of Sivas was predominantly Turkish that of the other five vilayets was 80 per cent Kurdish. The situation was further complicated by the overriding concern amounting almost to obsession on the part of Russia, Britain and France with the freeing of the Christian nations of the Balkans from Ottoman rule, a concern which led them to support the Armenian demands for local autonomy in the six vilayets. The Kurdish majority thus found itself in a difficult position: excluded from the proposed reforms designed to benefit the Armenian minority alone and dismissed as "marauding tribes" by Armenian propagandists and Christian missionaries, they were at the same time Muslims linked to the Turkish caliphate and preferring Turkish to Armenian rule and yet also a people which saw itself as forming a separate nation, and had for that reason frequently revolted against Turkish rule during the nineteenth century. One of the most important of these uprisings took place during the Crimean War in 1853–5, a timing which was deliberate. Its leader was Yezdan Sher, "who occupied Bitlis, Mosul and subsequently the entire region between Van and Baghdad" before being captured after betrayal by "a British consular agent, Nimroud Rassam" (Nikitine 1956, p. 159).

After Turkey's defeat in the Russo–Ottoman war of 1878, Russia obtained the independence of Romania and a Greater Bulgaria under the terms of the Treaty of San Stefano, which also contained an article (no. 16) providing for reforms in the eastern "provinces inhabited by the Armenians" and for a Turkish guarantee of their security "against the Kurds". Largely because Britain was reluctant to see Turkey placed under the virtual tutelage of Russia, the Treaty of San Stefano was superseded by that of Berlin within the same year (1898). Article 61 of the latter reproduced word for word Article 16 of the former with the addition of an undertaking by Turkey to "inform" the Great Powers of the progress of reform in the six eastern vilayets.

The Sultan was far from eager to introduce the reforms thus imposed. When G.J. Goschen, the senior European diplomat accredited to the Porte, in a memorandum of 11 June 1880, asked the Ottoman government on behalf of the Powers to report progress, he received a six-page reply dated 5 July from the Grand Vizier, Abidin Pasha, which concluded, "Je crois enfin superflu que la Sublime Porte donne avis aux Puissances signataires du Traité de Berlin des mesures prises par elle pour l'introduction successive des réformes dans les provinces du Kurdistan and d'Anatolie habitées aussi par des Arméniens" (Fany 1933, pp. 153–9).

Abidin Pasha's closing paragraph is significant in that it gives an undertaking by the Ottoman government to keep the Powers informed of the reforms to be effected "in the provinces of Kurdistan and Anatolia inhabited by Armenians". Not only were there no provinces inhabited by Armenians in Turkey, but Turkey itself was composed of two entities, Kurdistan and Anatolia, as witness the terms used by Abidin Pasha himself. Kurdistan did not become "Eastern Anatolia" until the Kemalist regime assumed power in Turkey, just as it was not until much later that southern Kurdistan became transformed into "Northern Iraq".

While this diplomatic exchange was taking place, the Kurds staged an armed uprising in Turkish Kurdistan and the northern areas of Persian Kurdistan with the aim of gaining independence. The leader of the revolt was Shaykh Ubaydullah of Nehri and Shemdinan, chairman of the Kurdish League whose manifesto opened with the declaration "The Kurds are a separate nation". Shaykh Ubaydullah sent copies of the manifesto to the representatives of the Western Powers and also endeavoured to guarantee the security of the Christian minorities in Kurdistan.[2] But as Olson points out, the Powers, Russia in particular, were as opposed to Kurdish independence as Persia and Turkey:

> At the end of this first stage of Kurdish nationalism, all of the European powers, as emphasized in the Treaty of Berlin, were opposed to Kurdish independence movements . . . Russia did not want to be robbed of the territories, some of which were largely Kurdish, in eastern Turkey that it had obtained by the Treaty of Berlin. Neither did it want a Kurdish state on its Caucasian borders, especially one animated by the religious fervour of the Nakşbandi order. Russia had its fill of such movements with Shah Şamil in the 1840s.
>
> (Olson 1989, p. 7)

Shaykh Ubaydullah's uprising failed. In 1881 he was taken prisoner and exiled to Mecca.

In 1891, Abdulhamid II, Sultan since 1878, raised the Hamidiye Light Cavalry Regiments (Hamidiye Hafif Süvari Alayları) composed entirely of Kurdish troopers under Kurdish officers, who were sons of tribal chieftains, trained in a military academy in Istanbul. Their formation caused tension amongst the Kurds as a whole because recruitment was restricted to Sunni Muslims, Alevis being excluded. In Olson's opinion (Olson 1989, p. 8), Abdulhamid saw the Hamidiye regiments as a means of tying the empire "more firmly to its Muslim roots" providing "a defense against Russia and the Armenians, both increasingly aggressive after 1878, and the Kurds . . . as a balance against the urban notables and the provincial governments" (ibid. p 8).

By 1895, there were 57 Hamidiye regiments each with a minimum strength of 512 men and a maximum of 1,512, a total of approximately 50,000 men constituting a corps under the Sultan's direct command entirely separate from the Ottoman army.

The Hamidiye regiments were responsible for the massacres of Armenians in 1895 and detachments also took part in the Balkan wars and the fighting with Syria. Their numbers were increased to 64 under the Young Turks in 1910 when, according to Olson, "there had not been such a concentration of Kurdish power and authority since 1874" (i.e. the fall of the Kurdish principality of Botan ruled by the Bedir-Khan family) and "the Hamidiye era was a necessary interlude in emergent Kurdish nationalism marking the third stage in its evolution. It contributed to feelings of solidarity among Sunni Kurds and offered leadership opportunities to many young Kurdish men. The Hamidiye also provided many Kurds with knowledge of military technology and equipment and the capabilities to use it" (Olson 1989, p. 10). And it is true to say that in Shaykh Sa'id's rebellion many of the leaders were former Hamidiye officers whereas the Alevi Kurds from the north scarcely took part.

The Armenian response to the massacres of 1895–6 was to massacre the Kurds in Armenia and north Kurdistan during the Russian incursions of 1914–15 into Bayazit, Erzurum, Eleşkirt, Van, Bitlis, Muş and as far south as the river Rawanduz. The Kurdish historian, Muhamed Amin Zaki (1880–1948), a native of Sulaimaniya who was serving as a staff officer in the Ottoman army at the time, writes of "large-scale massacres of the Kurdish population in these areas by well-armed bands of Armenians who acted as an advance force of the Russian army".[3] Zaki also mentions massacres of Kurds by forces under the command of Turkish officers inspired by pan-Turanist ideology. These, together with famine, epidemics and deportation, led Zaki to estimate the total deaths among non-combatants amongst the Kurds at 500,000. It is relevant here to point out that those principally responsible for the massacres of Armenians during the same period (1915–16), Talaat Pasha, Enver and Jamal, were also members of the pan-Turanist party, Union and Progress (İttihad ve Terakkî Cemiyeti).

Although Russian policy opposed Kurdish independence, St Petersburg became, from the middle of the nineteenth century, the leading centre of Kurdish studies. To be sure, the founder of this area of knowledge is generally acknowledged to have been the former missionary priest, Padre Maurizio Garzoni, who published his *Grammatica e Vocabolario della Lingua Kurda* at Rome in 1787, but in the same year Pallas's comparative dictionary containing several hundred Kurdish words was published in St Petersburg under the patronage of Catherine the Great and laid the foundations for subsequent studies by Russian, French and German Scholars.

Most of these published under the aegis of the Imperial Academy of Sciences and among them was the Russian Pole, A.D. Jaba, a former Russian consul at Erzurum, whose *Receuil de notices et extraits kurdes* appeared in 1860. Jaba also compiled a Kurdish–French dictionary, a conversational lexicon and an unpublished parallel French–Russian–Kurdish dictionary. A German scholar, Peter Lerch, published at St Petersburg in 1857 a selection of Kurdish texts, *Forschungen über die Kurden*, based on material collected during the Crimean War from Kurdish prisoners segregated in a camp at Smolensk for this purpose. Ferdinand Justi (*Kurdische Grammatik*, 1880), E. Prym and Albert Socin (*Kurdische Sammlungen*, 1890) also published studies of Kurdish material.

Perhaps the most important Kurdish material to be published in St Petersburg was the history of the Kurds originally compiled in 1596 by Sharaf Khan, "Prince of Bitlis, Moush, Khinis, Akhlat the Dependencies thereof and of all the Lands and Strongholds inherited by him from his Forefathers". This work, written in Persian, as its title *Sharaf-nameh* indicates, covers five centuries "so that the history of the great ruling dynasties of Kurdistan will not remain unknown". The original manuscript with corrections in the author's own hand dated and signed 1599 in the Royal Safavid Library at Ardabil was taken to St Petersburg with the rest of the library as part of Russia's spoils after the war with Persia in 1828. The Persian text was edited with an introduction in French by the Russian academician, V. Veliaminov-Zernov, under the title *Scheref-nameh ou histoire des kourdes* in 1860. A French edition in four volumes was published, also in St Petersburg, in 1869–75 under the title *Sheref-nameh ou Fastes de la Nation kourde* and was accompanied by an introduction and a formidable critical apparatus by its editor, François Charmoy.

This florescence of academic studies of the Kurds and their culture, disinterested as it may have been as far as individual scholars were concerned, was nevertheless a clear reflection of Russia's overriding territorial ambitions which envisaged the dismemberment of the Persian and Ottoman empire, access to "the warm seas", and the liberation of Christian minorities. Kurdish independence had no part in these ambitions and any encouragement shown from time to time was nothing more than an opportunistic move towards the realization of these ambitions on the part of Imperial Russia.

KURDS IN THE USSR: LENIN TO BREZHNEV

When the Bolsheviks assumed power in Petrograd in November 1917, Russia was still allied to Britain and France and at war with Germany and Turkey – an important factor contributing to the new central government's inability to extend its rule in any effective sense to the outlying regions of the Russian empire. Most of these territories were quick to declare themselves independent, among them Transcaucasia and Central Asia.

On 11 November, three days after the Bolsheviks took control, a Transcaucasian Assembly was set up. This brought together deputies from the various nationalities: Georgians who were mainly adherents of the Menshevik party; Armenians from the nationalist Tashnak movement; Tatars from the conservative Musavat (Equality) group. These were joined by a handful of Kurds.[4]

In 1918, on 22 April, the assembly proclaimed the establishment of the "Democratic Federal Republic of Transcaucasia". A month later it succumbed to disputes raised by its differing ethnic constituents. Georgia, with German encouragement, proclaimed its independence on May 26 to be followed next day by Azerbaijan supported by the Turks (Enver Pasha was in Baku at the time). On 30 May the Armenian National Council in Tbilisi claimed sovereignty over "the Armenian Provinces" without giving specific details of the territories designated by the term, an announcement which was immediately followed by a Georgian ultimatum to quit Tbilisi. The Armenian Tashnak government subsequently established itself in Yerevan where it was soon under attack by Ottoman forces who captured Alexandropol (modern Leninakan). The period 1918–20 saw the new-born Armenian republic embroiled in a series of conflicts in which resistance to invaders and massacres of minorities loomed large. Aram Manoukian, after his appointment as virtual dictator, was able to utilize the abilities of Russian-trained Armenian officers to launch a series of punitive expeditions against Kurdish and Azeri villages in the spring of 1918. These attacks were directed against regions where Armenians were in fact a minority of the population. In the summer of the same year General Andranich continued the attacks on Muslim communities (Ter Minassian 1989, pp. 73–6). From July to September 1920, Rouben Ter Minassian, a Turkish Armenian who had been named defence minister in Yerevan took over the anti-Muslim campaign with the aim of creating "une patrie par le fer et le sang" (ibid, pp. 215–18), despite his public declaration of admiration for the courage and code of honour of his Kurdish victims (ibid, p. 216).

Some eighteen months before the beginning of these campaigns, early in 1918, Enver Pasha despatched his brother Nuri Pasha to Baku. Shortly after his arrival a general uprising against the Russians and Armenians took place and Azerbaijan was proclaimed an independent republic. A few months later, on 15 September, the Ottoman army occupied Baku only to withdraw with the rest of the Turkish forces in Transcaucasia after the signing of the Mudros armistice on 30 October and the defeat of the Ottoman empire in a wider conflict of the First World War. The Turkish occupying forces were replaced by British troops in Azerbaijan who secured the British interest in Baku's oil wells.

It was in this context that Mustafa Kemal whose power in Turkey was in the ascendant, sought an alliance with the Soviet government to counter "Western imperialism". In 1919, he despatched two envoys, Enver's uncle Khalil Pasha and Fuad Sabi, to Baku for further negotiations which resulted in the Soviet–Turkish agreement of 29 November 1919, which included a Soviet undertaking to supply the new regime in Turkey with money and arms. Shortly afterwards, in the spring of 1920, a branch of the Turkish Communist Party was formed in Baku under the auspices of Mustafa Sufi, a leading member of the Communist Party in Turkey itself. Due largely to the efforts of the newly-established party, Azerbaijan became a Soviet republic without notable opposition on 27 April. Georgia followed suit on 7 May, becoming a full member of the Soviet Union in 1921. On 19 July 1920, the Turkish Foreign Minister, Beku Sami, led a delegation to Moscow. On 24 August, two weeks after the signing of the Treaty of Sèvres, a Soviet–Turkish agreement was concluded. In September, Turkish forces attacked Armenia and captured Alexandropol with tacit Soviet collaboration. Faced with this double opposition the Tashnak party lost control of Yerevan and by 29 November the independent republic of Armenia had ceased to exist; three days later Armenia became a Soviet Socialist Republic.

At this period the Kurds formed a majority in those areas of west Azerbaijan which marched with Armenia. They were for the most part farmers and urban tradesmen, Sunnis as compared with the Azeri Shi'ites. In the ancient city of Ganja, subseqently Kirovabad, the Kurds were almost completely assimilated, but this was not the case in the area which began forty kilometres to the south west and extended to the Araks and the Iranian border with Nagorny Karabakh to the east; approximately 5,200 square kilometres, this territory was almost entirely Kurdish. It included the capital Lachin together with the principal towns Kalbajar, Kubatli and Zangelan and the administrative sub-divisions of Karakushlak, Koturli, Murad-Khanli and Kurd-Haji. It was this area that subsequently formed the autonomous region (*uyezd*) of Kurdistan, known to the Kurds as "Red" Kurdistan (*Kurdistana sor*). One version of its genesis[5] has a letter from the leader of the south Kurdistan (now Iraq) national movement, Shaykh Mahmud Barzinji, to Lenin requesting Soviet aid in the struggle against British imperialism and drawing his attention to the "international significance of the Kurdish national question". Lenin is said to have expressed his awareness of the issue together with concern about the role of "Soviet Kurds".[6] Moreover, an autonomous Kurdistan was to be established and 40 million roubles was to be allocated to further this aim.

The Karabakh area had been divided before 1917 into seven Muslim, four Kurdish and three Azeri districts with the Armenian Christian area of Nagorny Karabakh isolated in their midst, albeit with "significant" Tatar and Kurdish minorities. The Armenian majority of Nagorny Karabakh was "reinforced" between 1917 and 1920 (Ter Minassian 1989, pp. 130–1). At the beginning of Soviet rule this area, with Nakhichevan, was disputed by Armenia and Azerbaijan, with further complications arising out of its close proximity to areas where Kurds predominated. It took the Soviet government three years to settle the Azeri–Armenian dispute. In 1920 a solution was deferred to a later date and the Red Army assumed administrative responsibility for the area in the meantime. Lenin's letter to Narimanov had implied that Lachin was to be included in Azerbaijan, but the authorities in Baku and Yerevan were given promises that were inevitably contradictory.

March 16 1921 saw the signing of a pact of non-aggression between Turkey and the Soviet Union. Two years later, on 4 July 1923, Moscow decreed that the Kurdish area of which Lachin was the capital was to become a part of the Azerbaijan SSR together with Nagorny Karabakh despite the status of both as autonomous regions. In February 1924, the enclave of Nakhichevan with Turkey, Iran and Armenia on three of its borders was also absorbed into Azerbaijan; it was however accorded the status of autonomous republic, one grade higher than *uyezd*.

These decisions established a series of five areas extending eastwards from Nakhichevan in an arc along the river Araks, all possessing distinct ethnic identities and with differing political status, viz the Nakhichevan ASSR (5,500 sq km) with an "Azeri–Kurdish majority" as Soviet statistics termed it and an Armenian minority population; the narrow southern strip of Armenian territory comprising Kafan, Goris and Yekhezghadzor; the autonomous region of Kurdistan (5,200 sq km) composed of four Kurdish districts; the Armenian autonomous region of Nagorny Karabakh (4,400 sq km), capital Stepanakert, whose Armenian majority was increased from 70 per cent to 94 per cent between 1919 and 1920; the remainder of the Azerbaijan SSR.

It cannot be denied that it would have been far more appropriate, given the ethnic constitution of the area as a whole, if Nagorny Karabakh had remained a part of Armenia, but at the same time it is hardly likely that Lenin, already ill and in his last year, could have envisaged the fate of "Red Kurdistan" under Stalin.

The undisclosed reason for the area's inclusion in Azerbaijan was the desire of the Soviet government to maintain friendly relations with the Kemalist regime in Turkey.[7] Armenian historians, among them Anahide Ter Minassian, assert that there were wider political aims, foremost among them the creation of "Greater Azerbaijan" extending from the Caspian to the Black Sea, as envisaged by the Azeri Musavat delegates to the Paris Peace Conference in 1919. Further, this was seen as a step on the road to a pan-Turanic entity,[8] an ideal which the establishment of Azerbaijan had by no means extinguished. Armenian commentators of today, however, tend to ignore the problem, comparable in all respects, of Kurdistan.

Kurdistan was able to survive as an autonomous region within Azerbaijan for roughly two years until 1925, the year which saw the beginning of Sheikh Sa'id's Kurdish uprising in Turkey. A Kurdish governing body was established, Kurdish schools and a teacher's training college were founded, books in Kurdish and a political periodical, *Sovyet Kurdustan*, were published.

This measure of self-government was of short duration. In 1929, the Baku government reduced Kurdistan from an *uyezd* to an *okrug* (district), the lowest territorial unit for the Soviet non-Russian nationalities. Eight years later Soviet Kurdistan's autonomy had entirely disappeared, again largely as a result of the desire to maintain good relations with Turkey where Kurdish insurgents remained a problem.[9]

To help understand subsequent events as they affected the Kurds as individuals and as families, it is worth citing an interview with Nadir K. Nadirov, a Kurdish member of the Kazakhstan Academy of Sciences, which appeared in the various foreign language editions of *Moscow News* at the beginning of 1990 (26 January–1 February). In his introductory resumé of his subject's background, the interviewer recalled that "Kurdistan" had been established in Azerbaijan in 1923 by order of the Central Committee and shortly afterwards became an autonomous district with Lachin as its capital. The leader of its first government was Gussi Gajev. The journal *Sovyetskiy Kurdistan* recalled as well as the teachers' training college at Shusha, the schools where Kurdish was the medium of instruction, and Kurdish-language broadcasting. In 1937 the Kurds, including Nadirov's family, were deported from Azerbaijan and Armenia. In 1944 the Georgian Kurds were also sent to the "special colonies", among them Nadirov's early home in Siberia, where they were resettled. Most adult males were deported separately and their fate is at present still unknown.

It should be emphasized that the deportations of 1937 referred to by Nadirov's interviewer were quite unrelated to the Second World War or its anticipation. Nor can the deportation of 1944 be connected with the war. In this respect they differ from the cases of the Crimean Tatars and the Volga Germans. According to Mihoyi, the deportations took place at the instigation of the head of the Azerbaijani government, Mir Jafar Bakirov, who had close connections with Stalin and the OGPU. While this may be true in the case of the Kurds deported from Azerbaijan, it fails to explain why Armenia and Georgia followed suit. Here again it would seem that the deportations were brought about by pressure from Turkey, which was resettling its Kurdish population at the same time (cf. the deportations from Dersim – modern Tunceli – in 1937–8). Not only did Turkey and Azerbaijan pursue an identical policy, both employed identical techniques, e.g. forced assimilation, manipulation of population figures, settlement of non-Kurds in areas predominantly Kurdish, suppression of publications and abolition of Kurdish as a medium of instruction in schools. A familiar Soviet technique was also used: Kurdish historical figures such as Sharaf Khan of Bitlis and Ahmad Khani and the Shaddadid dynasty as a whole were described as Azeris. Kurds who retained "Kurdish" as their nationality on their internal passports as opposed to "Azeri" were unable to find employment. The Kurdish department of the Institute of Oriental Studies at Baku was abolished as late as the 1960s although Kurdish studies continued in comparable institutions in Moscow, Leningrad and Yerevan. Strangely enough, *Sovyet Kurdustan* continued to be published in the 1930s, but not in Kurdish. A Turkic language, in a synthetic alphabet made up of Cyrillic as well as Roman letters, was used to provide coverage of issues unrelated to the Kurds and all too characteristic of *zastoya* (the period of stagnation).

Official Soviet statistics produced by the Azerbaijan SSR within the past two years show a decline in the number of Kurds within its borders according to census figures covering almost seventy years:

1921	32,780
1926	41,000
1939	6,000
1959	1,500
1970	5,000
1979	No Kurds recorded in Azerbaijan
1989	13,000

These figures are of dubious value and almost certainly inaccurate. It is scarcely credible that the figure for 1926 can be so low given that they include the population of "Red Kurdistan", when in 1921 the figure was only 8,000 fewer and did not include the autonomous region's population. The fluctuations between 1959 and 1989 are barely feasible. The official reasons given by the

Azerbaijani government are even less so. When, for instance, Soviet Kurds questioned them about "the disappearance of the Kurds" (*windabûna Kurdan*), the answer given was that "they had assimilated for objective reasons", i.e. because they were Muslims like the Azeris. It may be asked why this was the case in Azerbaijan when it was so evidently not so in Turkey, Iraq, Syria and Iran. Moreover, in 1988 some 10,000 of these "lost" Kurds returned their Azeri passports to Moscow with the request that the nationality description be changed to Kurdish. Professor Shakero Mihoyi estimated that the number of Kurds in Soviet Azerbaijan today is "at least 250,000". Mamo Khalit Darwishyan, a Kurdish ethnographer based in Yerevan, puts the figure even higher at 400,000. In 1988, Darwishyan wrote to Gorbachev to complain that the local authorities had prevented his investigating the situation in Lachin; in Kalbajar he was able to question Kurds because he had avoided making any request through official channels.[10] There are Kurdish communities to be found elsewhere in Azerbaijan: in Baku, Nakhichevan and Nagorny Karabakh.

The figures for Soviet Kurds in 1926, 1939, and 1959 census returns are cited by Bennigsen who comments that "most Soviet Kurdologists regard these as inadequate" and goes on to quote an estimate made by Aristova in 1954 of 160,000. The 1939 figure includes 15,000 Yazidi Kurds while those for 1959 include 21,000 Kurds in Armenia where in 1916 they numbered in the province of Yerevan alone, an area representing nearly 50 per cent of Soviet Armenia, more than 36,000. In Azerbaijan there were even greater numbers. The 1979 census figures given in *Processus ethniques en URSS* are not to be relied on. It may be asked how it was that the Kurdish population scarcely showed any increase between 1897 and 1979 when that of other Soviet nationalities increased four-, six- and in some cases eight-fold during the same period. Under Tsarist rule the Kurds increased in number by 32 per cent in the period 1897–1916.

Not all Transcaucasian Kurds were deported to be resettled in the other Soviet republics of Kazakhstan, Kirghizia, Tajikistan, Uzbekistan and Siberia, and some of these were subsequently able to return to Transcaucasia. The numbers deported are unknown. Some idea may be gained by considering what is known of deportations from "Red Kurdistan". Compared with Nagorny Karabakh, this is a larger, less mountainous, more fertile and more populous region. Given comparable increases of population over the same period, where Nagorny Karabakh in 1990 had a population of roughly 190,000, the four districts of Kurdistan might have a total population of 300–350,000 of whom some two-thirds would be Kurdish, and in Transcaucasia as a whole Kurds would have numbered close to one million, including 500,000 in Azerbaijan, had it not been for deportations and other forms of persecution.

This is not the place for a detailed analysis of Soviet estimates of the number of Kurds outside the USSR, but the 1970 census figure of 88,930 Soviet Kurds reflects – quite apart from any manipulation of the figures returned – the mass deportation of Kurds. Isayev's reference (see below) to their "assimiliation" because of their being "scattered among several other nationalities" is a typical Soviet euphemism for the forcible deportations of 1937 and 1944 and the resettlement in Soviet republics largely in Central Asia. What is true is that the ethnic situation in the Transcaucasus under Soviet rule is as complex as it was under the Tsars. Figures for 1959 give a total of 2,787,000 Armenians in the USSR as a whole, while the Armenian republic had 1,763,000 inhabitants consisting of 1,551,600 Armenians, 107,700 Azeris, 65,500 Russians, 25,600 Kurds (a figure higher than the 21,000 estimated by Bennigsen for the same year), 5,600 Ukrainians, 5,000 Assyrians, and 2,000 other nationalities. According to the 1970 census cited by Isayev, the total for Armenians was 3,559,151 of which 2,208,327 were in Soviet Armenia, 452,309 in Georgia, 483,250 in Azerbaijan and 298,718 in the Russian federation (Isayev also gives a figure of 1.5 million for the Armenians outside the USSR which should in fact be closer to 2 million). Soviet Armenia, which the Armenians themselves refer to as Eastern Armenia, is considerably smaller than the historical Armenia. The Soviet government with the support of the neighbouring republics adopted a policy of exclusion of those territories which had once had Armenian majorities, but which by 1920 had gained majorities of Georgians, Azeris or Kurds. Even taking into account the loss of Western Armenia, now part of Turkey, the Armenians can still count themselves fortunate compared with the Kurds for they at least have their own republic and have benefited in the long run from their membership of the USSR.

In other areas, particularly Turkmenia, the Kurds were as numerous as they were in Transcaucasia. The main areas of settlement were Kopet-Dag and Firyuza with smaller rural groups in Ciok-Tepe, Kakha and Kara-Kala with urban communities in Bagir, Bayram-Ali and in the capital, Ashkhabad.[11] But unlike the Kurds in Armenia, the Kurds of Turkmenia were subjected to an active campaign of assimilation and were granted no facilities for education in their own language. Nevertheless, they remained conscious of their identity and have participated in recent efforts by Soviet Kurds to obtain a restoration of the right to be acknowledged as a separate nationality.

The total number of Kurds living within the USSR today is unknown. Soviet Kurds themselves give estimates that range from approximately 300,000 to a precise figure of 1,120,000. As an example of the increase in numbers within the Kurdish diaspora in the Soviet Union, we may take the 3,000 Kurds resettled near Vladivostok in 1937 who today number 30,000 with their own schools using Kurdish as the medium of instruction and separate units such as *kolkhozy* within the Yakutsk ASSR. These Kurds are so conscious of their cultural identity that at the beginning of 1990 they sent a group of observers to the Düsseldorf trial of alleged PKK activists.

In the period since 1987, ethnic quarrels have forced many Kurds to leave Kirghizia, Tajikistan and Uzbekistan and move to Transcaucasia, the Krasnodar area in particular. In 1987–8, roughly 18,000 Kurds under threat in Armenia moved to the same area, although other Kurds left Azerbaijan for Armenia at the same time. The Kurds who have moved into the city boundaries of Krasnodar do not have valid internal passports and are not welcomed by the authorities with the result that in 1989 some 20,000 (of a rough total of 40,000) moved to Azerbaijan where a policy shift on the part of the government in Baku had made them relatively welcome.

The writer's own estimate of the number of Kurds in the USSR in 1990 is given in Table 10.2 of the Kurdish population in the republics or regions named. The figure for Azerbaijan includes between 10 and 20 per cent from rural areas who in part assimilated, but who have begun to rediscover their cultural identity under the more liberal rule initiated by Gorbachev's policy of *glasnost*.

The majority of those Kurds who were not deported from Georgia in 1944 have tended to congregate in or near the capital, Tbilisi, where they number approximately 34,000. A further 8,000 live in villages in the nearby region of Telavi. The Tbilisi Kurds, predominantly Yazidis, have established their own elementary and

Table 10.2 Estimate of the number of Kurds in the USSR, 1990

USSR republic/region	Numbers
Azerbaijan	180,000
Armenia	50,000
Georgia	40,000
Kazakhstan	30,000
Kirghizia	20,000
Uzbekistan	10,000
Tajikistan	3,000
Turkmenia	50,000
Siberia	35,000
Krasnodar	20,000
Other	12,000
Total	450,000

secondary school and a cultural centre where the languages of instruction and information are Kurdish, Georgian and Russian.

They have also formed their own theatre company and with the recent liberalization policies have begun to engage in private enterprise. Unlike the 100,000 Abkhazi Muslims in Georgia, Kurds are not perceived as a threat by the Georgians who see them as a tough and resilient people, much as Russians view Georgians.

Armenia, it must be conceded, is the only Soviet republic which preserved and protected Kurdish cultural infrastructures after the persecutions under Stalin. The Kurdish intelligentsia is mostly from Armenia, which is largely due to the fact that the Armenian Kurds have been able to be educated in their own language at primary and secondary level except in scientific subjects. The Writers' Union of Armenia has a Kurdish section and there is a flourishing department of Kurdish studies in the Oriental Studies Institute of the Armenian Academy of Sciences with a joint Armenian–Kurdish faculty board. A large number of books including textbooks, literary and scientific works as well as translations of foreign authors have been and continue to be published in Kurdish. Kurds arre represented politically on the Central Committee of the Armenian Communist Party, in parliament and in the government while the Armenian radio broadcasts news, music and other programmes in Kurdish.

In Armenia the main Kurdish settlements are in Alagöz and Tallin with others at Ashtarat, Zangibazar, Shamiran and Oktyabr as well as in Yerevan where the community numbers between 10,000 and 20,000.[12]

Among the older generation of Kurdish intellectuals born in Armenia one of the most prominent was the novelist, Ereb Shemo (1898–1978). Born into a poor family living in the neighbourhood of Yerevan, he left home in his early teens to work as a shepherd in the northern Caucasus where he experienced considerable hardship. Contacts with revolutionary soldiers and workers led him to join the Bolsheviks at sixteen and for the rest of his life he remained loyal to the Communist Party of the Soviet Union. From refugees who had fled to the northern Caucasus he learned of the atrocities being committed against Kurds by "the Tashnak counter-revolutionaries of the Armenian bourgeoisie" whose aim was to create a greater Armenia "from sea to sea". When he eventually returned home it was to find that his father had been killed by the Tashnaks and that his mother had died in the mountains she had fled to with his surviving sister, Chichek. Soviet rule brought improved conditions and Shemo was able to acquire an education, as he related in his autobiography, *Shvanê Kurmanja (The Kurdish Shepherd)*, which was published in Kurmanji Kurdish in Yerevan in 1935.

In 1937, despite his being a model communist author, Shemo was deported to Siberia and spent the next twenty years in a series of *gulags*. When he was allowed to return home under Krushchev he resumed writing, but never referred to his years in Siberia. He published four more novels in Kurdish of which the first was *Berbang (Dawn)* and the second, which appeared the following year, *Jîna Bextewar (Happy Life)*. Mamed Jemo[13] points out that the term "Kurdistan", which Shemo had used in his work published in the 1930s to designate the Kurdish regions of Transcaucasia, never appears in his later novels.

That Kurdish was very early recognized as one of the 130 languages of the Soviet Union is noted by the philologist M.I. Isayev in his "One Hundred and Thirty with Equal Rights" and he comments in a later work published in 1977, *National Languages of the USSR: Problems and Solutions*:

> Most Iranian languages and dialects are represented within Soviet territory including Tajik, Ossetic, Kurdish and Tat which also have a written form and those without any such as Talish, Baluchi,* Yaghnobi, Ishkashmi, Yazgulami and the Shughni-

Rushani sub-group of Pamiri.

* A written form of Baluchi is used in Pakistan (ed.).

Isayev draws on the figures given in the 1970 census when he describes Kurdish as:

> Spoken primarily in Armenia, Azerbaijan, and Turkmenia. The total number of Kurds in the USSR is 88,930 scattered among several other nationalities, a factor which contributes to their assimilation and the loss of ethnic identity. In Armenia, which has schools where Kurdish is the medium of instruction, where Kurdish books by Kurds and foreign authors are published and where there is a Kurdish newspaper, *Ria Taze (New Path)*, Kurds have preserved their cultural unity. The majority of Kurds, however, live outside the USSR: approximately 4 million in Turkey, 3.5 million in Iran, 2 million in Iraq and 250,000 in Syria. Their language is divided into several dialects, viz Sorani, Zaza, Luri, Gurani and Kurmanji, which is the dialect spoken by the Soviet Kurds. The language has had a written form from at least the twelfth century and today Kurds use both an Arabic-based alphabet in Iraq and Iran and Roman-based script in Syria. Soviet Kurds acquired a written form for their language after the 1917 Revolution. The first alphabet, devised in 1921, was based on Armenian and failed to come into general use. In 1929 it was superseded by a Roman-based alphabet, which was in turn replaced by Cyrillic in 1945. The literacy made possible by these developments has produced a significant number of writers engaged in important literary and socio-political activities including the creation of a literary language that is an instrument of social progress and communist education among this minority people. Foremost among these writers are A. Dzhindi, A. Avdal, A. Sharo, Dzh. Gendzho, U. Bako, A. Shamilov (Ereb Shemo) and V. Nadir.[14]

The French authority on the Kurds, Père Thomas Bois, published a study of Kurdish literature, *Coup d'oeil sur la littérature kurde*, in 1955. In it he points out that the writing of Soviet Kurds, although written in Kurdish, does not give expression to the nationalist feelings evident in writers from Kurdish regions outside the USSR. For Soviet Kurdish writers the homeland is the village, the valley, Armenia or the Soviet Union, not Kurdistan. Whether this is a deliberate choice or an awareness of the limits imposed by Soviet censorship it is hard to say and Père Bois did not live to see the revival of enthusiasm for Kurdistan among the Kurds of the USSR. Even from a technical point of view, though, according to Bois, Soviet Kurdish writing is stylistically at a much lower level of accomplishment than the Kumanji written by Syrian Kurdish authors such as Celadet and Kamuran Bedir-Khan, Osman Sabri, Cegerxwin or Nureddin Zaza, or those from Turkey such as M. Bozarslan, M. Uzun and M. Baksi. This view is more or less accepted today. The reason for this is, in part, political. In the early 1920s the Soviet authorities chose to encourage and support as the official written language of its Kurdish minority, of whom 95 per cent were illiterate, the colloquial Kurmanji of Transcaucasia rather than the literary language of scholars, writers and poets. Onto this vernacular was grafted a vocabulary needed to cope with modern conditions based largely on Russian. Outside Russia new formations are based on Kurdish root words. Credit cannot be denied to the Soviets for increasing the rate of literacy and for encouraging Kurdish studies, but even these achievements are ultimately outweighed, at least in the writer's view, by the massacres, enforced acculturation and deportations for which Stalin and Bakirov, together with their adherents, were responsible.

THE SOVIET KURDS AND *GLASNOST*: THE 1990 MOSCOW CONFERENCE

In the course of six visits to the USSR over a period of thirty-odd years beginning in 1959, the writer has been able to establish close ties with Soviet Kurds and can attest that never once was there any sense on either side of political or cultural alienation. To be sure, those encountered in the first five visits were predominantly intellectuals, but the last visit in 1990 extended contacts to all classes of Soviet Kurds. It is on the basis of this experience that the writer is able to state without reservation that Soviet Kurds perceive themselves as precisely that. They have a double allegiance: to their Kurdish identity and to the Soviet Union and it is noticeable that the latter, stronger perhaps in the older generation, is greater than any allegiance they might feel to the individual Soviet republics in which they live. In this respect, they may be seen as closely conforming to the Soviet ideal of citizenship. Nevertheless, it is the sense of being Kurdish that is foremost and many now look forward to an autonomous and united Kurdistan, for all Kurds, to be achieved with Soviet assistance.

In April 1983, I visited the USSR at the invitation of the Soviet Academy of Sciences and during the course of my stay spent many memorable evenings with Soviet and other Kurds studying or living in Moscow. On all these occasions there was an overwhelming sense of unity among all those present. At that particular time my hosts were euphoric. Yuri Andropov had succeeded Brezhnev as General Secretary of the Soviet Communist Party the previous autumn and he was seen as the first Soviet leader since Khrushchev to be willing to introduce a measure of reform into the system, and indeed, in his first public speech at the November 1982 meeting of the Supreme Soviet he had specifically mentioned the Kurds. What he had said was to the effect that in the Soviet Union there were national minorities belonging to peoples of whom the majority live beyond the borders of the USSR such as the Germans, Koreans and the Kurds. Although the Soviet Kurds were gratified by thus being singled out from among numerous other Soviet nationalities, they felt he had not gone far enough in recognizing their position and made the points that the Kurds are placed on the same footing as the Germans and Koreans, but these are minorities whose majorities live in their own established states outside the Soviet Union. It follows that the Kurds have, or should have, a Kurdistan where the majority lives.

The nationalist fervour unleashed among the minority peoples of the Soviet Union by Gorbachev's policies was not absent among the relatively small number of Kurds, but they differed from other minorities in that any alleviation of their situation could be achieved only with the aid of the Soviet central government. There is no doubt that the latter was fully aware of the Kurds' problems and was willing, up to a point, to provide a measure of assistance. That Andropov had cited them as an instance was scarcely fortuitous and Gorbachev, his protégé and successor, is a native of the Transcaucasian city of Stavropol, while in turn, one of his earliest and closest collaborators, Edvard Shevardnadze, is a Georgian. Neither could be other than well-informed about the Kurdish minority in those areas. But the question that remains unresolved, however much vague goodwill may exist among government leaders in Moscow, is that of imposing a solution or arriving at a consensus with republics on the national question and the proposed new constitution of the USSR.

In 1988, Kurdish delegations from Azerbaijan were participants in demonstrations in Yerevan provoked by the dispute over Nagorny Karabakh. In the following year, on 20 May, a large and orderly demonstration by Kurds took place in Moscow in Pushkin Square. Present were groups from nine Soviet republics and on the following day, as reported by the Soviet media, including television, they marched to Ismailovsky Park. Prominent among the demonstrators were women from the central Asian republics where most adult Kurds are female because of the deportations and "disappearances" of their menfolk during the past fifty years. A spokeswoman for this group, Mezihe Ghefûr, made the following statement:

> I come from Kirghizia. Where I live there are 10,000 Kurds and 6,000 of them are women, who have asked me to speak on their behalf. As you now know, under Stalin, we were deported and resettled all over Central Asia and in Kazakhstan. We have been strictly supervised in exile; our neighbours do not know why we were deported and are hostile. The word is that we were "enemies of the people" and we cannot shake off this reputation. How can Kurdish girls go to school and study in this kind of situation? And if they can't study how can they claim their rights as human beings let alone as Soviet citizens? All over the world women tell their children stories about the heroes of their countries, but this is denied to us Kurds – our heroes have been sent into oblivion. They have robbed us of our heroes. They have robbed us of our culture. It is hard to educate our children. We cannot bring them up to love their country and their people. We are ashamed to tell them that they are Kurds through their mothers. I believe nobody in all the world is as deprived of rights as Kurdish women in this country. We left our children at home and came to Moscow to ask for justice. Where we live our lives are in danger. We are afraid for our children. We are afraid of extremists who would not stop at murder. We hide in our homes, but when we do go out they shout at us "Go home!" But where can we go? We have no home.

Another speaker in Pushkin Square was Adil Celîl from Lachin. When he was a child in the 1920s he went to a Kurdish school. When the Azerbaijani authorities filled in "Azeri" as his nationality on his internal passport in 1979 he refused to accept it and made strenuous efforts, like many other Kurds at the time, to get it changed to "Kurdish". "The Kurds of Azerbaijan" he told the rally "refuse to die". His mother, he added, told him before he left for Moscow, "Go to Moscow, son. If they are real democrats they will give us back our independence. If they don't we'll give up believing in any of it: *perestroika*, Gorbachev or Lenin".[15] These and other statements were reported in the Soviet media. In addition to asking the Soviet central government to make the day-to-day existence of Soviet Kurds secure, the demonstrators also demanded the restoration of Kurdistan as constituted in 1923 as an autonomous region in Azerbaijan. Some delegates proposed an autonomous Kurdistan in the Krasnodar region, but they were met with incredulity on the part of other delegates who told them that the Russians would never hand over land as fertile as that. The Baku government had proposed a restoration of Kurdistan but not in the same areas. The proposed new Kurdistan was to be in Jeyran, a semi-desert. This was rejected by the Kurds. It was rumoured also that the governments of Byelorussia and Kazakhstan were prepared to offer the Kurds territory within their borders.

Two months later, on 17 August, the Supreme Soviet promulgated a law under which all Soviet citizens who had been deported under Stalin were to be repatriated with their previous rights restored.[16] However just the principle underlying this law, its application encountered insurmountable problems. Peoples like the Volga Germans were able to return to a country that made them welcome, but in the case of others such as the Krim Tatars and the Kurds, their former homelands had been colonized by Russians and in the case of the Kurds by Azeris.

A spokesman for the Soviet Kurds, the poet Ali Abdul Rahman, was subsequently received by the member of the Politburo responsible for nationalities, Chebrikov (later replaced), who advised that the Kurds should be represented by a single organization. This came into effect with remarkable rapidity on 20 September at a meeting of Kurdish leaders which concluded with the formation of Yekbûn (Union) and the election as chairman of Mohamed Sulaiman Babayev, a retired agronomist from Baku who had occupied important positions in the Ministry of Agriculture. The committee included Academican Nadir K. Nadirov, Professor Shakero Mihoyi, Ali Abdul Rahman, Tosen Rashid, an engineer, and Colonel Wakil of the *militsia*. It was agreed jointly between the secretariat of the Central Committee of the Communist Party of the USSR and Yekbûn to organize a general conference of Kurds in Moscow and a seven-member steering committee was nominated including four Kurds, viz: N.K. Nadirov, chairman; Ivan Kitaev, Deputy Director of the Central Committee's Marxist–Leninist Institute, co-chairman; M. Babayev and A. Avdali, joint secretaries; Shakero Mihoyi, E.A. Bagramov, also from the Marxist–Leninist Institute, and G.E. Taperznikov of the Institute for Inter-ethnic Relations. The conference was to have as title, "The Kurds of the Soviet Union: Past and Present" and was originally scheduled for June, then 25–6 July 1990. The sponsors were listed on the official programme as follows: the Marxist–Leninist Institute, the Institutes for the History of the Communist Party in the republics of Armenia, Azerbaijan and Kazahkstan. Twenty lecturers were listed, for the most part Soviet Kurds; non-Soviet Kurds were unlisted.

There were apparently considerable behind-the-scenes negotiations between the party and Yekbûn over the Kurds to be invited from outside the USSR. The former wanted them to be limited to three to five known historians, writers or "cultural activists". The Kurds proposed thirty-eight names representative of the political and cultural establishment of the Kurdish diaspora. A compromise was reached and eighteen were accepted, many of them in fact leading members of Kurdish political parties from Iran, Iraq and Syria. They included Jalal Talabani, who would not or could not come and who was represented by Dr Kamal Fu'ad. Mas'ud Barzani was represented by Dr Mohamed Salih Guma. The Iraqi Kurds were also represented by Mohamed Aziz, general secretary of the Iraqi communist party, who lived in Moscow and by Sami Abdul Rahman, leader of the People's Democratic Party, as well as Dr Mahmud Othman of the Kurdish Socialist Party. From Iran came Dr Sa'id Sharaf Kandi, who had succeeded the late Dr A. Ghassemlou as general secretary of the KDP-Iran, and Salah Bedreddin represented Syria. The Institut Kurde de Paris was represented by Kendal Nezan. Others included Mehmet Ali Aslan, a lawyer from Turkey; the writer Dr Cemşid Heyderi, Said Molla and Ehmed Karamus, all from Sweden, and Riza Colpan, a writer resident in Australia.

The conference was held at the Marxist–Leninist Institute and six hundred attended, mostly Kurds from nine Soviet republics representing all classes, including workers and peasants as well as the intelligentsia. The opening speech was by I. Kitaev, followed by N.K. Nadirov and Boris Nikolaevich on behalf of the Nationalities

Council of the USSR. All the Soviet delegates gave their papers in Russian for which no translation was provided, while those from abroad were in Kurdish, French or English of which a translation into Russian was made. Within the two days of the conference a total of thirty papers or short addresses were delivered, which left no time for public debate. The Soviet Kurds read scholarly papers or outlined political desiderata, but at one point there were interruptions from Kurdish peasants and workers who made impassioned speeches about national liberation and their own poverty, one going so far as to declare that he didn't want schools and didn't care about culture, but did want enough food to feed his children and a chance to live unharassed.

One of the conference's finest moments was the public reconciliation with a warm embrace of the young Kurdish Sunni Muslim chieftain, Sayid Shaykh Hasan, mufti of the Kazakhstan SSR, and the head of the Yazidi community, Shaykh Broyan Muraz Shirinovich, from Tbilisi. The first declared that he was a Kurd first and a Muslim second and the latter that he placed being Kurdish well in advance of his being a Yazidi. Another splendid moment was when Yekbûn's chairman, Mohamed Babayev and Academician Nadirov were also persuaded to embrace and forget the differences which had arisen from the former's popularity among workers and the latter's among intellectuals.

A final resolution was passed and given to the press and the other media at a press conference, and a letter was sent to President Gorbachev. This final resolution was drawn up and signed by the steering committee, but, strangely enough, it was not submitted to the conference for approval. This may have been because there was no time to do so. It was said that there was only one copy in Russian available and that there were no translations ready. I was told at the close of the conference that it made reference to the resolution adopted by the symposium on Kurdistan held in Lausanne on 27–9 April 1990, which had been attended by about 800 Kurds representing all political groupings including the PKK, as well as official representatives from the Swiss parliament. What that resolution had stated may be summed up as follows: that the Kurdish people constitute a single nation; that Kurdistan had been divided without any reference to its inhabitants between Iran, Iraq, Turkey and Syria; that the Kurdish question, including that of the Soviet Kurds, should be referred to the United Nations in the hope of a solution based on the right to self-determination. At the time, several Kurds told me how overjoyed they were that the Moscow conference had adopted the Lausanne resolution. But when the Moscow resolution was published in the West a month or so later[17] it was no great surprise to find that all mention of the Lausanne symposium or of any other conference on Kurdistan[18] or indeed of the treaties of Sèvres and Lausanne was omitted. Even under "the new thinking" the USSR was not ready to face the issue squarely. The participation of non-Soviet Kurds was dismissed with the bland formula: "the conference was attended by Soviet and foreign scientific researchers into the Kurdish question, by sociologists, writers and other intellectuals as well as by representatives of the Kurdish intelligentsia from outside the USSR".

We ought not, however, to lose sight of the significance of the fact that the conference was primarily concerned with the Soviet Kurds and that it was the first of its kind to be organized and sponsored by the highest levels of authority within the Soviet Union. The final resolution is not therefore to be dismissed and not least because, invoking "the spirit of the new democratic tendencies" it emphasized "the flagrant perversion of national policy under Stalin in the period of stagnation (*zastoya*) with reference to the Kurdish people, namely, the dissolution in 1929 of the autonomous region of Kurdistan, the forced assimilation of Kurds, the deportations of 1937 and 1944, the closing of Kurdish schools and publishing houses and the falsification of population figures". It continues, "even in the era of *perestroika* the Kurdish problem remains unsolved and there has been no restoration of former rights". It stressed the need to develop publishing and broadcasting in Kurdish, to overcome the numerous obstacles to the teaching of Kurdish language and literature. It noted that there is only one periodical in Kurdish, that broadcasting in Armenia and in Georgia is inadequate and that "there is no co-ordination of any of the efforts being made to provide for the national and spiritual aspirations of the Kurdish people". Furthermore, it pointed to a de facto deterioration of the position of the Kurds: "for many years Kurds have been unrepresented at the highest levels of government and since the last elections there are no Kurdish representatives in the legislative assemblies of the various republics". Concern was also expressed about "the almost complete absence of cultural relations between Kurds in the USSR and those resident in other countries", and this included Kurdish publications from abroad. The committee therefore urged that Kurdish publications, using the Roman-based alphabet of non-Soviet Kurdish communities, should be established in the USSR and the removal of all barriers to the reception of foreign-based Kurdish publications.

The conference committee also noted the growing interest of Soviet Kurds in their fellow Kurds abroad and their struggle for self-determination and noted with regret that the Kurdish question remained of little significance in the "new thinking" and in international affairs with particular reference to East–West relations. "Incredulity" was expressed at the Soviet government's lack of response to atrocities committed against the Kurds and in particular the use of chemical weapons by the Iraqi government in 1988:

> We regard it as anomalous that aid and support of any sort should be given to regimes which used these and other means to oppose Kurdish struggles to achieve self-determination . . . It is our conviction that the Soviet Union in the spirit of "the new thinking" should take the initiative in bringing to the urgent attention of international organizations, particularly the United Nations, the sufferings of the Kurdish people.

In conclusion, the resolution urged the setting up of a "Kurdish Federal Association" to include representatives from all the Soviet republics concerned, together with a Kurdish Cultural Centre based in Moscow, to include a publishing house, as a prelude to the establishment of an autonomous Kurdistan in a suitable area. The final words of the resolution gave warm support to the "policy of democratic change and liberalization in the political, social and national life of the USSR" and at the same time rejected "chauvinism and aggression" while stressing "the historic ties" between the Kurds and neighbouring peoples in the Soviet Union.

What steps the Soviet government will take remains to be seen. What is certain is that the Soviet Kurds, tenacious in their adherence to their language, culture and traditions, share with their fellow Kurds beyond the USSR the ultimate dream: a sovereign and independent Kurdistan.

Notes

2 Kurdish society, ethnicity, nationalism and refugee problems

1 The inclusion of the Zaza and Guran among the Kurds is not an innovation of modern Kurdish nationalism. The late sixteenth-century Kurdish author Sharaf Khan Bidlisi already considers both as subgroups among the Kurds, and so does the seventeenth-century Turkish traveller Evliya Çelebi. Even earlier we find references to Guran explicitly identifying themselves as Kurds, such as the fourteenth-century mystic Jalaluddin b Yusuf al-Kurani at-Tamliji al-Kurdi (who wrote in Arabic, see C. Brockelmann's *Geschichte der arabischen Literatur*, Supplement and II p. 262). Many Kurdish nationalists prefer to ignore the fact that Zaza and Gurani are in fact different languages, and wish to minimize the differences. When several Kurdish journals published in western Europe recently began including sections in Zaza besides Kurmanji and/or Sorani, this aroused some protest by some of those whose perceive a threat to Kurdish unity. Unlike Zaza, Gurani has a long literary tradition, which is, however, virtually extinct now. (See also Chapter 5, this volume, ed.)

2 On the beliefs of the Ahl-e Haqq, see Minorsky 1920, 1921; Edmonds 1969; Mokri 1970. Several basic ideas seem typically Iranian (Mazdean or Zoroastrian), while Roux (1969) has pointed to the presence of many elements of old Turkish religion.

3 On Yazidi doctrines and history see Menzel 1911; Lescot 1938.

4 On the institution of this form of ritual co-parenthood among the Kurds, see Kudat: 1971. I heard about the existence of such *krîv* relations between tribal Kurds and Christians in the Cizre and Tur Abdin regions.

5 This tribe, the *Ermeni-Varto*, with winter quarters near Silopi (southeastern Turkey) had by the 1950s gradually merged into the Kurdish tribe Teyyan, and spoke only Kurdish (Hütteroth 1959, p. 57).

6 By "Kurds" we mean those commonly called thus since the sixteenth–seventeenth centuries. In earlier sources, however, the term "Kurd" seems to refer to a particular type of pastoral nomads, *not* to all speakers of Kurdish (and Gurani and Zaza).

7 Even then the Turkish candidate for the left-wing Worker's Party of Turkey, which was surprisingly successful in the 1960s, belonged to the *aghawat* stratum. In the late 1970s, when the Kurdish movement had gained much strength in Turkey, several independent candidates (i.e., not affiliated to any party) challenged and defeated the established party machines in the elections, by appealing both to traditional loyalties and to Kurdish nationalist sentiment. These men obviously depended much less on state patronage.

8 A graphic description of this situation is given in Ümit Kaftancıoğlu's documentary novel *Tüfekliler* (*Men with Guns*). The author worked as a school teacher in the town of Derik near Mardin in the 1960s, and describes events that he witnessed: the power and brutal behaviour of local chieftains and their armed retinues, violent feuds, the oppression and exploitation of the peasantry, and the connivance of the local government authorities in all this. His observations are still representative of the situation in many parts of Kurdistan.

9 The name "*guran*" obviously connects these peasants with the tribal confederacy *Guran* and the *gurani* language, but they were regarded as entirely different social groups. "*Kurmanj*", the term used for non-tribal peasants in northern Kurdistan, was used in southern Kurdistan for a segment of the tribal élite. *Miskên* and *Klawspi* mean "poor" and "white-cap" respectively, the latter apparently after a distinctive headgear which had already gone out of use by the nineteenth century, while the name stuck.

10 The word *millî*, by which Atatürk designated his movement, and usually translated as "national", referred to the Muslim rather than the Turkish nation. Only later did it acquire ethnic–nationalist overtones.

11 I borrow this French term following Smith (1986) for those ethnic communities with a strong sence of identity, but lacking the political institutions characterizing a nation.

12 *Mem û Zîn*, critical edition by M.B. Rudenko (Akademija Nauk SSSR, Moskva, 1962) pp. 30–5. The passage sounds so modern that one wonders whether it could be a later interpolation. However, the manuscripts on which the cited edition is based, though not very old, predate the emergence of modern nationalism.

13 On the factions in these early Kurdish organizations, and the issues dividing them, see also van Bruinessen 1978, pp. 369–76 and 1985, pp. 129–36.

14 On developments in the Kurdish movement in Turkey during the 1970s and 1980s, see van Bruinessen 1986 and 1988a.

15 See Kutschera 1979; Chaliand 1980; McDowall 1985 and Hyman 1988 for general overviews; Jawad 1981 and Ibrahim 1983 specifically for Iraq; van Bruinessen 1984 and 1988a; and Laber and Whitman 1988 for Turkey; van Bruinessen 1981 and 1986 and Entessar 1984 for Iran. Recent developments can be followed through the useful bi-monthly bulletin of news clippings *Bulletin de Liason et d'Information* published by the Kurdish Institute of Paris.

16 The KDP was the party which, with Mulla Mustafa Barzani as its president, led the Turkish movement until its collapse in 1975. With

the defeat, the party disintegrated and several of its former leaders established new, mutually competing, political formations. Barzani's sons Idris and Mas'ud, based in Iran, attempted to resuscitate the KDP (initially under the name of "Provisional Leadership of the KDP"), this was mainly supported by Kurmanji-speaking, tribal elements from northernmost Iraq. Barzani's long-time rival, Jalal Talabani, initially based in Syria, established the PUK, which drew support from Sorani speakers further to the south. Two of Barzani's right-hand men, Mahmud Osman and Sami Abd al-Rahman, also established their own, more ephemeral parties.

17 On the Turkish reactions to the arrival of these refugees, their treatment and the political problems their presence generated, see Aslan 1988.

18 Abd al-Rahman Ghassemlou and two other representatives of the KDP-Iran were shot dead even while they were negotiating with the representatives of the Iranian government. The precise circumstances of the murders remain unclear, since the Iranian negotiators left the country without being properly interrogated by the police. Iran accused Iraq of the murders, but the evidence strongly suggests that the Iranians helped the unidentified murderer to enter the building. See the careful journalistic investigation by Marc Kravetz in the Paris daily *Libération*, 7 August 1989.

19 In 1990, the PKK was accused of two violent attacks on Kurdish villages in which tens of innocent civilians were killed. Unlike earlier attacks on families of "village guards", which it had proudly acknowledged, the PKK rejected responsibility for these attacks and claimed that they were deliberate provocations by Turkish security troops, a view that appears to be shared by the Turkish Human Rights Associations.

20 See the observations by the Polish anthropologist Leszek Dziegiel (1981), who worked on one of these development projects

21 Medico International mentions fifteen strategic villages, housing between 20,000 and 40,000 people each (1990, p. 63).

4 Humanitarian legal order and the Kurdish question

1 Wilson, H.A. (1988) *International Law and the Use of Force by National Liberation Movements*, Clarendon Press, Oxford, p. 36.

2 Higgins, R. (1972) International Law and Civil Conflict, in E. Luard (ed.), *The International Regulation of Civil Wars*, Thames & Hudson, London, pp. 160, 170–1.

3 Wilson 1988, pp. 25–8, 36–7.

4 Wilson 1988, p. 27.

5 Were the argument to be pursued and the Kurds to be considered belligerents in any of the states under consideration, all the provisions of the four 1949 Geneva Conventions would apply to the conflict, Iran, Iraq, Turkey and Syria all being States Parties.

6 The 1949 Geneva Conventions were ratified by Iran on 20 February 1957, Syria on 2 November 1953, Turkey 10 February 1954 and acceded to by Iraq on 14 February 1956.

7 On 21 March 1986 a UN Security Council statement (S/PV.2667) stongly condemned the use by Iraqi forces of chemical weapons against Iranian forces in the Iran–Iraq war, while on 26 August 1988 the UN Security Council adopted a resolution condemning the use of such weapons in the same conflict.

8 Wilson, 1988, pp. 2, 45 suggests that Article 3 was a substantial step, states for the first time declaring international responsibility in internal conflict.

9 (1958) Stevens & Sons, London, pp. 15–16.

10 Wilson 1988, pp. 2, 47.

11 Wilson 1988, pp. 47; see also Bond, J.E. (1974) *The Rules of Riot*, Princeton University Press, Princeton, p. 123 with respect to Pakistan and Ceylon.

12 Wilson 1988, p. 47.

13 Article 1: "the High Contracting Parties undertake to respect and to ensure respect for the present Convention in all circumstances".

14 Wilson 1988, p. 136: "The authority of national liberation movements to use force is not agreed upon as a matter of international law. Such authority is actively supported by the newly independent States and the Eastern bloc States, but has never been accepted by an established government confronting a liberation movement, or by the Western States. Practice in the UN particularly the Declaration on the Principles of International law and the Declaration on Aggression, both adopted without vote, does not resolve the fundamental differences over the status of national liberation movements and the extent of their authority as a matter of law. However, the trend over the last four decades and since 1960 in particular, has been toward the extension of the authority to use force in national liberation movements." See, generally, Wilson, pp. 91–136 and also Asmal, K. (1983). The Legal Status of National Liberation Movements with Particular Reference to South Africa, *Zambia Law Journal*, 15, pp. 37, 45–50.

15 The ICCPR was ratified by Iran on 24 January 1975 and Syria and Iraq, both with reservations, on 21 April 1969 and 25 January 1971.

16 See, for example, General Assembly Resolution 2625 (XXV), the Declaration of Principles of International Law Concerning Friendly Relations and Co-operation among States in Accordance with the Charter of the United Nations, adopted by consensus in 1970; The Helsinki Declaration; Resolution 1514 (XV) UNGA, 14 December 1960, Declaration on Colonialism.

17 Wilson 1988, pp. 58–78; *Western Sahara Advisory Opinion*, ICJ Rep 1975, pp. 12, 31–3; *Namibia Advisory Opinion*, ICJ Rep 1971, pp. 3, 31.

18 Crawford, J. (1979) *The Creation of States*, Clarendon Press, Oxford, pp. 84–106, 356–84.

19 See, UNGA Resolution 1541 (XV), 15 December 1960: "The authors of the Charter . . . had in mind that Chapter XI should be applicable to territories which were then known to be of the colonial type".

20 Nanda, V.P. (1972) Self Determination in International Law, *AJIL*, 66, p. 321; Nawaz, M.K. (1971) Editorial Comment: Bangladesh and

International Law, *Indian Law Journal*, 11, p. 251.

21 McNemar, D.W. (1971) The Post Independence War in the Congo, in Falk, R. (ed.), *The International Law of Civil War*, Johns Hopkins University Press, London, p. 244; Riesman, M. (1973) Humanitarian Intervention to Protect the Ibos, in Lillich, R. (ed.), *Humanitarian Intervention and the United Nations*, University of Virginia Press, Charlottesville, p. 167.

22 Sim, R. (1980) Kurdistan: The Search for Recognition, *Conflict Studies*, 124; Harris, G.S. (1981) Ethnic Conflict and the Kurds, *Annals of the American Academy*, p. 112; McDowall, D. (1989) *The Kurds*, London, Minority Rights Group, no. 23. This cultural, linguistic and religious disunity is paralleled by Kurdish political divisiveness which makes it almost impossible to locate a unified struggle for self-determination.

23 Kintominas, P. (1984) Can the Right to "Self-determination" in International Human Rights Instruments be Used to Advance the Position of Indigenous People? Sydney University, Sydney, unpublished, reaches the conclusion that the Kurds are a people for the purposes of self-determination.

24 Wilson 1988, pp. 151–62.

25 Bothe, M. (1982) Article 3 and Protocol 11: Case Studies of Nigeria and El Salvador, *American University Law Review*, 31, p. 899.

26 For the background to this provision see Cassese, A. (1967) A Tentative Appraisal of the Old and New Humanitarian Law of Armed Conflict, in Cassese, A. (ed.), *The New Humanitarian Law of Armed Conflict*, 1, Editoriale Scientifica, Naples, p. 467.

27 Accession on 14 November 1983, although Iran has signed. The conflict must be against a High Contracting Party for the Article to apply: Article 96(3).

28 Article 96(3).

29 Article 43.

30 Fleiner-Gerster, T. and Meyer, M. (1985) New Developments in Humanitarian Law: A Challenge to the Concept of Sovereignty, *International and Comparative Law Quarterly*, 34, pp. 267, 275, suggest that the Article is, in practice, limited to those confronting the governments of Israel and South Africa.

31 Wilson 1988, pp. 173–8.

32 See, for example, the FLN which in 1960 sent an instrument of accession to all four Geneva Conventions to the Swiss government. Various other liberation movements have declared their intention to abide by the Conventions and Protocols: ANC, 28 November 1980, SWAPO, 25 August 1981; EPLF, 25 February 1977; UNITA, 25 July 1980; ANLF, 24 December 1981; Hezbi Islami, 7 November 1980; Islamic Society of Afghanistan, 6 January 1960; See, further, Wilson, 1988, p. 171 and Asmal, K. (1983), The Legal Status of National Liberation Movements, *Zambia Law Journal*, 15, pp. 37, 55–7, which describes the position of the ANC and SWAPO with regard to the Conventions and Protocol on Non International Armed Conflicts, *International and Comparative Law Quarterly*, 30, p. 416.

33 Asmal, K. 1983, p. 55.
34 Meron, T. (1987) The Geneva Conventions as Customary Law, *American Journal of International Law*, 81, pp. 348, 350–1.
35 Cassesse, A. (1981) The Status of Rebels Under the 1977 Geneva Protocol on Non-International Armed Conflicts, *International and Comparative Law Quarterly*, 30, p. 416.
36 Cassesse, op. cit., p. 419.
37 With respect to the Red Cross see Veuthey, M. (1983), Implementation and Enforcement of Humanitarian Law and Human Rights Law in Non-International Armed Conflicts: the Role of the International Committee of the Red Cross, *American University Law Review*, 33, pp. 83, 92–3. See also Wilson, note 1, pp. 2, 137–46. Note also the attempts of the PLO to be admitted to WHO.
38 The Convention on the Prevention and Punishment of Genocide, 1948, has been ratified by Turkey, Syria, Iran and Iraq. The Convention on the Elimination of All Forms of Racial Discrimination has been ratified by Iran, Iraq and Syria, while Turkey has signed the 1988 Convention on Protection for Torture or other Cruel, Inhuman or Degrading Treatment or Punishment.
39 Cameron, I. (1988) Turkey and Article 25 of the European Convention on Human Rights, *International and Comparative Law Quarterly*, 37, p. 887.
40 Hampson, F. (1989) Human Rights and Humanitarian Law in Internal Conflicts in Meyer, M.A., *Armed Conflict and the New Law: Aspects of the 1977 Geneva Protocols and the 1981 Weapons Convention*, British Institute of International and Comparative Law, London, p. 55.
41 This mechanism has been invoked in the context of both Greece and Turkey: Denmark, Norway, Sweden and the Netherlands v Greece, 3321–3/67; 3344/67; YB 12 bis; France, Norway, Denmark, Sweden, the Netherlands v Turkey 9940–9944/82, 35 D & R 143 with respect to torture. The Commission found Greece had violated the provisions of the Convention, but Greece withdrew from the organization, while Turkey reached a "friendly settlement" with the complaining states, giving assurances.
42 Hampson, F. (1989) Using International Human Rights Machinery to Promote Respect for International Humanitarian Law, unpublished, suggests that although the existing machinery as represented by the UN Sub-Commission on the Prevention of Discrimination and Protection of Minorities and the UN Commission on Human Rights have proved to be unwilling to act in the context of the Kurds, refusing to pass a resolution condemning the use of gas by Iraq against the Kurds (Decision on Human Rights, 45th Session, 1989/111: Situation of Human Rights in Iraq – to take no decision on draft resolution 1989/L. 82) this does not mean that all such machinery will refuse to act. She cites particularly the monitoring body under the ICCPR which could prove to be a more useful forum. This body, unlike the Commission, is comprised of independent experts. Hampson suggests that this Committee be used in concert with an effective monitoring and informing strategy, roles which could be played by national and

international non-governmental organizations, even individuals. This suggestion is a valuable one and these tactics need not be confined to this Committees, but could be used equally with respect to other independent monitoring Committees, such as the Committee set up under the Convention to Eliminate All Forms of Discrimination Against Women, 1979, or the new Convention on the Rights of the Child. A useful indication of how such tactics can be used in another context, which could be drawn on by those interested in the Kurdish problem, can be seen in Byrnes, A. (1989), The "Other" Human Rights Treaty Body: The Work of the Committee on the Elimination of Discrimination Against Women, *Yale Journal of International Law*, 14, p. 1. It is to be noted that, in its most recent session, however, the Human Rights Commission did authorize an investigation of the Human Rights situation in Iraq.

5 Political aspects of the Kurdish problem in contemporary Turkey

1 This chapter was translated into English from the original French for this volume (ed.).
2 For these aspects, see Seker, M., *Güneydoğu Anadolu Projesi*, Siyasal ve Ekonomik Sorunlar, Istanbul, 1987, V. Yayınları; Jafer, M.R., *Underdevelopment: a Regional Case Study of the Kurdish Area in Turkey*, Helsinki, 1976, Painoprint Oy; Nezan, K. La culture kurde en Turquie à l'épreuve du second choc, *Studia Kurdica*, 7–12, 1988, pp. 63–76.
3 Cf. Libaridian, G. Etude des relations arméno-kurdes et leurs problèmes, *Studia Kurdica*, 1–5, 1988, pp. 63–76.
4 See my article, Traditionalism or Nationalism: Kurdish Responses to the Kemalist Regime, *CEMOTI* (Paris), 6, June 1988, pp. 107–28.
5 See my article, Les révoltes kurdes en Turquie kemaliste (Quelques aspects), *Guerres mondiales et conflits contemporains*, 151, 1988, pp. 121–36.
6 Thus P. Gentizon could write in 1937 that "Insofar as one can judge, the Kurdish issue is really one of policing". Cited in Rambeau, L., *Les Kurdes et le droit*, Paris, 1937, p. 37.
7 On this see Beşikçi, I., *Doğu Anadolu'nun Düzeni*, Istanbul, 1969, E. Yayınları, pp. 131–32.
8 See Ahmad, F. and B.T., *Türkiye' de Çok Partili Politikanın Açıklamalı Kronolojisi 1945–1971*, Ankara, 1976, Bilgi Yayınları, p. 266.
9 On this party, see Vedat, S., *Türkiye' de Kürtçülük Hareketleri ve İsyanlar*, Ankara, 1980, Kon Yayınları.
10 Beşikçi, I., *Doğu Anadolu'nun Düzeni*, Istanbul, 1969, E. Yayınları, pp. 131–2.
11 For these centres see *DDKO Dava Dosyası*, Ankara, 1976, Komal Yayınları; and Diyarbakır Askeri Sıkıyönetim Savcılığı, *DDKO Davası, Gerekçeli Karar*, Diyarbakır, 1972.
12 Most notably M. Zana who was elected mayor of Diyarbakır and who is still in prison.

13   On the PKK see van Bruinessen, M., Between Guerilla War and Political Murder: the Workers Party of Kurdistan, *MERIP Reports*, July–August 1988, pp. 40–6.

14   See, for example, the accounts of the terror contained in the Annals of *Cumhuriyet* between 1978 and 1980.

15   See the dossier in *Güneş ne Zaman Doğacak*, Yeni Ülke, 9, 1989.

16   For further details on the Kemalist attitude towards the Kurdish problem see my Mémoire for EHESS, Le Problème national kurde en Turquie kemaliste, prepared under the supervision of R. Paris, September 1986.

17   By this term I mean an underlying force which is often lacking in formal structure but is always supra-political and which often determines the major policy choices of the state itself. This party includes some Kemalist propagandists, the secret police, part of the bureaucracy and, of course, the army.

18   Preface by C. Gürsel to Fırat, M.S., *Doğu İlleri ve Varto Tarihi*, MEB Yayınları, 1961, Ankara.

19   Beşikçi, op. cit., pp. 328–36.

20   N. Atsız, quoted in *Yeni Akis*, 1, August 1966.

21   Ismail Cem, *Türkiye Röportajları*, Istanbul, 1970, Cem Yayınları.

22   See *CIA, MIT ve Kontr-Gerilla*, Istanbul, 1979, Aydınlık Yayınları.

23   See the verdict of the military tribunal at Diyarbakir, *DDKO Davası Gerekçeli Karar*, Diyarbakir, 1972.

24   See the recollections and comments of one such person; in Ayvaz, I., *Buhranın Kaynağında*, Istanbul, 1980, Ötüken Yayınları.

25   See Birand, M.A., *12 Eylül, Saat:04;00*, where he also tries to analyse the mentality of the "guardians of the regime", Istanbul, 1985, Milliyet Yayınları.

26   For these manoeuvres, see Öymen, O. *Türkiye' de Anarşi*, Istanbul, 1979, Aydınlık Yayınları, p. 101.

27   See, for example, *Le Chronique de l'Amnistie Internationale*, February 1989.

28   See, for example, *Hürriyet*, 21.4.81, for the case of the administration of the town of Mardin, and 4–5 of the journal *Demokrat*, published in Norway, 1981, p. 8.

29   *Cumhuriyet*, 15.2.88; Tercüman, 11.2.86; Milliyet, 3.4.86.

30   *Yeni Gündem*, 21.2.88.

31   *Info-Turk*, October 1984; *Libération*, 17.10.84; *Milliyet*, 18.10.84; *Tercüman*, 26.2.88; *Cumhuriyet*, 26.2.87.

32   See the interview with Talabani in *Hürriyet*, 11.10.88.

33   *Le Monde*, 26.10.84; *Tercüman*, 22.10.84; *Bulletin de Liaison et d'Information* of the Kurdish Institute in Paris, 28, July 1987.

34   Artunkal, T., *La vie politique turque*, Cahiers de la Pastorale des Migrants, 31, 1988, p. 30.

35   Particularly *Medya Güneşi* and *Özgürlüklü Gelecek*.

36   *Milliyet*, 22.7.87.

37   *Yeni Gündem*, 26.4.87.

38   *2000'e Doğru*, 1.7.87; 13.12.87.

39   Kirka, C. Uslanmayanın Hakkı, *Hürriyet*, 13.10.88.

40 See the special issue of the *Bulletin de Liaison et d'Information* of the Kurdish Institute in Paris, Mme Mitterrand au Kurdistan, May 1989.
41 In 1975 Ecevit described all Kurdish ethnic demands as racist.
42 *Cumhuriyet*, 6.9.88.
43 See *Tempo*, 42, 1988.
44 See the interview with N. Yılmaz in *Tempo*, 42, 1988, pp. 26–7.
45 Cf. *Bulletin de Liaison et d'Information*, 43–6, 1989.
46 The inhabitants of this village were forced to eat human excrement. A trial is still pending. Cf. *Cumhuriyet*, 25.1.89.
47 *2000'e Doğru*, 11.9.88 and *Cumhuriyet*, 9.4.87.
48 Cf. M. Barzani in *Tempo*, 8.9.88 and J. Talabani in *2000'e Doğru*, 11.9.88.
49 Y. Döğün in *Cumhuriyet*, 16.9.88.
50 M.A. Birand, *Tempo*, 18.9.88.
51 Cf. KFD-S, 'Facts about Kurdish refugees from Iraq in Turkey, Stockholm, 1989, *Bulletin de Liaison et d'Information*, 43–5; Bozarslan, H., Kurdish Refugees as Agents of Social Change, *Arbeitsheft*, Berliner Institut für vergleichende Sozialforschung.
52 ANAP is the Motherland Party (Anavatan Partisi), SHP the Social Democratic Popular Party (Sosyal Demokrat Halkçı Parti), DYP the True Path Party (Doğru Yol Partisi) and RP the Welfare Party (Refah Partisi).
53 The MÇP is the Nationalist Labour Party (Milliyetçi Calışma Partisi).
54 See my report Kurdologie pa Turkiska, *Svensk-Kurdisk Journal*, (Stockholm), 3, 1985.
55 Gellner, E., *Muslim Society*, Cambridge, London and New York, Cambridge University Press, 1985, p. 60.
56 *2000'e Doğru*, 13.9.87, p. 32; C. Başangıç *Kanlı Bilmece: Güney Doğu*, V. Yayınları, 1988.
57 *Milliyet*, 15.1.86.
58 This is the name given to the faction of the ANAP closest to the extreme right. It particularly brings together many of the former powers-behind-the-throne.
59 Postscript (August 1990): Since the time of writing several things in Turkey have changed dramatically. The conflict between the authorities and the PKK has nearly assumed the dimensions of civil war, and the following of the PKK has increased considerably, as has that of the Islamic Party of Kurdistan. Official Turkish policies, however, continue to maintain a balance between the influence of the "Party of State" and considerations of political regionalism.

6 The situation of Kurds in Iraq and Turkey: current trends and prospects

1 See: Nasser, M.H. (1985), "Iraq: Ethnic Minorities and their Impact on Politics", *Journal of South Asian and Middle Eastern Studies*, 8, (3), p. 25.
2 This point was mentioned on various occasions by the leaders of the ruling Ba'th Party in public speeches, in particular by President Ahmad

Hasan Al-Bakr (ruled 1968–79).

3   The point was highlighted in a report by the League of Nations. See: The League of Nations, *A Report Submitted to the League of Nations by the Council Resolution of the 30th September, 1924*, p. 90.

4   In fact, Britain doubled the amount of credit made available to the Iraqi government shortly after the Halabja massacre.

5   During the Israeli raid on Lebanon in 1982, various Kurdish organizations, chiefly the PKK (Kurdish Workers Party) announced the loss of comrades fighting against advancing Israeli troops. It seems more likely that these individuals were receiving training in Palestinian camps when the Israeli incursion occurred.

6   Many would regard the Yazidis as part of the Kurdish people (ed.).

7   When Ba'th returned to power in Iraq in 1968, one of the two communist parties in Iraq (Iraqi Communist Party, "Armed Struggle") was led by Aziz (Ali Haydar) al-Haj, a Faili Kurd from Baghdad. Another Faili Kurd, again from Baghdad, Habib (Mohammed Karim) al-Faili, was the Secretary of the Kurdistan Democratic Party of Iraq until 1975.

7 The Kurdish movement in Iraq: 1975–88

1   In this perspective, so-called "Kurdish cultural rights in Iraq" can be considered to be the result of this traditionalist/modernist alliance, historically achieved, rather than a voluntary creation of the current Iraqi regime, as the latter occasionally pretends: the right of schooling in the Kurdish language in primary schools, which was obtained in 1931, as well as the operation of Kurdish publishing houses, was the result of a series of petitions sent by the Kurds to the League of Nations in 1929, criticizing the Iraqi government for not implementing the measures promised to the Kurds by the League in 1925. The foundation of the Centre for Kurdish Studies at the University of Baghdad in 1959 was achieved after the legalization of the KDP following the collapse of the monarchy in 1958. The opening of Kurdish language high schools (1970) and the creation of the Kurdish Academy (1973), were the result of the peace treaty of 1970, signed between Mustafa Barzani and the current Iraqi regime.

2   Two important dates have to be recalled. In 1970, an Iraqi–Kurdish accord was reached. The KDP, led by Barzani, represented the Kurdish position. The accord consisted of a project of Kurdish autonomy, to be proclaimed within four years. But in 1974, the year in which an autonomous Iraqi Kurdistan was to be proclaimed, the two parties failed to reach agreement. The KDP demanded a centralized Kurdish administration, endowed with economic autonomy through sharing of revenues from the oil fields located in Kurdish regions, especially the rich zone of Kirkuk. These demands were ignored by the Iraqi government, which proclaimed a law that granted Kurdistan only very restricted autonomy, since it made it directly dependent on Baghdad. This led to a new and a violent front war. This war, as is well known, was terminated by a political agreement between Iran and Iraq, stipulating a halt to all Iranian aid to the Kurdish movement. The movement, which

for several decades had depended on the charisma of Mustafa Barzani, collapsed within a week. Beginning in April 1975, for the first time in decades Iraqi Kurdistan was completely occupied by the Iraqi army.

3 It should be added that some Iraqi non-Kurdish groups have found refuge and protection in the Kurdish mountains. These include the Iraqi Communist Party, in opposition to the Iraqi government since 1979, and the pro-Syrian Ba'th Party, which entered the opposition and began operating in Kurdistan in the early 1980s.

4 A large proportion of this tribe was exterminated by the Iraqi government in 1983. It should also be mentioned that another proportion of Barzani tribesmen is known to constitute the main support of one of the three Islamic parties, Hizbullah Kurd, led by Shaikh Khalid, Mas'ud's uncle. He is also considered a Barzani tribal leader.

8 The Kurds in Syria and Lebanon

1 For some relevant publications see the list of references below. See also further works by I.C. Vanly cited in this chapter.

2 See the nine classical authors edited, with Arabic text, in eight volumes, by M.J. de Goeje, *Bibliotheca Geographorum Arabicorum* (hereafter *BGA*) Leiden, 1870–93 (2nd edition, 1906). See also Guy Le Strange, *The Lands of the Eastern Caliphate*, London, 1905 (which includes some useful maps).

3 See references by I.C. Vanly, in "Regards sur l'histoire des Kurdes . . .", *Studia Kurdica*, Institut Kurde de Paris, autumn 1980.

4 See *BGA*, *Géographie d'Aboulfeda*, or *Taqwīm al-Buldān*, Arabic text edited with an introduction in French by M. Reinaud, Paris, 1840.

5 For more details see Jean Pichon, *Le partage du Proche-Orient*, Paris, 1938.

6 The official minutes of this conference were published by the French Ministère des affaires étrangères under the title *Documents diplomatiques: Conférence de Lausanne*, Paris, 1923. Excerpts from the minutes are cited, with commentary, in I.C. Vanly, *Le Kurdistan irakien entité nationale*, Neuchatel, 1970 (the published version of my doctoral thesis, *La Question nationale du Kurdistan irakien: étude de la révolution de 1961*, University of Lausanne).

7 I.C. Vanly, "The Kurds in Syria" (published under the pseudonym Mustafa Nazdar) in G. Chaliand (ed.) *People without a Country*, London, 1980.

8 Steven Runciman, *A History of the Crusades*, vol. I, Cambridge, 1951 (repr. 1980), p. 269.

9 Amin Maalouf, *Les Croisades vues par les Arabes*, Paris, 1983, p. 57.

10 Carsten Niebuhr, *Reisebeschreibungen nach Arabien und anderen umliegenden Ländern* (4 vols), Kopenhagen, 1774–8, vol. II. (French edition, Amsterdam, 1776, English edition, Edinburgh, 1792.)

11 N. Elisséeff, *Nûr ad-Dîn, un grand prince musulman de Syrie au temps des croisades* (3 vols), Damascus, Institut Français de Damas, 1967, vol. III, p. 836.

12 Idem, vol. III, pp. 605–7, 721 ff.
13 A. Raymand (ed.) Paris, 1980, p. 103. This authoritative work was sponsored by the CNRS.
14 The 1970 census gave the population of Syria then as 6,305,000.
15 In 1933, about 9,000 Christian Assyrians forcibly expelled from Iraq were settled by the French among the Kurds in the Jazira, but the majority later emigrated to Europe or the United States. Most of the Christians living in the region at present are merchants and have close ties with the Kurds.
16 *La Syrie*, p. 13.
17 See "Les tribus montagnardes . . .", *Bulletin d'études orientales*, 6, 1936, pp. 9–10.
18 W.R. Hay, *Two Years in Kurdistan*, London, 1921. Hay wrote (p. 92): "Where Kurdish and Arabic villages adjoin, we find the former with their available acreage fully cultivated and asking for more, while the Arabs have only scratched the soil in a few placess and left the rest of their village lands fallow. The result is that the Kurds are continually expanding at their expense, and I have little doubt that they will eventually squeeze them out of the district."
19 If my memory serves me correctly, the Kurd-Dagh is represented by five members of the Syrian parliament, all of them Kurds.
20 C. Bedir-Khan is the posthumous co-author with the French Kurdologist Roger Lescot of an extensive *Grammaire kurde, dialecte kurmandji*, Paris, 1970. A German edition was published in Bonn in 1986 as *Kurdische Grammatik*.
21 In 1952 Dr Bedir-Khan left Beirut for Paris where he became Professor of Kurdish at the French National Institute of Oriental Languages and Civilisations (INALCO). It was at his instigation that the present writer joined the Institute to teach Kurdish civilization from 1959 to 1962.
22 Beirut, 1986.
23 Musalli correctly cites (p. 233) as Kurds or of "Kurdish origin": the first Syrian prime minister, Abd al-Rahman Pasha al-Yousef (originally from Damascus) under King Faysal in 1920; and ministers of different periods, including Mohamed Kurd-Ali (a leading historian), Hussain Ibesh, and Ali Bozo (all from Damascus), and Rashad Barmada (from Aleppo). After independence, three instigators of the *coup d'état* who became chiefs of state were of Kurdish origin: Marshal Husni al-Za'im (from Damascus) in 1949, Colonel Adib al-Shishakly (from Hama) in 1951, and shortly afterwards, Colonel Fawzi Silo (originally from Kurd-Dagh). Marshal al-Za'im's prime minister was a Kurd from Hama, Husni Barazi, while Colonel Shishakly had as his prime minister Husni's brother, Dr Mohsen Barazi, a university professor who had worked with Prince Celadet on the latinization of the Kurdish alphabet.
24 Information that placed the numbers of these "Kurdish infiltrators" at 120,000 was supplied to me by the KDPS.
25 My own family home in the Kurdish quarter of Damascus was among those covered in anti-Kurdish graffiti at that time.

26 The oil production of Qarachok was 9.7 million tonnes in 1986, more than sufficient for Syrian home consumption. Since then better-quality oil has been extracted in the Arab area of Deirezzor.

27 Musalli, *'Arab wa-Akrad*, p. 455.

28 Other sources give a figure of 17,000.

29 These manoeuvres provoked a protest note from Mr Gromyko, then Soviet minister of foreign affairs, "against the military intervention by Syria in northern Iraq", which was delivered to the Syrian Ambassador in Moscow on 9 July 1963. For further details, see Vanly, *Le Kurdistan irakien entité nationale*, pp. 208–10.

30 See the organ of the Syrian army, published in Damascus, *Al-Jundi* (*The Soldier*), 636, 14 January 1964.

31 I.C. Vanly, *The Persecution of the Kurdish People by the Baath Dictatorship in Syria*, subtitled, *The Syrian Mein Kampf against the Kurds*, Amsterdam, 1968 (38 pp.).

32 I.C. Vanly, *Interview sur le Kurdistan et la Question Kurde*, given in 1959 in my capacity as chairman of the *New Observer* in Athens, published in French and Greek, Athens, 1960 (32 pp).

33 Judgment no. 23 of the Court of the Military Governor, published in the official records of the Syrian Arab Republic dated 3 July 1965. I only knew of the judgment a year later.

34 See *Le Monde* of 14–15 January 1990 for an article on "L'Euphrate de la discorde".

35 See Charles Saint-Prot, *Les Mysterès syriens*, Paris, 1984, which takes a pro-Iraqi Ba'th stand.

36 It was reported that the Kurdish soldiers in Hama spared the life of any inhabitant who claimed to be a Kurd or of Kurdish descent.

37 In addition to those of my works already mentioned, see on the Kurdish situation in Syria, Vanly, "The Kurdish Problem in Syria: Plans for the Genocide of a National Minority" (in English and French), published by the Committee for the Defence of Kurdish People's Rights; and *Kurdistan und die Kurden*, Band 3, Göttingen, 1988.

38 More detailed information is given in the work of the Kurdish historian Mohamad Amn Zaki on Kurdistan's history, published in Arabic translation by Mohamed Ali Awni, Cairo, 1945.

39 See on this subject, Vanly, *Kurdistan und die Kurden*, Band 3.

40 "Akrad Lubnan: tanzimuhum al-ijtima'i wa'l-siyasi", (c. 300 pp.) Lebanese University of Beirut (unpublished).

41 Details of the case are given in the thesis cited in the preceding note.

42 See Michel Seurat (1980) *Les Populations l'état, la societé*, pp. 87–141.

43 The three Jazira MPs are: Fuad Aliko (secretary of the "People's Union", Hamid Derwish (secretary of the "Progressive KDPS") and Kamal Ahmed (secretary of the KDPS).

9 The development of nationalism in Iranian Kurdistan

1 It was the tribal armed men, together with the armed forces brought in by Mustafa Barzani, which made up the Republic's army.
2 On this see further Anderson 1983. Nairn (1977), *The Break-up of Britain*, NLB, London, offers similar reasons for the absence of Scottish nationalism.
3 The term "cultural autonomy" was not clearly defined. It was assumed to imply a recognition of the Kurdish language, and of the status of the Kurds as a religious minority.
4 At Ghassemlou's funeral on 20 July 1989 at Père Lachaise in Paris, Mr Abdollah Hassanzadeh, a member of the political office of the KPDI, revealed some details of the assassination, and announced the party's general policies after Ghassemlou's death.

10 The Kurds in the Soviet Union

1 This chapter is a greatly condensed version of a monograph-length paper on the subject which, it is to be hoped, the author will publish in full elsewhere (ed.).
2 Cf. Jalil, Jalil, *The Kurdish Uprising of 1880*, Moscow, 1966 (in Russian); Beirut 1979 (in Arabic). Cf. also HM Government's *Blue Book*, London, 1881.
3 Zaki, Mohamed Amin, *A Short History of the Kurds and Kurdistan*, Dar al-Islami, Baghdad, 1931 (in Sorani Kurdish); Arabic translation by Awni, M. Ali, Cairo, 1936, (repr. London, 1961).
4 The ethnic composition of Transcaucasia was complex. By 1917, Georgians numbered 1.4 million, almost all within Georgia itself; Armenians totalled 1.7 million, throughout Russia with approximately 1 million in Transcaucasia: Tatars, of whom a significant number lived in Armenia, numbered about 2 million. The latter, known since 1920 as Azeris, formed the Muslim Turkic-speaking population of Transcaucasia and Azerbaijan. Russian statistics of the period provide the following approximate figures. For the province of Yerevan in 1916 a total of 1,220,242 comprising Armenians (669,871), Tatars (373,582), Kurds (36,508), Russians (16,103), Gypsies (12,642). Yerevan, the capital, was relatively small with a population of 30,000. Baku (pop. 260,000) included 79,000 Russians, 69,300 Tatars (mostly workers and artisans) and 63,000 Armenians (mainly in industry and commerce). Tbilisi (in 1897) had a total population of 159,000 comprised of approximately 60,500 Armenians, 42,000 Georgians and 39,000 Russians. In 1916, the province of Nakhichevan comprised a total population of 135,000 broadly divided between 54,000 Armenians and 81,000 Kurds and Tatars. (Figures according to Anahide Ter Minassian, *La République d'Arménie*, Paris, 1989. Cf. Y. Ternom, *La Cause arménienne*, Paris, 1982.)
5 Mihoyi, S.K. "The Kurdish Question in Soviet Azerbaijan", originally published in Russian. Translation into Kurdish by Bavê Nazê in *Berbang*, 59, August 1989.

6 Mihoyi quotes a letter from Lenin to N. Narimanov, Secretary of the
   Baku Communist Party (Lenin, *Works*, vol. 4, pt. 3, p. 100).

7 Carrère d'Encausse, H., *La Gloire des nations ou la fin de l'empire
   soviétique*, Paris, 1990, p. 90.

8 Carrère d'Encausse, p. 132.

9 In spite of this, Soviet studies of the Kurds in Azerbaijan and
   autonomous Kurdistan were published in the 1930s, e.g. Bukchpan,
   K., *Azerbaijanskiye Kurdy*, Baku, 1924 and K. Pchelina's "Po Kurdis-
   tanskomu uyezdu Azerbaijana", *Sovyetskaya Etnografiya*, 4, 1932,
   pp. 108–21. Bennigsen (1960) also mentions studies by G.F. Chursin
   and B.V. Miller.

10 Letter published in *Bulletin* of the Institut Kurde de Paris, October–
   December issue 1989.

11 On the Kurds in Turkmenia see Sokolova, V., *Kurdskiy Yazyk*, Ch. 2,
   Moscow-Leningrad, 1953, on Khorasanian Kurmanji; Gubanov, S.M.
   in *Turkmenovedenie*, vols 5–6, Ashkabad, 1928; Kozuhov, A.,
   Machinskiy, B. and Pabet, E.I., *Sovyetskiy Turkmenistan*, Ashkabad,
   1930.

12 On the Georgian and Armenian Kurds see Lyayster, A.F. and Khrsin,
   G.F., *Geografiya Kavkasa*, Tbilisi, 1924, and *Geografiya Zakavkasa*,
   Tbilisi, 1929; Shaginyan, M., *Sovyetskoye Zakavkaze*, Leningrad,
   1931, pp. 33–50; Ambaryan, A., *Kordere Sovetakan Hayastanun (The
   Kurds in Soviet Armenia)*, Yerevan, 1957. A full bibliography is given
   by Bennigsen.

13 Unpublished thesis, "Vie, et oeuvre romanesque d'Erebe Şemo",
   INALCO Institut, Paris.

14 Isayev, M.I., *National Languages in the USSR: Problems and Solutions*, trans. P. Medov and I. Saiko, Moscow, 1977, pp. 63, 68–9.

15 For these and other statements, cf. Bavê Nazê, "*Kurdên sovyetistanê
   doza mafên xwe dikin*" (Soviet Kurds demand their Rights) in
   Berbang, 59, Stockholm, 1989.

16 *Pravda*, 17 August 1989.

17 *Berbang*, 66, Stockholm, September 1990. The text of the resolution
   was accompanied by an article on the conference by Dr Cemsid
   Heyderi. The August-September issue of Armanc also published it
   with an article by Bavê Nazê and a French version of the text
   appeared in the July *Bulletin* of the Institut Kurde in Paris.

18 Those held at Bremen in April 1989, at Paris in October of the same
   year and at Florence in March 1990.

Bibliography

Amnesty International (1990) Iraqi Kurds: at Risk of Forcible Repatriation from Turkey and Human Rights Violations in Iraq (AI Index: MDE 14/06/90), London.

Anderson, P. (1983) *Imagined Communities. Reflections on the Origins and Spread of Nationalism*, Verso & NLB, London.

Andrews, P.A. (1989) *Ethnic Groups in the Republic of Turkey*, Ludwig Reichert, Wiesbaden.

Anschütz, H. (1984) *Die syrischen Christen vom Tur 'Abdin*, Augustinus, Würzburg.

Anter, M. (1965) *Birîna Reś/Kara Yara [The Black Wound]*, Istanbul.

Aslan, M.A. (1988) *Kürt Mülteciler [Kurdish Refugees]*, Demokrasi yayinlari, Ankara.

Asmal, K. (1983) The Legal Status of National Liberation Movements with Particular Reference to South Africa, *Zambia Law Journal* 15.

Barth, F. (1953) *Principles of Social Organisation in Southern Kurdistan*, Brødrene Jørgensen, Oslo.

Barth, F. (1961) *Nomads of South Persia. The Basseri Tribe of the Khamseh Confederacy*, Allen & Unwin, London.

Batatu, H. (1978) *The Old Social Classes and the Revolutionary Movements of Iraq*, Princeton University Press, Princeton.

Bedir Khan Dj. and Lescot, R. (1970) *Grammaire kurde (dialecte kurmandji)*, Adrien Maisonneuve, Paris.

Bennigsen, A. (1960) Les Kurdes et la kurdologie en Union Soviétique, *Cahiers du monde russe et soviétique* 3, Ecole Pratique de Hautes Etudes, Paris.

Beşikçi, I. (1969) *Doğu Anadolu'nun düzeni [The Way Eastern Anatolia is Organized]*, E Yayınları, Istanbul.

Beşikçi, I. (1972) *Kürtlerin mecburi iskani [The Forced Settlement of the Kurds]*, Komal, Ankara.

Blau, J. (1965) *Le Kurde d'Amadiya et de Djabal Sindjar*, Klincksieck, Paris.

Blau, J. (1984) *Mémoires du Kurdistan. Recueil de la tradition littéraire orale et écrite*, Editions Findlaky, Paris.

Blau, J. (1989a) Le Kurde, in Schmitt, R. (ed.) *Compendium Linguarum*

Iranicarum, Ludwig Reichert, Wiesbaden.

Blau, J. (1989b) Gurânî et Zaza, in Schmitt, R. (ed.) *Compendium Linguarum Iranicarum*, Ludwig Reichert, Wiesbaden.

Bois, Th. (1986) Kurds and Kurdistān: History from 1920 to the present, in Bosworth, C.E. *et al.* (eds) *Encyclopaedia of Islam*, new edition, Tome V, Brill, Leiden.

Bond, J.E. (1974) *The Rules of Riot*, Princeton University Press, Princeton.

Bothe, M. (1982) Article 3 and Protocol 11: Case Studies of Nigeria and El Salvador, *American University Law Review* 31.

Bozarslan, H. (1988a) Traditionalism or Nationalism: Kurdish Responses to the Kemalist Regime, *CEMOTI* 6, Paris, pp. 107–28.

Bozarslan, H. (1988b) Les Revoltes kurdes en Turquie kemaliste (Quelques aspects), *Guerres mondiales et conflits contemporains* 151, pp. 121–36.

Bruinessen, M. van (1978) *Agha, Shaikh and State: On the Social and Political Organization of Kurdistan*, Thesis, State University of Utrecht (reprint 1987, Express Edition, Berlin).

Bruinessen, M. van (1981) Nationalismus und religiöser Konflikt: der kurdische Widerstand im Iran, in Greussing, K. (ed.) *Religion und Politik im Iran*, Syndikat, Frankfurt am Main.

Bruinessen, M. van (1983) Kurdish Tribes and the State of Iran: The Case of Simko's Revolt, in Tapper, R. (ed.) *The Conflict of Tribe and State in Iran and Afghanistan*, Croom Helm, London.

Bruinessen, M. van (1984) The Kurds in Turkey, *MERIP Reports* 121.

Bruinessen, M. van (1985) Vom Osmanismus zum Separatismus: religiöse und ethnische Hintergründe der Rebellion des Scheich Said, in Blaschke, J. and Bruinessen, M. van (eds) *Islam und Politik in der Türkei*, Express Edition, Berlin.

Bruinessen, M. van (1986) The Kurds between Iran and Iraq, *Middle East Report* 141.

Bruinessen, M. van (1988a) Between Guerrilla War and Political Murder: the Workers' Party of Kurdistan, *Middle East Report* 153.

Bruinessen, M. van (1988b) Les Kurdes et leur langue au XVIIème siècle: notes d'Evliya Çelebi sur les dialectes kurdes, *Studia Kurdica* I–5, Institut Kurde, Paris.

Bruinessen, M. van (1989a) The Ethnic Identity of the Kurds, in Andrews, P.A. (ed.) *Ethnic Groups in the Republic of Turkey*, Ludwig Reichert, Wiesbaden.

Bruinessen, M. van (1989b) *Agha, Scheich und Staat. Politik und Gesellschaft Kurdistans*, Parabolis, Berlin (revised translation of van Bruinessen 1978).

Bruinessen, M. van (1990) The Kurds of Turkey. Further Restrictions of Basic Rights, *The Review* (International Commission of Jurists) 45, pp. 46–52.

Byrnes, A. (1989) The "Other" Human Rights Treaty Body: The Work of the Committee on the Elimination of Discrimination Against Women, *Yale Journal of International Law* 14.

Cameron, I. (1988) Turkey and Article 25 of the European Convention on Human Rights, *International and Comparative Law Quarterly* 37.

Cassesse, A. (1967) *The New Humanitarian Law of Armed Conflict*, Editoriale Scientifica, Naples.

Cassesse, A. (1981) The Status of Rebels under the 1977 Geneva Protocol on Non-International Armed Conflicts, *International and Comparative Law Quarterly* 30.

Chabry, A. and L. (1987) *Minorités et politique au proche-Orient. Les raisons d'une explosion*, Maisonneuve & Larose, Paris.

Chaliand, G. (1978) *Les Kurdes et le Kurdistan. La Question nationale kurde au Proche-Orient*, Maspero, Paris.

Chaliand, G. (1980) *People without a Country, The Kurds and Kurdestan*, Zed Books, London.

Chevalier, M. (1985) *Les Montagnards chrétiens du Hakkâri et du Kurdistan septentrional*, Département de Géographie de l'Universite de Paris-Sorbonne, Paris.

Crawford, J. (1979) *The Creation of States*, Clarendon Press, Oxford.

Draper, G.I.A.D. (1958) *The Red Cross Conventions*, Stevens & Sons, London.

Driver, G.R. (1923), The Name Kurd and its Philological Connexions, *Journal of the Royal Asiatic Society*.

Dziegiel, L. (1981) *Rural Community of Contemporary Iraqi Kurdistan Facing Modernization*, Agricultural Academy, Crakow.

Eagleton, W. (1963) *The Kurdish Republic of 1946*, Oxford University Press, London.

Edmonds, C.J. (1925) A Kurdish Newspaper: *Rozh-i Kurdistan, Journal of the Royal Central Asian Society* 12.

Edmonds, C.J. (1957) *Kurds, Turks and Arabs*, Oxford University Press, London.

Edmonds, C.J. (1969) The Beliefs and Practices of the Ahl-i Haqq of Iraq, *Iran* 7.

Entessar, N. (1984) The Kurds in Post-Revolutionary Iran and Iraq, *Third World Quarterly* 6.

Esman, M.J. and Rabinovich, I. (1988) *Ethnicity, Pluralism and the State in the Middle East*, Cornell University Press, New York and London.

Eyyubi, K.R. and Smirnova, I.A. (1968) *Kurdskiy Dialekt Mukri*, Izdatel'stvo Nauka, Leningrad.

Falk, R. (1971) *The International Law of Civil War*, Johns Hopkins University Press, London.

Fany, M. (1933) *La Nation Kurde et son évolution sociale*, Paris.

Fırat, M.Ş. (1970) *Doğu illeri ve Varto Tarihi [Eastern Cities and the History of Varto]*, 3rd edn, Ankara.

Firuzan, T. (1983) *About the Composition and Structure of Tribes. Īlāt va 'Ašāyer*, Ketāb-e Âgāh, Tehran.

Fleiner-Gerster, T. and Meyer, M. (1985) New Developments in Humanitarian Law: A Challenge to the Concept of Sovereignty, *International and Comparative Law Quarterly* 34.

Franz, E. (1986) *Kurden und Kurdentum*, Deutsches Orient-Institut, Hamburg.

Gellner, E. (1983) *Nations and Nationalism*, Basil Blackwell, Oxford.

Ghassemlou, A.R. (1965), *Kurdistan and the Kurds*, Czechoslovak Academy of Sciences, Prague.

Guest, J.S. (1987) *The Yezidis. A Study in Survival*, KPI, London.

Hadank, K. (1930) *Mundarten der Gûrân*, Walter de Gruyter, Berlin.

Hadank, K. (1932) *Mundarten der Zâzâ*, Walter de Gruyter, Berlin.

al-Hamawandi, M. (1985) *Fikrat al-Hukm adh-Dhātī wa'l-Aqalliyyāt al-'Irāqiyya: Dirāsa Taṭbīqiyya fī'l-Waṭan al-'Arabī* (*The Idea of Autonomy and Ethnic Minorities: A Study Applied to the Arabic World*), Cairo.

Hampson, F. (1989) Using International Human Rights: Machinery to Promote Respect for International Humanitarian Law, unpublished paper.

Harris, G.S. (1981) Ethnic Conflict and the Kurds, Annals of the American Academy.

Hawrāmī, M.A. (1974) *Seretayēk le Fīlolozhī Zimanī Kurdī, al-Ma'ārif* [*A First Study of the Philology of the Kurdish Language*], Baghdad.

Hay, W.R. (1921) *Two Years in Kurdistan. Experiences of a Political Officer*, Sidgwick & Jackson, London.

Heinrich, L.A. (1988) Die Arbeiterpartei Kurdistans (PKK). Kult des Opfers und Kult der Tat als Programm, *Orient* (Hamburg) 29, pp. 423–39.

Hourani, A. (1947) *Minorities in the Arab World*, Oxford University Press, London.

Hütteroth, W.D. (1959) *Bergnomaden und Yaylabauern im mittleren kurdischen Taurus*, Diss. Marburg.

Hyman, A. (1988) *Elusive Kurdistan: The Struggle for Recognition*, Centre for Security and Conflict Studies, London.

Ibrahim, F. (1983) *Die kurdische Nationalbewegung im Irak. Eine Fallstudie zur Problematik ethnischer Konflikte in der Dritten Welt*, Klaus Schwarz, Berlin.

İnsan, Hakları Derneği [Human Rights Association] (1990), *Halepçe'den Kamplara... Kürtler... [From Halabia to the Camps... the Kurds...]*, Alan-Belge (and twelve other publishers), Istanbul.

Jawad, S. (1981) *Iraq and the Kurdish Question*, Ithaca Press, London.

Jebarī, A.M. (1970) *Mēzhūy Rozhnamegerī Kurdī [History of Kurdish Journalism]*, Zhīn, Sulaimaniya.

Joseph, J. (1961) *The Nestorians and their Muslim Neighbours*, Princeton University Press, Princeton.

Kaftancıoğlu, Ü. (1974) *Tüfekliler [Men with Guns]*, Remizi, Ankara.

King, R. (1987) *Irak–Iran: la guerre paralysée*, Edns Bosquets, Mayenne.

Kintominas, P. (1984) Can the Right to "Self-determination" in International Human Rights Instruments be Used to Advance the Position of Indigenous People? University of Sydney, unpublished paper, Sydney.

Kishavarz, A.H. (1985) *Some Aspects of the Social Structure and Economy of Iranian Tribes*, Centre for Iranian Documentation and Research, Paris.

Kudat, A. (1971) Ritual Kinship in Eastern Turkey, *Anthropological Quarterly* 44.

Kurdish Medical Association in Sweden (1989) *Facts about Kurdish*

Refugees from Iraq to Turkey, Stockholm.

Kurdo, Q. (1983) *Tarîxa Edebiyata Kurdî, Roja Nû* [History of Kurdish Literature], Stockholm.

Kurdoev, E. (1978) *Grammatika kurdskogo yazyka, na materiale dialektov kurmandji i sorani [A grammar of the Kurdish language, based on material in the Kurmanji and Sorani dialects]*, Izdatel'stvo AN SSSR, Moscow.

Kutschera, C. (1979) *Le Mouvement national kurde*, Flammarion, Paris.

Laber, J. and Whitman, L. (1988) *Destroying Ethnic Identity: The Kurds of Turkey*, Helsinki Watch, New York and Washington.

Laçiner, Ö. (1985) Der Konflikt zwischen Sunniten und Aleviten in der Türkei, in Blaschke, J. and van Bruinessen, M. (eds) *Islam und Politik in der Türkei*, Express Edition, Berlin.

Lambton, A. (1953) *Landlord and Peasant in Persia*, Oxford University Press, London.

Lambton, A. (1969) *The Persian Land Reform 1962–1966*, Clarendon Press, Oxford.

Lenczowski, G. (1979) *Political Elites in the Middle East*, 3rd edn, American Enterprise Institute, Washington.

Lescot, R. (1938) Enquête sur les Yezidis de Syrie et du Djebel Sindjar, Institut Français de Damas, Beirut.

Lillich, R. (1973) *Humanitarian Intervention and the United Nations*, University of Virginia Press, Charlottesville.

Luard, E. (1972) *The International Regulation of Civil Wars*, Thames & Hudson, London.

Luke, H.C. (1925) *Mosul and its Minorities*, Hopkinson, London.

McCarus, E. (1958) *A Kurdish Grammar: Descriptive Analysis of the Kurdish of Sulaymaniya, Iraq*, American Council of Learned Societies, New York.

MacDonald, C.G. (1988) The Kurdish Question in the 1980s, in Esman, M.E. and Robinovitch, I. (eds) *Ethnicity, Pluralism and State in the Middle East*, Cornell University Press, New York, pp. 233–52.

McDowall, D. (1985) *The Kurds*, Minority Rights Group Report 23, London (rev. edn 1989).

MacKenzie, D.N. (1961a) The Origins of Kurdish, *Transactions of the Philological Society*.

MacKenzie, D.N. (1961b, 1962) *Kurdish Dialect Studies*, 2 vols, Oxford University Press, London.

Malek, M. (1989) Kurdistan and the Iran–Iraq War, *New Left Review* 175.

Medico International (1990) Deportations in Iraqi Kurdistan and Kurdish Refugees in Iran, *The Kurdish Academy Yearbook 1990*, pp. 59–77, Berlin.

Mélikoff, I. (1982) Recherches sur les composantes du syncrétisme Bektachi-Alevi, in *Studia turcologica memoriae Alexii Bombaci dedicata*, Naples.

Menzel, T. (1911) Ein Beitrag zur Kenntnis der Jeziden, in Grothe, H., (ed.) *Meine Vorderasienexpedition 1906, 1907*, Bd I, Hiersemann, Leipzig.

Meron, T. (1987) The Geneva Conventions as Customary Law, *American Journal of International Law* 81.

Meyer, M.A. (1989) *Armed Conflict and the New Law: Aspects of the 1977 Geneva Protocols and the 1981 Weapons Convention*, British Institute of International and Comparative Law, London.

Mgoi Sh. Kh. (1977) *Problema Natsional'noi Avtonomii Kurdskogo Naroda v Irakskoi Respublike* (1958–70 gg) *[The Problem of National Autonomy of the Kurdish People in the Iraqui Republic, 1958–1977]*, Izdatel'stvo AN SSR, Yerevan.

Middle East Watch (1990) *Human Rights in Iraq*, Yale University Press, New Haven and London.

Minorsky, V. (1920, 1921) Notes sur la secte des Ahlé Haqq, *Revue du Monde Musulman* 40–1, 44–5.

Minorsky, V. (1943) The Gûrân, *Bulletin of the School of Oriental and African Studies* 12.

Mokri, M. (1970) *Contribution scientifique aux études iraniennes: Recherches de kurdologie*, Klincksieck, Paris.

Molyneux-Seel, L. (1914) A Journey in Dersim, *Geographical Journal* 44.

More, Ch. (1984) *Les Kurdes aujourd'hui. Mouvement national et partis politiques;* Harmatan, Paris.

Müller, K.E. (1967) *Kulturhistorische Studien zur Genese pseudoislamischer Sektengebilde in Vorderasien*, Franz Steiner Verlag, Wiesbaden.

Musaelyan, Zh. S. (1963) *Bibliografiya po Kurdovedeniyu [Kurdological Bibliography]*, Akademiya Nauk SSSR, Institut Narodov Azii, Moscow.

al-Musalli, M. (1986) *'Arab wa-Akrād, Ru'ya 'Arabiyya lil-Qadiyya al-Kurdiyya [Arabs and Kurds. An Arab View of the Kurdish Question]*, Beirut.

Nairn, T. (1977) *The Break-up of Britain*, NLB, London.

Nanda, V.P. (1972) Self Determination in International Law, *American Journal of International Law* 66.

Nawaz, M.K. (1971) Editorial Comment: Bangladesh and International Law, *Indian Law Journal* 11.

Nebez, J. (1957) *Nūsīnī Kurdī be Latīnī* [Writing Kurdish in Roman Script], al-Ma'ārif, Baghdad.

Nebez, J. (1969) *Kurdische Schriftsprache: Eine Chrestomathie Moderner Texte*, Buske, Hamburg.

Nebez, J. (1975) Die Schriftsprache der Kurden, in Duchesne-Guillemin, J. (ed.) *Monumentum H.S. Nyberg*, vol. 2, *Acta Iranica* 5, Tehran and Liege.

Nerīman, M.S.E. (1977) *Bībliyografyay Kitēbī Kurdī [A Bibliography of Kurdish Books]*, al-Majma' al-'Ilmī al-Kurdī, Baghdad.

Nikitine, B. (1956) *Les Kurdes: étude sociologique et historique*, Klincksieck, Paris.

O'Ballance, E. (1973) *The Kurdish Revolt: 1961–1970*, Faber & Faber, London.

Olson, R. (1989) *The Emergence of Kurdish Nationalism and the Sheikh Said Rebellion, 1920–1925*, University of Texas Press, Austin.

Oranskij, I.M. (1977) *Les Langues iraniennes*, Klincksieck, Paris.

Orient (1988, special issue) *Conflit du Golfe*, Paris.

Parmaksızoğlu, I (1983) *Tarih Boyunca Kürttürkleri ve Türkmenler [Kurdish Turks and Turcomans Throughout History]*, Türk Kültürünü Araştırma Enstitüsü, Ankara.

Patriotic Union of Kurdistan (1976) *Revolution in Kurdistan. The Essential Documents of the Patriotic Union of Kurdistan*, PUK Publications, New York.

Pelletiere, S.C. (1984) *The Kurds: An Unstable Element in the Gulf*, Westview Press, Boulder and London.

Planning and Budget Organization (1979) *An Introduction to the Consideration of the Economic and Social Problem of Tribal Society of Kurdestan*, Tehran.

Planning and Budget Organization, Statistical Centre (1960) *Âmārgīrī-ye Keshāvarz-e Ostān-e Kordestān [Agricultural Statistics of the Province of Kurdistan]*, Tehran.

Planning and Budget Organization, Stastistical Centre (1985) *Âmārnāme-ye Ostān-e Kordestān [A Statistical Survey of the Province of Kurdistan]*, Tehran.

Politique Etrangère (1988 special issue) *Irak–Iran: La diplomatie de conflit*, Institut Français des Relations Internationales, Paris.

Press Reviews (1983–89), *Bulletin de liaison et d'information* 1–50, Institut Kurde de Paris, Paris.

Rasool, Sh. M. (1990) *Forever Kurdish. Statistics of Atrocities in Iraqi Kurdistan*, n. p.

Rondot, P. (1936) Trois essays de latinisation de l'alphabet kurde: Iraq, Syrie, URSS, *Bulletin d'Etudes Orientales* 5, Cairo, pp.1–31.

Rondot, P. (1937) Les Tribus montagnardes de l'asie antérieure. Quelques aspects sociaux des populations kurdes et assyriennes, *Bulletin d'Etudes Orientales* 6, Cairo, pp. 1–50.

Rooy, S. van and Tamboer, K. (1968) *ISK's Kurdish Bibliography Nr 1*, 2 vols, International Society Kurdistan, Amsterdam.

Roux, J.P. (1969) Les Fidèles de Vérité et les croyances religieuses des Turcs, *Revue de l'Histoire des Religions* 175.

Salzmann, P. (1971) National Integration of the Tribes in Modern Iran, *The Middle East Journal* 25.

Schneider, R. (1984) *Die kurdischen Yezidi. Ein Volk auf dem Weg in den Untergang*, Gesellschaft für Bedrohte Völker, Göttingen.

Şemo, E. (1983) *Dimdim*, Roja Nû, Stockholm.

Seurat, M. (1980) *La Syrie d'aujourd'hui*, A. Raymand, Paris.

Sim, R. (1980) Kurdistan: The Search for Recognition, *Conflict Studies* 124, Institute for the Study of Conflict, London.

Smith, A.D. (1986) *The Ethnic Origins of Nations*, Basil Blackwell, Oxford.

Soran, H.S. (1979) *Kitēbxaney Soran* (A Kurdish Bibliography), n. p.

Staff Report to the Committee on Foreign Relations, United States Senate (1987) *War in the Persian Gulf: The US Takes Sides*, Washington.

Tehran University, the Institute of Social Study and Research (1969) *Barrasī-ye Natāyej-e Eslāhātī-ye Arzī [A Study of the Results of Land Reforms]*, Tehran.

Ter, Minassian A. (1989) *La République d'Arménie*, Editions Complexe, Brussels.

Uzun, M. (1984) *Tu* [*You*], Dengê Komal, Stockholm.

Valensi, L. (1987) La Tour de Babel: relations ethniques et religieuses au Moyen Orient et en Afrique du Nord, *Les Annales*, July–August, Paris.

Vanly, I.C. (1968) *The Persecution of the Kurdish People by the Baath Dictatorship in Syria*, Amsterdam.

Vanly, I.C. (1970) *Le Kurdistan irakien, entité nationale. Étude de la revolution de 1961*, De la Bacconiere, Neuchatel.

Vanly, I.C. (1980) Regards sur l'histoire des Kurdes, *Studia Kurdica*, Institut Kurde, Paris.

Veuthey, M. (1983) Implementation and Enforcement of Humanitarian Law and Human Rights Law in Non International Armed Conflicts: The Role of the International Committee of the Red Cross, *American University Law Review* 33.

Walker, C. (1980) *Armenia. The Survival of a Nation*, Croom Helm, London.

Whitman, L. (1990) *Destroying Ethnic Identity. The Kurds of Turkey, an Update*, Helsinki Watch, New York and Washington.

Wilson, H.A. (1988) *International Law and the Use of Force by National Liberation Movements*, Clarendon Press, Oxford.

Index